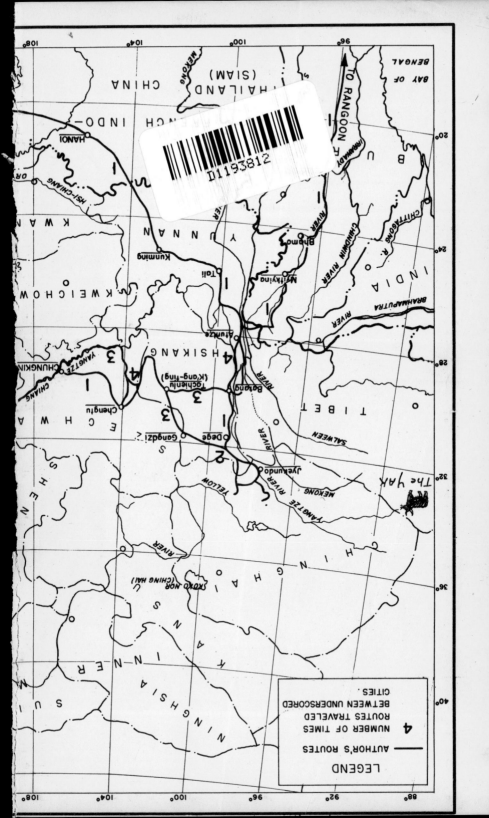

LEGEND

——— AUTHOR'S ROUTES

4 NUMBER OF TIMES
ROUTES TRAVELED
BETWEEN UNDERSCORED
CITIES.

The Yangtze and The Yak
Adventurous Trails
In and Out of Tibet

By

Marion H. Duncan
Missionary, Geographer and Explorer

Alexandria, Virginia
1952

Copyright 1952
Marion H. Duncan

Lithoprinted in U.S.A.
EDWARDS BROTHERS, INC.
ANN ARBOR, MICHIGAN
1952

TABLE OF CONTENTS

LIST OF ILLUSTRATIONS

CHAPTER I

CHAPTER II

CHAPTER III

CHAPTER IV

CHAPTER V

CHAPTER VIII

CHAPTER IX

CHAPTER X

CHAPTER XI

CHAPTER XII

CHAPTER XIII

CHAPTER XIV

CHAPTER XV

MAPS

INTRODUCTION

Some years ago the first half of this Tibetan story covering the years 1921-28 was published under the title of "The Mountain of Silver Snow." This second half embracing the years from 1929 to 1936 records ventures more venturesome and dangers more dangerous than those reported in the first volume. The scenes of the first adventures were in Batang and in the areas southward, mostly in Yunnan, Burma and the southeastern portion of the Tibetan Tableland. The incidents of this book center in Batang and in the regions to the north and east upon the Tibetan Plateau with the entrance through the Yangtze Gorges into Tibet.

To a greater extent than in "The Mountain of Silver Snow" the tracing of the travelled routes throughout the Eastern Tibetan Highlands are not the chronicle of a single journey between stated points. Portions of the route here recorded were traced four times such as the trip through the Yangtze Gorges. The trails between Tachienlu and Batang, and from Tachienlu to Dzochen were traversed upon three occasions. Although each trip had events worthy of record, for the sake of brevity and interest, the outstanding incidents of multiple trips over the same route are combined into one account. Numerals and asterisks upon the maps will show the number of trips over any route. My companions upon these journeys were not always the same but these variations are indicated and are irrelevant since adventures and not personalities are the theme of this volume.

The author spent fifteen years when in Tibet, and many hours since studying the Tibetan language and the different systems of transliteration adopted by seven different Tibetan authorities. As this book and its maps are for the use of both scholars and the general public the author has attempted to romanize the place names, as spelled by his teacher Gegan Atring who investigated the proper Tibetan characters on the spot, with two objects in view. First, to create a name which adheres to the Tibetan enunciation, is pronounceable and has the appearance of an English word. Second, to hold closely enough to a scientific transliteration so that a Tibetan scholar with the aid of a Tibetan-English dictionary, such as Das, can discover the original Tibetan characters. The author believes he has succeeded reasonably well in this almost insurmountable task although recovery of the Tibetan characters in some cases may require a little searching.

In the transliteration, diacritical marks have been avoided as they are easily lost in printing and are not understood by the average reader. The chart (Appendix No. 4), on the sound of English letters, has been kept as simple and brief as possible.

Finally, although this volume may not fulfill the Tibetan standard of good writing of "To be free from the three faults of,—too much, too little and mistakes" yet the author hopes that it may give the reader the feeling expressed in another Tibetan proverb that it is "Arrow to the target and words to the meaning."

MR. MARION H. DUNCAN

Chapter I

WESTWARD TO THE YANGTZE

Among perpetual snow mountains in the highest recesses of Inner Tibet, legend places a long-haired wild yak of immense size. From its opened mouth over a long protruding red tongue comes a never-ending stream of water which Tibetans affirm is the source of the Dri (Dre) Chu or Wild Yak River which is known to most of the world as the Yangtze.

For its first four hundred miles the Dri Chu flows through the almost uninhabited and bitterly cold Jyangthang (Chang-tang), the elevated undulating plains of northern Tibet upon which graze thousands of wild yak. In the second four hundred miles the monotonous grassy Jyangthang is replaced by forested ravines and cultivated valleys intermingled with grasslands; in these parts the wild yak yields to the product of its mating with domesticated cattle—found in the various blends of tame yak which supplies the nomad with a complete livelihood and the valley dwellers with work and dairy stock.

For the remainder of its mountainous course the Yangtze, as the Chinsha Chiang or River of Golden Sand, continues to step downward by furious rapids in a great half-circle of eight hundred miles before leaving the Tibetan Plateau to enter the heavily cultivated Chinese farms of the Red Basin. More gentle, but with wild stretches in the Gorges, the Yangtze, now known as the Great or Long River, courses the flatter land of the water buffalo and rice paddies for its final sixteen hundred miles to the sea.

To reach the Land of the Yangtze and the Yak from America we take ship at a Pacific port, having set forth on our different trips from Vancouver, Seattle and Los Angeles. However, we have returned home through the ports of San Francisco and New York.

The departure of a ship is the beginning of a dynasty of time. To the seasoned traveler it is a holiday and to the novice an epoch. One leaves the familiar democracy of an intimate environment, bidding farewell to America, and becomes the temporary subject of an absolute monarch, the captain of the ship, who in turn must be guided by the shifty currents of wind and water.

On shore the prospective passenger only vaguely senses, that the ship, which is about to leave its easy slurping movements alongside the wharf to gallop with a steady, twisting rocking upon unfettered seas, is to be his sole tie to a stable life. As the hour of embarking approaches the seriousness of the voyage begins to thrill and yet to appall. One tries incoherently to think of final directions for relatives and friends whose uneasy chatter enhances the confusion of sailors and dockmen making ready to cast off.

The seeming chaos however is orderly. Each person has his assigned task. The band plays joyful music but changes to such sad tunes as "Farewell to Thee" when the time for departure draws nigh. The passengers grab the many-colored rolls of paper from the deck steward and hurl them shoreward forming a rainbow arcade of flimsy lines which the farewellers on shore grasp to keep a final tie that does not bind. Late arrivals must now press and push to reach the crouching gangplank. Dockmen are unhurriedly filling the last net with belated baggage and the crane swings creakingly aboard where sailors dump the pieces outside the hold as they fasten winches, cranes and tackle firmly in their couches where storms will not be able to disturb.

As the time of departure draws near there begins a continuous ringing of bells. Ship officers rush to and fro in final inspections while boatswains quietly speak forceful impetus to tardy workers. Tugs appear alongside to push the giant away from its wharf. Dock laborers release middle ropes as the engines begin to throb and then stand-by to cast off the end hawsers. As the tugs inch the ship away, the end hawsers are unfastened and pulled on deck. The passengers wave frantically as the streamer arcade stretches and breaks, to fall and become sodden discolored fragments. The giant ship gains headway under its own power and soon the tugs withdraw leaving a bit of man-made world steaming in solitary state toward a distant port.

My fiancee Kate Louise Habecker and I were married at mid-semester on Feb. 2, 1921 while in missionary training school and consequently postponed our formal honeymoon until we boarded the old Empress of Japan of 7000 tons on August 13th. To the landlubber bridegroom an ocean voyage seems to be the ideal honeymoon until he encounters the seasick wave. Then romantic moonlight strolls and spooning upon darkened decks vanish into hurried staggers to the ship's railing and to drowsy dopey reclining upon a deck chair. The endearing tones of passionate love avowals which the bride has heard are replaced by incoherent mutterings that the ship might sink or strike a rock or do something which will stop the everlasting dipping, rolling and squirming motions. My wife fortunately enjoys our formal honeymoon but I struggle until we reach land.

About 1880 Jules Verne is reputed to have circled the globe in eighty days. Aeroplanes take eighty hours but ships are still a slow leisurely means of travel and the radio has not overcome altogether the physical isolation of a ship at sea. Hence an ocean trip involves days of thought and preparation on the part of both passengers and the ship's personnel to insure comfort and happiness. Yet more nerve wracking than equipping a round the world cruise are the preparations which my wife Louise and I have made for our six-year term in an isolated outpost near the Yangtze on the Tibetan Plateau in the Land of the Yak. Lest we forget an important item we take the catalogs of the huge mail-order houses and check through them page by page until our stock is complete for at least a two year residence without replenishment. Securing supplies for the additional four years will require constant foresight as Batang our intended station is so remote that letters take 3 to 6 months and magazines 6 to 12 months to arrive. Freight packages reach the station in an average time of two years.

Life was still so primitive in the Orient in 1921 that stoves and iron beds could not be bought in Shanghai and Hongkong. The farther inland one traveled the less one could buy. Purchasing from the large mail order houses and shipping goods to the Tibetan Plateau tripled the cost of equipment such as beds and stoves and made sugar worth a dollar a pound and coal oil a dollar a gallon when laid down in Batang. Fortunately the cheapness of native foods, which we use largely, such as yak beef at five cents a pound and eggs less than a cent apiece with vegetables in proportion equalize living expenses so that one can live in semi-foreign style a little more cheaply than in America.

Out of sight of land one has time to note the denizens of the sea. Constantly tailing us are gulls plucking refuse dumped over the side, until sensing we are leading them across the ocean, they disappear so quietly and suddenly that one is not aware of their departure. A hundred or more miles from shore the gap left by the gulls is filled by gunies who appear everywhere and anytime. Brownish with white bands around the base of the tail the gunies are a small species of albatross, some of whose members have white bodies and heads, while others seen only in the southern seas have the longest wing spread for birds, reaching to 11 feet. Three of the smaller species with wings three feet long and not over nine inches wide float effortlessly over the wake of our ship to catch fish churned to the surface by the propellers. Whales occasionally spout and schools of porpoises race the ship springing clear of the water in long horizontal leaps. As one approaches Japan sometimes the long slender, whitish bodies of flying fish hurl above the waves supported by two large upper fins spread out like wings. Some sail as far as 200 feet under their initial momentum.

Life aboard ship settles down into a fixed routine of five meals a day, the three regular ones assisted by broth in mid-morning and tea in mid-afternoon. In between meals the occupational castes complete their rites. The deck promenaders walk so many miles with ten times around the deck equalling a mile; the bridge enthusiasts bid four hearts in preference to watching the silver sheen of moonlight on the ocean; the lovelorn seek out an isolated nook to spoon and sigh, treating everything else as casual; the socialite bitter-enders create a drunken noise every night in spite of ship regulations and the discomfort of others; the garrulous conversationalist tires you but never himself; the silent mysterious hide their identity with the air of an important personage or a seasoned traveller; worst of all is the activist who is never satisfied unless a concert, a lecture, a tournament or a dance is kept going by your cooperation lest one be unoccupied, have a moment's leisure, or show signs of being lonesome.

Humor on board ship assumes two unvarying forms, (1) jests centered around seasickness and (2) tomfoolery to worry and deceive even the sophisticated. Seasickness afflicts about twenty-five percent upon an ordinary voyage with a little rough weather; but if a storm should strike early before the majority have acquired their sea-legs or a certain tolerance to the endless motion, perhaps ninety percent will suffer from a mild to a violent condition in which they strive after tranquillity in keeping their meals down, but find that they must exercise their meals up. The jests play around such verbal thrusts as "What's the matter, got a weak stomach?" with the answer "No, I'm throwing it as far as the rest of them"; and the Frenchman travelling on an English ship. The Frenchman had learned enough English to take it literally. He was aroused one night by his friend who occupied the berth above him. His friend suddenly was nauseated and yelled "Look out below"; and the Frenchman obediently stuck out his head in time to receive a deluge.

Seasick jokes soon subside as the subject and its activities are limited. Not so with the tomfoolish tongue which ever invents a new rumour or a new "cock and bull" story to worry the unwary. These rumours range from statements "that the boat is going to turn back to America" or that "a plane will come out to meet the boat in order to take off an important personage urgently needed in government work," to the cry that "the indistinct loud speaker has just announced a meeting of all passengers in the lounge." Such statements always given with straight face and oily tongue soon convince the novice that everyone is a liar and he wonders why everyone should pick on him.

Some read books which they otherwise would never have opened, and some play bridge or pinochle to which they would not give spare time on land. The socially minded make casual friendships with people they would not think of associating with at home. The wanton engage in flirtations uninhibited by family and friends' supervision which had kept them in a straighter path in the hometown. Life aboard ship is a great leveler of society, breaking down the barriers of race and nationality and softening the antipathies of religious conviction.

Certain days stand out most distinctly. The two big parties are the Captain's Dinner and the Hard Times Party. The Captain's Dinner or Dress-up Night brings out the most gorgeous evening gowns on the ladies and formal dress or dark suits for the men. Special orchestra music, singing by male quartet, gaudy decorations, and dancing until the sleepy hours wind up with a final moonlight walk upon the top deck. The Hard Times Party is the favored evening in which all revert to the primitive, by wearing poverty-stricken costume. Those who feel poorest wear the least and are happy. Without design I won a prize once at such a time. As usual I waited until just before dinner time to think about my "Hard Times" suit. Under sudden inspiration and a certain admiration of Gandhi I decided to imitate the Hindu sage. Stripping to an athletic strap I grabbed a sheet from the bed and, with the help of safety pins, a handkerchif tied around my head and a pair of dark spectacles, transformed my thin bony frame, sloping forehead and absent-minded gaze into a recognizable image of Gandhi.

Unknown to me the Hindu leader had a short time previously made a voyage on our boat the President Lincoln. Consequently upon stepping into the dining room the hubbub of the waiters changed into clapping, while I sought my seat pulling a paper goat tied to the end of a string. After dinner in the parade staged before the judges, in which all Hard Dressers participated, I won the prize as being the hardest up. Since Gandhi was a teetotaler the prize was in keeping with his habits and a bottle of buttermilk was shared with my table companions.

The present-day steamships strive to give passengers all the facilities of their home life. A gymnasium is supplemented by a 15 by 30 foot swimming pool and games, such as shuffleboard, played on deck. A wellstocked library for the studious and an inexhaustible bar for the thirsty offer a contrast in mental and physical relaxation. Chapel services on the recognized days offer religious comfort. Lectures by some of the more distinguished passengers, whose experiences and life have been unusual, are delivered to those interested. A daily newspaper of important news is published and distributed in time for the evening meal. There are limited facilities for the sending and receiving of radio messages to any part of the world yet in spite of all comforts and contacts one never quite overcomes the feeling of ebbing away from the world. Our temporary isolation engenders a sense of helplessness and insecurity for the ship is a world to itself and the law of the sea is dominant.

National and religious holidays are kept with the proper spirit. If the ship is to be at sea over Christmas, toys and food luxuries are not forgotten by the ship's supply officer. On Christmas Day gay decorations with a Christmas tree and appropriate gifts for every child, besides candy and fruit in which even the adults share, are part of the festivities. Two of our most pleasant and distinctively remembered Christmas Days were spent upon the ocean, one in the Red Sea where our British hosts piped in the flaming pudding as the final touch for Christmas Eve.

Unless the ship takes the direct northern route by the short circle almost touching the Aleutians and consuming fourteen days to Yokohama, the first stop is a day in Honolulu which gives one a taste of tropical Hawaii. Then to Japan with a day in Yokohama, through the inland sea for a day at Kobe and maybe a stopover night at Nagasaki. From here it is two more days through the discolored waters of the Yellow Sea whose hue has been created by the Yangtze. The ship enters the mouth of this tremendous stream whose upper ends drain the yak-lands of Tibet. One docks at Shanghai after a two hour trip up the Whangpu river. Shanghai is the chief port of China and funnels Yangtze river-trade inland, part of which finally reaches the grasslands of Tibet where it is carried upon the backs of yak.

Figure 1
The Panchen Lama, highest spiritual authority in Tibet, and the author

Figure 2
China, America and Tibet—represented by Lo Tai Tai, Mrs. Louise Duncan
and Jamkuzhoh Baodren in Batang, Tibetan Border

Chapter II

YARNS OF THE YANGTZE GORGES

North of Shanghai the Yangtze River Dragon, with a mouth full of islands, pushes tongues of chocolate waters for two hundred miles into the clean Pacific. This silt-laden flood races with romance. The first thousand miles barely moves fast enough to be called a current so that real enchantment begins at the Gorges above bustling Ichang and ends two hundred and fifty miles westward at Chungking. Some farther upper reaches of the Yangtze have still more rugged canyons within the borders of Tibet, but their magnificence is wasted on burly yaks and sheep-skinned Tibetans.

Less than forty years ago up-river travellers sat in bamboo chairs three feet above the water on launch-sized junks; now square-sterned steamers eighty-five to one hundred and ninety feet long pushed by double-powered engines hoist one over turbulent swirls and cut easily around jutting rocks. Although these modern vessels give greater safety to life and goods, they permit no leisurely inspection of bewitching temples and storied landmarks as was possible when chanting coolies with measured tread spent hours pulling one's junk over raging rapids.

Far up in the snow-covered mountains of Tibet the Yangtze starts as a tiny rivulet; after tumbling and winding fifteen hundred miles to Chungking the river has become a quarter of a mile in width. Below Chungking this vast spread of waters is force-pumped into a chasm often a hundred to two hundred yards wide; in low water season rushing and roaring over hidden rocks; in high water boiling around right-angle turns with cyclonic force.

Four times, twice up and twice down, we have travelled on the Yangtze across China. On our first trip, naturally the most vivid in recollection, we take passage on the British ship Kingwo recently repaired after scraping a rock on a downward voyage in the Gorges. The Kingwo is built especially for the Yangtze service,

measures 148 feet long, 28 feet wide and has a draft of 6 feet 8
inches. She is a vessel of 284 tons with a speed of 14.5 knots.

We pull anchor at Shanghai in the first tinges of dawn. Out of
the Whangpu into the Yangtze we meander upstream against the
sluggish, silt-surfeited current, several times backing off from mud
banks which threaten to suck us beneath the surface. It is April
and the water is at its lowest. The Yangtze shrinks from a width
of ten to fifty miles at its mouth to over a half mile wide at Hankow some six hundred miles inland. We pass Foochow junks,
reputed to be the largest of their type, guided by a pair of eyes in
the bow and carrying cloth, kerosene and manufactured products
inland which they will exchange for woodoil, tea, and rice from
the Changsha bowl, and famed ware from Kiukiang. The junks
need all of their ragged ribbed sails to push against the current.
We halt briefly at Nanking and Wuhu; and at Kiukiang long
enough to buy a set of bowls with rice grains embedded in the
ware and to wish we could have time to visit Kuling a day's
journey up the mountain for a stay in China's most famous summer resort. We swing around Orphan's Island crowned by a monastery and delay long enough at Hankow to go shopping and to
pay our respects to the American Consul.

Embarking once more we push toward Shasi where much tung
oil is loaded by downriver boats for export to America. On a
later trip in 1934 within this stretch occurred a remarkable dem-
onstration of belief in a superstition. We were on the S.S. *Ichang*
which had formerly been commanded by a Capt. Nichols, an Eng-
lishman of long experience upon the river. However, he had incurred the hatred of his crew or at least a part of the men. He
disappeared enroute to Shasi on July 13, 1930 presumably by
being thrown overboard, although it is barely possible he fell or
jumped off the steamer. An investigation failed to reveal the
exact cause of his disappearance as the Chinese insisted the river
dragon had pulled him into the water. The Chinese then pre-
dicted that a man would fall overboard every year from this boat
in July. As the forecast had been fulfilled by a member of the
crew or a passenger vanishing every year it was firmly stated
someone would go overboard from our ship between the first and
15th of this month. The 15th arrived and so strong was my belief

in the duplicity of the Chinese mind which would see that someone was pushed overboard to maintain the prophecy that I slept
inside the cabin rather than my usual place next to the railing
where one could be easily shoved off. True to the schedule a man
went overboard that night but whether he fell over or was pushed
off the crowded boat where doorways opened out to the waters
with no railing, the river dragon will not tell. At least I slept
soundly with locked door.

Travelling only by day and anchoring each night we arrive at
Ichang after nine days from Shanghai. Ichang lies just above the
first gorge and is featured by a pagoda which is, however, overshadowed in interest by a series of pyramid hills across the river.

Water below the zero level which is the mark for safe navigation delays us five days in Ichang. Then we push through a drifting fog past a series of conical and pyramidal peaks forming a
row of menacing lower teeth for the Tiger's Tooth Gorge. The
fog lifts under the rising sun as we enter the limestone cliffs of the
Huang-mao-hsia or Yellow Cat Gorge which merges into the Lamp-
shine Gorge; the names were created by the shape and shine of
the crouching rocks. Not quite halfway through on the right bank
(right is facing the mouth of a stream) is a water-worn "Dragon's
Cave" which is reputed to run inland for miles to an outlet;
definitely seen within its mouth is the limestone rock dragon
guarding his lair.

These gorges are within the first sixteen miles above Ichang.
Just beyond is the Zigzag Reach, one broad stretch of granite
rocks and rubble at low water as now, but at mid-level creating
the dangerous Otter Rapid. Hardy fishermen are using trained
otters and cormorants to catch fish in the swift waters. On the
right are chalky white precipices resembling the cliffs of Dover
and known as the Yellow Cow Cliffs. These cliffs intrigue the eye
but the boatmen are much more concerned with the maze of
rapids, swirls and narrow channels twisting between huge clumps
of boulders and reefs. On the rocky shore junks bottom up are
being repaired while piles of goods testify to the strength of the
current and the sharpness of the reefs. Unwound bales of cotton
cloth drying on the hillside cover acres with bands of white, black
and blue.

As we enter the beginnings of the Zigzag Reaches up three hundred feet from the water on the face of the left cliff are seen the queer rock projections of the Ox-liver Horse-lung Gorge. While we gaze at these accurately-shaped liver and lung-outcroppings we almost miss the cartoon of a human face in white on the opposite grey cliff. This figure is the Clown of the Yangtze. Meanwhile the Chinese pilot is tensely watching the midstream where crouches the dreaded Kongling, a black mass of rock thrusting a head fifty feet high during low water. At its feet lie the Pearl Rocks submerged and scattered but thick enough to make the channel hazardous and crooked. One of the first steamers to try the rapids slashed her bottom here on her maiden voyage in 1900 and sank a short distance downstream.

Above this gorge is the first series of rapids that tests the driving power of our boat. These Hsintan or New Rapids, although formed by a landslide some three hundred years ago, are considered young; so short a space of time in China could not create age when traditional history goes back five thousand years. Such immense masses of rocks and earth were pushed into the Yangtze that the river was dammed for a time; later breaking through in great sluices with terrific currents. Even now three hundred men are needed to pull the largest junks past the three rapids.

Our own ship throws out a steel cable (Photo No. 4) which sixty men fasten around a huge rock; then with full steam ahead, squeaking in every plank, her bow deep in water and seeming to stand still for awful moments, the ship inch by inch winds herself over the rapids which fall six feet within a hundred and fifty feet of distance. Our anxiety dies when we reach the quieter waters near the anchored rock. Up the slope are the temporary straw huts, readily movable as the water rises, which serve as squalid homes for the Hsintan coolies.

For these last few years at the Hsintan and other dangerous rapids there have been trim red lifeboats which save many a life that formerly stayed in the clasp of the river dragon.

In working a junk over the Hsintan only the toughest bamboo hawsers two to three inches in diameter are used. The inboard end is bound firmly round the mast near the deck and the other end hitched to lines slung from the shoulder and waist of half-naked men. With a toggle or button wound in a loose hitch around the hawser the coolies bend on all fours and creeping to the cadence of a beating drum, with almost invisible paces, inch the boat through a gap in the reef. A faulty cable, a slippery hitch or slowness of the steersman at the crucial moment and the boat ends upon a jagged reef, or joins again the scores of junks moored below the rapid where some have waited for days.

Past the three rapids into the Kueichou Reach, deriving its name from the picturesque walled town on the left bank, our boat enters the succession of minor rapids, races and whirlpools which, in the absence of fair winds, will delay junks for a day or more until they reach Roller Point where bamboo cables six hundred yards long are needed. Huge rollers of wood have been wedged into the rock so the cables can slide on them rather than be frayed through on the toothed rock-edges. Even then there are places where the rock is worn down in grooves several inches deep by centuries of cables.

As we approach the hamlet of Laokueichou our cabin boy who knows some English tells us our first yarn of the Yangtze Gorges. Pointing to a temple on the left bank opposite the city he speaks haltingly.

"Mister, temple of Chuyuanfu, long time, seven hundred years gone, Chinese Emperor not like him. He jump in water. Big fish take him in mouth. Throw him on bank to sister. Sister fix body into idol and build temple. Big fish still here, make three bad, round and round pool called Chuyuansanbao, mean three jewels of Chunyuan. When river too high, swallow boat."

"Is that really true," I queried unwisely.

"True, not true, take boat down, not see boat anymore," he retorted with a shrug of his shoulders.

In a short time the Yehtan Rapid looms before us; tame in low water as now, but on our other trip up when the water was above the thirty-foot level, the rapid was fearful to see and harrowing to surmount. The boiling and rushing current is produced by a great fan-shaped bar of detritus piled up by a mountain torrent on the north bank. This accumulated pile of rocks pens the tributary into a channel that shoots the water into the Yangtze with such force that it tests the power of man and steam. Wild is the wail of the master whose boat breaks loose and is swept down-stream for when he pulls up far below he must go to the bottom of the line and await his turn over again.

The charm of the canyons compensates for the risks of the river. Bands of grey limestone cliffs alternate with red sandstone upended and curved in every type of incline while along the water's edge spits and shingles of sand and gravel pile up in the center of concave curves. Arched bridges and tiled temples peeping out of steeply wooded ravines cause the mind to dream of armored knights battling fire-spouting dragons in order to rescue charming princesses.

One hour's run brings us to the Buffalo Mouth Reach where another rapid, famous for great whirlpools which toss the ship almost out of control at high level, is entered through blood-red cliffs known as the Shihmen or Stone Gates. Many a junk and a few foreign boats have been swept upon the rocks so that some red boats are stationed here to save the unfortunate. Such passages have caused engineers to recommend that all upper Yangtze ships have three rudders and double bottoms.

Another six miles and our boat climbs almost to a standstill in mounting another rapid the Chingtsopiao which has a long and tumultous approach that erases from our thoughts the quaint Patung Pagoda and village, which is important because not many of the towns visible in the gorges are big enough to warrant a pagoda.

A long stretch of comparatively smooth water brings us to the longest and by many considered to be the grandest gorge of all. This is the Wushan Tahsia or Witches Mountain Great Gorge with twenty-five to thirty miles of silent stately mountain slopes in rainbow colors. On its steep sides cling little stone houses whose inhabitants live by dipping fish with small conical nets, dipping with the current. The solid rock cliffs from low water to high water level are pockmarked by countless pot-holes bored like the holes of a cookstove upon the cliff-face; these were formed by the numberless stabs of boatmen's prongs and hooks as they pushed and pulled their junks at the different water-levels during the last few thousand years. The eerie quietness is broken by the gurgle of a whirlpool or the whistle of the junkmen as they

invoke the aid of the God of Wind. More and more the weirdness
of endless ridges and valleys is broken by the sonorous blast of a
steamer as she, with a long tail of black smoke fading behind her,
ploughs up waves that threaten to swamp junks, whose owners
frantically row to one side while cursing the ancestors of the foreign devils.

In the Wushan Gorge vertical cliffs rise up a thousand feet and
more, with some of the peaks a mile high, their tips flirting
among wisps of clouds during bright sunshine and bathed in
gloom during the rainy weather. The gorge is quiet and melan-
choly during the present low water; when the big freshets come
down, urged by melting snows in Tibet, the waters, a hundred feet
higher, transform the sullen river into a mighty demon. Silty
yellow waters rush in zigzag fashion, dashing from wall to wall,
sputtering and boiling around half-submerged rocks, breaking into
all kinds and shapes of backwashes and whirlpools which transform the gorge into a gyrating mass of turbulent water, so dangerous that calloused Chinese junkmen of long experience will not
enter, waiting until the river has somewhat subsided. Junks bound
upstream may spend a week passing this gorge which at low water
narrows to a hundred or one hundred fifty yards wide in a long,
red sandstone defile.

One can disembark on the Hupeh-Szechwan boundary halfway
through the gorge at Paishih on the right bank and take a good
walk toward the western end of the Wushan, that is if one likes a
trail cut along the face of the cliff a few feet above surging water.
Wonderful views are obtained, especially at Clear Water Cave
where, at a sharp bend, one can count the twelve Fantastic Peaks
piercing the sky like filed teeth (Photo No. 5). Just before the
bend on the left bank not far above the water is Kongmingbai a
large circular indention of hard slate-like rock showing at least
six layers of stone. The Chinese steward had a ready explana-
tion (Photo No. 6).

"Teacher, history is written upon that rock and at the end of
each dynasty the stone peels off ready for a new record."

"I can see cracks criss-crossing all over the face and they look
like Chinese characters but one must have a better imagination
than I have, to read them," was my sober reply.

At Wushan the first walled town in Szechwan province, the river broadens. Nevertheless it is still one series of cascades featured by Dismount Rapid created from detritus brought down by a tributary; and so named because here is a cave where the passing horsemen must dismount and bow down to the old Dragon who resided here. Safely past this causeway of rapids, some dangerous at low water, others at mid-level, and a few at high water, our boat is ready to enter the most spectacular gorge of all, the four mile long Wind-box or Fenghsianghsia.

Some 3,450 years ago Yuwang the God of the Yangtze sat on Wushan Mountain, directing the course of the waters, when the rocks of the stretch here called the False Gorge, resisted his power. Then the wizard Wutse, in the form of an ape, aided him, cleaving the hills further westward by a fearful blast of wind from his nostrils to form the Wind-box Gorge generally about a hundred and fifty yards wide. Wutse also had a share in molding the Wushan Gorge which was named after him.

The portals of the Wind-box are guarded by the Cat Rock which lies at the extremity of a race created by the Long Snake Reef (Photo No. 7). A tremendous current is set up whose power shudders our steamer; it has been the cause of wrecking many a junk during low water in less than an hour; but when summer freshets are at their height, sometimes a hundred and fifty feet higher, terrible is the raging of the waters as they swirl madly from one cliff to the other trying to squeeze through this over one half mile high canyon which at one point is estimated to be about eighty yards wide. Since the precipitous cliff faces are a thousand feet straight up, the river must take the passage carved for it by the wizard Wutse.

Terraced shelves of black rocks and giant foot-spurs, ominous enough at low water, produce dangerous passages at high level. Wise travellers on junks will take the advise of their Laobans or boat-captains and wait until the floods have subsided before entering the Wind-box, the most awesome and historical of all. Half-way through and high up in fissures on the sheer left face are narrow wooden boxes which resemble Chinese blacksmith bellows. They are reported to be either windboxes, or coffins which they also resemble, but why placed there only a Chinese could understand and they are unsatisfactory in their answers.

"Do you see that zigzag of square holes cut into the face of the right cliff?" asks our genial Scotch engineer, pointing his finger upward.

"A famous general of Hupeh called Mengliang was checked by his enemies. He chipped out these holes, inserted wooden beams and formed a stairway to scale the cliff and take his foes by surprise. A few hundred yards upstream are two iron posts projecting from a flat rock on the left bank. Here were hung iron chains to prevent salt junks from passing into Hupeh in the reign of Taohuang, Emperor of Shu in the Ching Dynasty. Those chaps were as resourceful and adventurous as we," continued the engineer who often regaled us with bits of history as we chugged slowly upstream.

Guarding the western entrance of the four and one half mile long Wind-box Gorge is the Yenyushih or Goose-tail Rock (Photo No. 8) which towers sixty feet above low water; when awash or slightly submerged in summer its jagged points are so dangerous that craft wait at Kueifu when going downward until the water rises or falls. The common saying is, "If the Yenyushih appears as a horse the downward passage should not be attempted; if like an elephant the channel should not be forced upward." The Goose-tail Rock rests on an immense tripod of rock beneath which is the famous dragon castle of Kueilongkong. Only the strongest men can move this rock and make it swing so as to open the gate of the castle.

Out of the Wind-box with its legends we pass the Stinking Salt Streams (Photo No. 9) which are natural salt springs said to have been discovered by a begger in the reign of Hsienfeng. Flowing up from a great bed of shingle the salt water is evaporated in large iron pans. Salt is recovered by men from the nearby temporary village only when the water is not too high to cover the flats. Close by is the Venice of the Yangtze, the city of Kueifu, once the seat of kings and still romantic with sing-song girls in sampans and many gondola-like boats that ply the nearby sidestreams.

As we leave we look back to a dreamy hill on the left, once the site of the ancient stronghold of the White Emperor's City which flourished in the days of Liubai Emperor of the Shu in the times of the Three Kingdoms. Here are antique temples and stone tablets, at present marred by the semi-foreign palace of the late Wu Pei Fu, a former warlord ruling China a few years ago, who retired amidst this grandeur of nature as a solace from his former glory.

Ever-changing colors keep our eyes from tiring. Here are blue and silver-fissured limestone cliffs cut up and down like shoemaker's wax by threads; over there are barriers of sandstone-rouged lips pierced by silver sprays where a cascading stream cleaves a canyon to the Yangtze. Beyond Kueifu we enter a double channel, the narrow inner one is not over 150 yards wide with sandstone walls whose tops are on a level with our deck; the outer about three times wider arches to the foothills which at high water may bring disaster to a ship. We behold one such example of misfortune, a fine large steamer beached on this upper shelf some seven months ago (Photo No. 10). Rapidly falling water left her there, unharmed but useless for yet another three months, when high water will float her again. Here the Yangtze constricted into perhaps its longest narrow channel is about one hundred fifty yards wide but two to four hundred feet deep. So narrow it has to be deep to carry the tremendous volume of water that drains from a half million square miles of land above the gorges.

Although there are four low-water rapids from Kueifu to Yunyang (town of Clouded Sun) the most fascinating spectacle was watching coolies coal ship with baskets carried aboard from junks lashed alongside. Their sing-song cries, to lighten the load while bearing two baskets on the end of a pole supported by one shoulder, will cease as they hand a tally stick to the man at the door.

The one rapid of unusual attraction is the Tongyangtse formed from rocks spread fan-shaped by a tributary stream. Above their mouth for a considerable distance upstream many of these affluents are navigable but where they empty into the Yangtze they are usually impassable rapids. Some fifty years ago the Chinese

built dams to prevent the formation of detrital cones and to guide
the mouths of the tributaries so as to throw the waters in a downstream direction. The most permanent results of such efforts are
characters on rocks reading, "By chiselling away, still the waves."

Opposite Yunyang is the most impressive temple seen along
the river, properly labelled with the high-sounding title of
"Temple of the Ethereal Bell of a Thousand Ages" (Photo No.
11). Here junkmen stop to burn incense, light candles and shoot
off firecrackers. Steamers do not permit us to enjoy close views of
such rites nor grant time to reminisce over a thousand other
scenes but rush us by with a casual glance. The temple is a favored picnic spot but to reach it requires the climbing of a hundred
steps to find that it was erected in honor of Changfei, a bold warrior of the Han Dynasty. When Changfei died his head was cut
off and placed in a tub of oil to preserve it. Ladies in trouble
over their love affairs visit the temple, toss a few coppers into the
oil and Changfei's head rises up to advise them. The present
temple replaces the old one which was swept away when the
Yangtze rose 200 feet during the great flood of 1870.

Eight miles above Clouded Sun is the last bad low water
rapid, the Hsinlongtan or New Dragon Rapid. In 1896 a tremendous landslide of the left bank constricted the river channel from
eight hundred to two hundred yards wide, creating a race which
costs the lives of three men a day in February and March. The
total yearly loss of life on the river each year in all the gorges is
calculated to be around a thousand. Falling a foot in fifty feet at
the New Dragon Rapid, the Yangtze has such vicious eddies and
whirlpools that boatmen are happy to pass it safely.

In this part where the sandstone benches of the high water
channel extends for forty miles the signals of the Chinese mari-
time customs, prominent on high poles, show the traffic conditions
up and down. A red triangular kite with the longest apex pointing
upwards, indicates a steamer going up and with apex downward
the reverse. Two kites denote two steamers and if a junk is present red balls are suspended.

Our ship ties up for the first night at Hsiaochang where a
tributary enters the Great River. If possible vessels choose a quiet
bay in which to anchor for each night. Unlucky is the boat caught

by darkness which must stop in swift waters that may swing her
on a rock. A wise skipper will anchor early in the afternoon
rather than risk a long stretch of dangerous water to the next
harbor.

Eight Cliff Gorge is the last part of the standstone plateau.
It is a corridor hazardous at mid-level, when the thirty feet high
walls are submerged and it is difficult to find the main channel
which is about a hundred and fifty yards wide. In the distance
we see the anti-foreign town of Wanhsien (the Myriad City)
guarded by two nine-storied pagodas. Soon we anchor in midstream and at once a multitude of junks from the city fasten their
hooks into us.

The gesticulation and babble of the junkmen for prize passengers and baggage almost erase from our minds the annoyance of
the custom officers who want to snoop into our belongings. That
they have cause is evident in the many smuggled boxes of cigarettes, bottles of opium and four revolvers which were found. One
revolver is concealed in a large fish and we muse in pity upon the
probable fate of the mute owner as he is hustled by guards into a
sampan. He will be lucky to keep his head while the tobacco
owners may get off with taxes and fines that will take more than
all of the enormous profits which would have been obtained if
they had been successful. We were vexed to find afterwards that
one of the drawers of our washstands had concealed cigarettes for
our cabin boy who knew from experience the exemptions from
search which foreigner's cabins receive.

Wanhsien is noted not only as the port for a large trade with
eastern Szechwan but also for its irregular and striking location.
Backed by shrubbed hills with misty peaks the city rises high
above stone stairways which are flanked by the arched and tow-
ered gates of a high wall. The main part of the city is placed
above the highest flood. Buddhist temples with belled towers and
moon-arch bridges break the monotony of low tiled roofs green
with moss. Files of water carriers drip continuous streams upon
the slippery stone steps. Lining the river's edge are bamboo huts,
moving upward as the water rises but ever feeding and smoking
the countless coolies from junks and steamers.

Wanhsien builds junks out of the cypress wood found in the hills and supplies the sailors with pretty girls so that it is a boatman's paradise. In misty twilight the multitude of flickering lights, the gurgle of water swirling around the junks and the musical tones of Chinese voices are to the romantic a realm of enchantment fit for Arabian Nights. Nor does the steady rat-a-tat-tat of stone mason's chisels cutting limestone blocks and other daylight industry dispel the charms of the nights. If one can philosophize the poverty and squalor, a walk among the crowded lanes with their smells of burning grease and sweetish opium smoke is an unforgettable dream.

An hour above Wanhsien we pass the jutting reefs that form the mid-level and high water level Tiger Rapid of which there is no trace in winter. Three hours more (about twenty five miles) brings us to the Shihpaochai or Precious Stone Castle, a limestone column thrusting precipitiously upward for two hundred feet (Photo No. 12). It is crowned by a monastic Buddhist temple reached by a pagoda of nine stories which clings to the riverside face of the rock. A village crouches below it near the water's edge. Situated on the left bank at a sharp bend this storied rock presents itself as the medieval castle of the Gorges.

"What is the story of the rock?" I inquire of the chief engineer who is always willing to vary the monotony of his duties with yarns of the Gorges.

"It's a tale like the killing of the goose that laid the golden egg. Near the summit is a hole through which, many years ago, there trickled down into a scooped out cavity enough rice for the daily needs of the monks who lived in the temple. This kept up for a number of years. Finally a lazy and greedy monk chipped the hole larger in order to secure two day's supply of food. The flow of rice abruptly ceased and never flowed down again," replied the chief engineer.

For the next thirty miles we have a maze of reefs and rapids in low water bordered with drying shingles out of which gold is being washed by bare-waisted prospectors. All vanish when the river rises to present a broad expanse of smooth but swift water. The canyon walls shift to a series of pyramidal peaks divided by foamy creeks tumbling into the Yangtze. Soon we are at the Iron Doorstep where the junks must cross to the other side by means of tying one end of the tracking rope to the rock and the other end to the mast just above the deck. All hands man the sweeps. Shouting in unison with the boat-captain's pounding of the drum but oblivious to the captain's screaming racing commands, the crew row furiously, sometimes stimulated with blows from the wet mop by the boatswain, until the boat has made slack water. At the right moment the rope is cast from the rock anchor unless there has been a miscue when the bamboo cable snaps with singing twang. Now and then the current carries an unlucky boat upon the protruding reefs below when fortunate is the captain who can get his cargo ashore before the junk sinks.

An hour's steaming finds us at Tientseshan, the Mount of Heaven near Fengtu. Here is a temple to the God of Hades who, on her wedding day, abducted a maiden and made her his queen. Her masked and clothed skeleton still sits enthroned beside her Lord of the Dead. Travellers continue to climb the hill to the temple to buy passports to heaven which are said to admit one through the Holy Gate without question. Stamped by the local Mandarin (Magistrate) and the Abbot, and with the seals of the Great Bear's seven stars, it costs only a dollar, certainly a valuable document for the money and for most people.

On the way up to the temple one can try his strength and skill on the Heartless Stone, a round rock mounted on a short post. Heartless Stone must have metal in it as the stone is very heavy for its size and, as the Chinese say, works against the will. Not many can rotate Heartless Stone.

A few miles above the Mount of Heaven are the great reefs of Buddha's Face and the Goddess of Mercy. They are just another group of rocks at low water but covered at thirty feet in summer, to create a hazardous rapid full of powerful whirlpools which cast steamers about like driftwood. The first steamboat to attempt the gorge at flood level rested forty days on the Buddha Face Reef where a maelstrom had tossed her.

Our next forty miles are uneventful but on another trip during the flood stage we enjoyed the tremendous whirlpools which always vary the monotony of climbing rapids. Arriving at the fair-sized city of Fuchou where a large tributary from the south pours into the gorge we are amazed to see boats with such crooked sterns that the after-deck is almost perpendicular to the fore-castle. Many reasons are given for this construction, the most common argument being that this type best rides the rapids around sharp bends among the cliffs. Probably the real reason is the legendary superstition of an ancient master, whose boat, built of green timbers which had warped into this twisted shape, was unusually lucky in riding the tortuous rapids of the Kongtan Ho.

The river has been broadening with less perilous swirls but it is here we see a junk perched on a rock by its upper end; a small boat is just leaving with goods and trackers from the doomed ves-sel. Before we are out of sight it appears as if the unfortunate boatman is clinging to the tip of the bow as the rescuers row to save him.

From Fuchou to Changsho taking two days by junk but only four hours by our steamer we pierce again a region of romance. Our Scotch engineer backed by the stimulus of his daily refresh-ments is anxious to tell us the best yarn of the Yangtze.

"Changsho, a warrior of renown and a nobleman, lived in these parts a hundred years ago. He had a lovely daughter who was sought by many lords in marriage. Her parents proud and jealous were loth to lose her. In the course of time the girl began to pine and fade away. Her parents could not discover the cause and much alarmed they sent for the wise old women but they could not cure her. Finally by much questioning of the girl the mother obtained the confession that a fairy named Moyu, in the shape of a man, visited her at midnight. Changsho was very angry but failed to find the fairy after prolonged searching. The mother continued to consult the oracles and at last received in-formation that her daughter's visitor was Yin Moyu who dwelt in a prominent rock at the mouth of a small sidestream which en-tered the Yangtze below the city. The father Changsho hired men to break up the rock, and when it was split in the center, a stream of blood gushed out. By this means Yin Moyu was destroyed but the tributary still bears his name. I can't say whether the maid recovered or not, but this is her father's city of Changsho."

Abounding in shingle banks and sand spits, the river widens

in many places during the next forty miles sometimes reaching four hundred yards or more. The gorge is transformed into gentle slopes of cultivated land with fields of pink, red, white and purple poppies. Only the low water rapid of Yelotse or Wild Mule Rapid is a little nasty because of a high wind. In the last stretch the slope roughens so gradually that we almost pass unnoticed the Brass Gong and Moonlight Gorges through which rushes a strong current that produces a booming sound during high water. Just beyond at Taipingkan on an island near the left bank sit three gold leafed Buddhas in niches at the top of a large rock. According to custom the central figure is the largest.

After a further eight miles around a great horseshoe bend the junk traveller heaves a sigh of relief. Here is the Harbour Master (Photo No. 13)—a huge Buddha encircled by a rampart of incense sticks created by the worship of countless Laobans rejoicing over the safe delivery of their ships from the river dragon of the gorges. Nearby is a second smaller gilded figure the assistant Harbour Master who secures less attention but yet is not forgotten. The sighting of this great stone Buddha is also the signal for the junk crew spokesman to remind their foreign guest, if they are lucky to have one, that the last feast of pork is due. At the passing of every major rapid he has been touched for a feed of pork which seems to be a daily occurence, until the end of the voyage, four to six weeks after leaving Ichang. After such a long risky voyage the foreigner pours out his last gift, supplemented by wine money, with thanksgiving.

On the left bank opposite the large Buddha is the Bridge of Sighs, three moss-covered spans of stone, so called because it was the last bridge crossed by students coming to Chungking for the ancient literary examinations.

Past the last Buddha on the right bank are large black rocks Tantseshih and Fukueishih where dwell the mother and wife of Yuwang the Father of the Yangtze. Introduced by these and smaller rocks the commanding heights of Chungking rise above us crowning a hilly peninsula formed by the curving Yangtze and its affluent the Kialing. Chungking seems to be a series of street steps and tiled terraces. Amidst a creaking city of anchored junks

our steamer pushes itself against the wharf and we leave the
Yangtze behind us.

Yet we will always dream of those days through twilight gorges
and over foaming rapids; of swaying copper-colored trackers
chanting "Hay-lo" when stepping easily with smooth water, or
panting "Hi-way" when bent double, creeping along like turtles;
of a hundred men tugging at the end of a bamboo cable while at
the other end hangs a junk, half a mile away, backing under the
rush of angry water like a spider at the end of his gauzy thread.
We will ever hear the shanties of the trackers punctured by the
furious tapping of the captain's drum as he signals the pace and
the pull; suddenly the medley is drowned by the twanging snap-
ping of the cable at the crest of the rapid which hurls the under-
manned craft into staggering downstream. In this crisis we see
the cooks jump up from the steaming rice-pot and every passenger on deck, including the opium-smoking soldiers comman-
deering a free ride, seize the long sweeps to row frantically, that
the screaming master at the rudder may regain control and bring
them all safe into a backwater rather than into the death-embrace
of the Yangtze Dragon.

In these upper Yangtze gorges for unrecorded centuries daring
youthful trackers have shivered in shadowy canyons, chanted to
the roar of raging rapids and whistling winds, and sweltered on
sun-baked rocks with quivering tread, inexorably conquering the
angry water for a wage of ten cents a day. Above and around them
in silent grandeur templed valleys and terraced heights recall tales
of superstitious exploits, which they tell to one another while eating their simple meal of rice and cabbage with a bit of pork.

Figure 3

Yak emerging tired after swimming the Yangtze at Lamdah, typifying the

Yangtze and the Yak

Figure 4

The Kingwo pulling itself over the Hsintan Rapids by cable fastened to rock

Figure 5
Wushan Gorge in the region of the Twelve Fantastic Peaks

Figure 6
Kongmingbai—layers of rock where history is inscribed and peeled off

Figure 7
Long Snake Reef in Windbox Gorge

Figure 8
Goose-tail Rock at western entrance of Wind-box Gorge during low water

Figure 9
Stinking Salt streams near Kueifu

Figure 10
Steamer beached on sandstone below terraced slopes near Kueifu

Figure 11
Temple of Changfei or Ethereal Bell of a Thousand Ages

Figure 12
Shihpaochai or Precious Stone Castle, above Wanhsien

Chapter III

RAMBLES THROUGH THE RED BASIN

Westward toward Tibet from Chungking, one may go through the Red Basin by land or around it by water. Overland it is a two to three days journey in an overcrowded bus or for the wealthier an overloaded, decrepit automobile. In spite of protests by the one who charters the bus the broken-down auto will carry extra guests under the guise of assistant drivers or guards to protect against bandits. Two of these extras will have precarious seats on the scarred fenders. Luggage will be tied and draped around the outside until it resembles the moving vehicle of a transient worker.

Once we took this trip overland and in two days of about twenty-eight hours driving covered the two hundred and eighty miles between Chungking and Chengtu. The road is a continuous process of dropping into deep mudholes and bumping over misplaced rocks. We swung around sharp curves so fast we did not have time to worry about precipices and we turned out so many times to push our car out of sticky red clay depressions that we did not tire of the cramped quarters in the back seat. In 1934 there were three of us each holding either a chronometer or a heavy camera upon our laps and Barbel our hunting dog in the back seat, three drivers in the front seat and two soldiers on the front bumpers. Our luck was not good. The river at Neichiang was high and we lost a day ferrying over the flood which was so swift that another auto slid between the banks and the improperly docked ferryboat into the river where it would stay until the water dropped. We needed the week's rest in Chengtu to recover as we prepared for a further three day's bus ride toward Yaan (Yachow).

Enroute from Chungking to Chengtu the bus and the auto have not entirely superseded the ancient mode of using nine days in a sedan chair or its poor relative the hwa-gan. The hwa-gan is only a rope seat, softened by bedding, slung between two light bamboo poles and carried by two to three men. The sedan chair is an enclosed chair to protect the occupant from the weather. Its two heavier bamboo poles are supported on the shoulders of three to six men. The sedan chair mode demands nine nights in bedbug inns aerated by opium smoke, but the leisurely scenic delights of everchanging landscape and the intimate insight into Chinese home life are a worthwhile compensation.

"Three foreign devils are going to Yaan and I am the number one boy. Mr. Dickinson has spoken to you about hiring men but if you will grant me a little favor say about twenty cents per man a day I will see that you get the contract in preference to another shop who have also put in a bid. I will also see that your men are properly tipped at the end of the trip so you can pay them less wages and thereby make a little profit in that way. The foreigners have put large sums of money into my hands," argued Lee our boy as he sat in the office of the shop which hires coolies for packing goods to other cities. The attempt to secure a portion of the profits is good Chinese custom and it is difficult to thwart this type of commission on the part of one's servants. Our cook Tsang is also said to have supported Lee in his endeavors but I was never able to find out how much, if any, our two men were able to wrangle out of the contract. One thing is certain, any servants utilized in the contract negotiations obtained some sort of fee for their connections with the deal.

Irrespective of the servant graft-commissions involved we hire our coolies to Yaan through the kindness of Mr. F. Dickinson, at whose home we were staying. Bus service is supposed to be possible to Yaan but it is an intensification of our previous bus sufferings and most of the time is only available for one third of the way. The river ferries are more numerous, bridges are frequently washed out, the mud is deeper and the steep grades of the hills treble the knocks of abused engines until they fail to knock once more. Mud and flood struggle with us five weary days in making the eighty miles from Chengtu to Yaan. We retrogress from bus to ricksha to hwagan to walking and the last was the surest and least annoying.

However, for real adventurous variety and restful romance between Chungking and Yaan one must go by river skirting the Red

Basin by using the Yangtze and its tributaries. By water from Chungking one has the choice of either a turtle-gaited junk which reaches Ipin (Suifu) in three weeks or of waiting two weeks for an unscheduled steamer and then arriving at the end of the third week in Ipin. By junk one wastes one's heart on possible bandits; by steamer one worries about board bills and lost time with the prospect of finally having to go by junk. One warlord suddenly commandeers the first steamer to transport troops to fight another warlord not far from the terminal of the steamer's route. Repair and custom taxes delay the next steamer from Wednesday to Thursday to Friday to Saturday until we hate to call on the agent and are equally reluctant for him to call on us in the "calming of our mind" business. The ship wins by two days over the junk which would have been the victor if rains had not created higher water in the Yangtze.

We hire a cook at Chungking, Tsang Wun Ch'in who served us faithfully for seven years. My wife Louise and two children John Kenneth and Marian Louise with myself and the cook give us five fares which enable us to rope off sufficient room for cots and baggage which have to pass the fourth inspection since leaving Hankow. In passing inspections and arrangement of passage we are aided by the indefatigable Gordon Jones whose family made our stay in Chungking pleasant and successful upon four different occasions enroute in and out of Tibet. Incidentally baggage inspection becomes a daily uncertainty at every stopping place on the river. Soft talk, melted in a little hard cash and a few cigarettes, put us through these trials until opening our trunks becomes only a gesture and the presentation of our calling cards. The ship's officers help their cause and ours by passing out cigarettes as the soldiers step on board.

Government officials with female escorts have engaged the ship's cabins to our delight as we prefer the purer air and the lack of insects found upon the deck. Tsang prepares our food in foreign fashion and we eat alone. In spite of the savory odors from the ship's food, the constant crowding of Chinese to secure a seat at the limited tables, do not arouse our envy for the other passengers have time to eat but twice a day.

No gorges above Chungking, such as exist below it, require

our constant watch lest we miss some scene for here there are only low muddy banks, rolling hills or an occasional bluff. Terraced farm land replaces cliffs and mountains; gurgling whirlpools substitute for leaping rapids. In this stretch to Ipin the Yangtze is wider, usually one fourth of a mile and broadening to one half a mile. It is so shallow in places during dry weather that steamers must draw less than six feet lest they plough into a mud-bank, and be as helpless, if not as endangered, as when snagging a jagged rock in the gorges.

Our ship ties up at night as our pilot needs daylight to follow the evershifting channel. Because of bandit-soldiers roaming the countryside we stop for the nights at the larger towns which often causes a short run. On the fourth evening we anchor at Nanki, a long walled town in the midst of a low marshy plain. Nanki has large beautiful temples which present exquisitely carved gates towering above the unbroken level of tiled shops and homes. The other three nights give us only quaint, sleepy towns except bustling Luchow, 135 miles above Chungking.

Five days up the swirling yellow waters find us at Ipin, 201 miles from Chungking. About ten o'clock in the misty morning our ship the Kiafoo enters the mouth of the Min river to turn around and then dock at the wharf. We are happy and relieved. Soldiers have crowded on for free rides at the various ports until the deck is an open can of sardines, oily and greasy. The incessant chatter and slopping of people who talk and eat all day and half the night has wrecked our nervous system. Then the sun shining hotter each day was slowly baking us under the canvas-covered deck like pigs in blankets.

Amidst a well-rounded missionary establishment of hospital, school, church and residences, Dr. C. E. Tompkins, a veteran of 27 years in China, treats 15,000 patients a year. He is unable to meet us at the boat because he is saving the life of a Chinese woman who protested the transfer of her soldier husband to another region, by taking opium. One and a half hours of artificial respiration with stimulants restores the woman although Dr. Tompkins despaired of saving her for a time. I watch the process for the technique may come in handy.

We sojourn a day in Ipin at the Tompkins' who engage a small river junk to transport ourselves and goods six days upriver to Loshan (Kiating). We delay another day to travel with the Pao Shang Tue or Protective Merchants Association who dispatch their junks in a group for protection. We share their security for the sum of ten dollars which probably represents a sizable portion of the sum paid by the merchants to the district ruler for soldiers. In any event we would need a soldier escort of three to one hundred men per day, the number depending upon the road risk from armed bands of freebooters. Tea money averages ten cents per soldier a day which makes our present arrangement cheaper and safer, as twenty soldiers a day is the average escort for a foreign caravan.

Our junk cost 35 dollars of Szechwan currency or 15 dollars in American money for the eighty-seven miles to Loshan, the trip to be made in six days. This is higher than the Chinese pay but we are rated as rich foreigners and must pay more to obtain the same accommodations, which also consists of food, if we desire to eat the rice and cabbage fare of captain and crew. In the convoy are thirteen other boats some larger but none smaller than ours. One boat contains goods for the missionaries at Chengtu but we are the only foreigners amidst a multitude of Chinese.

Our goods fill most of the hold below deck. The captain as usual has promised that no other goods will be loaded upon the boat but we know and he knows that this promise is to keep him from overloading the boat, since we can cast out other goods when the boat has reached the proper level. We find it wise to ignore the presence of sundry baggage, an occasional passenger or of smuggled contraband passing through customs with the exempted foreigner's goods. Besides the crew of eight men as trackers, the laoban or captain, the cook, the bowsman and two soldiers, we have a runner with the official pass from the Mayor of Ipin. This runner is charged with the protection and any necessary aid needed by us to our destination.

We watch the cook formally sprinkle the blood of the freshly killed cock over the bows of the junk while the men put aboard a new bamboo rope. It is a bright day in the middle of May when

we cast off. Our crew of six men row across the Min to the left
bank and the trackers are put ashore to pull the boat on its tedi-
ous trip upstream. Our largest boat has twenty-five trackers but
additional men are hired for the dangerous rapids; at one time
we had thirteen men tracking. In addition to the trackers each
boat has a steersman who is usually the captain and often the
owner of the craft. In the bow is the bowsman who on the smaller
craft as our own acts as cook in the intervals of peaceful waters
but in dangerous places he drops the cleaver and grabs the boat-
hook to keep us off the rocks, to sound the depth of water in the
shallows or pull us around a sharp cliff. On the larger junks a
third boatman assists the bowsman and does the cooking. The
bowsman wields a bamboo pole about fifteen feet long and shod
with an iron point and an iron hook. In the course of centuries
the iron poles of the river boatmen have made millions of holes
in the sandstone rocks lining the shore, pockmarking the cliffs in
rows in accordance with the level of the water. The bowsman and
cook will also handle the bowsweep—a long spar 25 feet long
with two narrow, thick blades at its water-end. The bowsweep is
essential in properly heading the boat to the current in dangerous waters, especially in going downstream.

Each of the junks in our Pao Shang Tue, including our own,
has a small red flag with Chinese characters to aid in identifica-
tion, not only among ourselves, but also to would-be bandits who
otherwise could not know we had paid the proper protection
money. This is my analysis of the protection by the merchants
associations as the junks, under the stress of current and unavoidable delays of wind and men, soon become widely scattered,
and stretch along the river for miles, and, interspersed with miscellaneous craft, will be unable to aid one another in the event of
a bandit attack. I easily recognize that our two sometimes unarmed soldiers were largely front. They change with every magistrate who uses his discretion regarding arms as he might lose them
to the bandits.

Our boat is about 35 feet long, about eight feet wide and draws
about 14 inches to two feet when fully loaded (Photo No. 14).
The hold is composed of six or seven bulkheads which are three
feet deep so at the bow we are about one foot above the water. It

is said to be made of a laurel evergreen called Lanmu, a fine yellow hardwood and caulked with a mixture of wood oil, lime and chopped hemp. Its capacity is about 6 tons downstream and 3 tons upstream. The bottom is flat and the bow gradually slopes to a high stern so that we resemble a Dutch wooden shoe tied to a cord, when the trackers are pulling us upstream. Bamboo mats, in circular form, roof over the 15 feet amidships making a covered section seven feet wide and six feet high where we live in comfort; the crew eat and sleep in the twelve foot length of bow, and in the stern whose last few feet are also roofed with bamboo mats. The long wooden handle of the rudder projects beyond the stern cabin where it is manipulated by the captain perched on a bench high enough for him to see over both mat roofs. Here the captain screams out his curses, pounds his drum, and in dangerous spots dances up and down like a maniac while we loll in blissful laziness upon the foredeck.

We become accustomed to letting our life hang by a thread for our long braided bamboo cable not much over a fourth of an inch in diameter sometimes stretches more than a quarter of a mile long and the trackers may be out of sight in a low spot or around the slope of a hill. The biggest cables for the largest junks on the Min River are about two inches in diameter and a half mile long, and they support a craft eighty-five feet long carrying fifty tons. A new rope is always purchased at the beginning of a trip as they are not available at many intermediate points. The latest old rope is carried along as a spare. Most of the time the greater part of the length lies curled upon the stern as a few hundred feet usually suffice for ordinary water and depth. For the longer lengths one of the trackers will support the cable in the middle for small craft such as ours but a sampan is used for the larger junks.

One end of the cable is attached to a round projecting beam that crosses the width of the boat to the rear of the center line and about fifteen feet from the stern. From here it runs diagonally over our mast roof through a bamboo ring which slides up and down on a mast, as the heighth of the shore demands. In the passing of rapids the cable is brought down and tied to the mast near its base. Sometimes the Min river at this low water season is so shallow that our craft must be steered far from the bank as the trackers wade through the water (Photo No. 15). Then the long cable sinks into the water so that to the casual observer a distant craft may seem to have no connection to the shore, for the trackers, bent double, may be hidden by bushes and bluffs.

Slowly (the average tracking speed is two miles an hour in ordinary water and on some days ten miles is creditable), so slowly that at times our onward movement cannot be detected with the eye, our trackers crawl upstream to the measured cadence of swinging chants. Each man has a breast and shoulder strap whose two ends are attached to a toggle which is so curled once around the cable that it is quickly attached and easily detached. The boss tracker runs up and down the cable to keep it free from obstructions and at intervals taps the taut tugs to sense the pull of each tracker. If his light bamboo whip detects slackness it comes down lightly upon the back of the tracker.

The strain and pace are set by the captain from his perch by voice and drum as he aids the crew with his rudder twisting it so as to push against the changing current. Within sound of his voice the captain lets loose a torrent of language most of which (fortunately) my command of Chinese is not able to decipher. Beyond range of his shouts and amidst the noise of boiling rapids the captain taps his commands upon a drum. "Stop" is a short sharp beat; "slow" is indicated by a slow even rhythm; and "full speed" is called for by constant rapid drumming. The bowsman must also be alert, pushing or pulling with his pole in a swift current close to shore or poling the bottom when the water is shallow and fast.

The chanting of the trackers is musical with a sad and weary note. As they step lively along in placid reaches "Haylo" resounds in unison to be snappily broken by the leader who sings out what sounds like "I ay ay hay ay" to which the rest respond with a prolonged long a and then an oh. A pause and then the continuous repetition of "haylo" will sound again. Sometimes they will vary this with responding to the leader's cry by an "oh" with a secondary responser shouting "oh ho" rising up and down in tone. Then all repeat "Oh lah hway go, Oh lah dao, Gao toh." To this the leader responds with "Oh ay" and the rest repeat the long chant above. When the current is strong their tune changes to one of slower rhythm alternating "i-way and hi-way" in different pitches. In the swiftest currents all trackers must get down on all "fours" using the hands to grasp rocks and brush, then straining every muscle they make steady jerks in unison and emit a groaning sound, and as the boat breaks into easier water again they shout "i-e" in unison as if relieved from strain. Another less frequent call when walking slowly sounds like "ay-chow" alternated with "ow-ee."

In the dangerous whirlpools and rapids the encouraging shouts of the pilot-captain will change to frothy cursing and frenzied pounding on the drum, and sometimes in his rage he will dance up and down on his bench and pound his fist upon the roof of the mat-shed, especially if the trackers slacken their straining tug with the current at a critical point. Surmounting the Chukent'an (Rapids) the junk immediately ahead smashes her rudder against a rock. Instantly rendered unmanageable the boat swings broadside to the current and jerks its cable from the trackers who are thrown in all directions but released by their easily detached toggles. The careening boat is carried swiftly downstream and plunges into our cable jerking it from our trackers. The execrations of our pilot now changes to fear and all of us spring up to wield the oars in order to keep the boat from going on the rocks. I grab an oar and even the lethargic Chinese soldiers pale and spring up to aid the bowsman and myself in rowing. Our efforts do not have much rhythm but enable the pilot to control the boat with the rudder, keeping us in deep water until we pass the projecting rocks and pull to shore far below, at least a quarter of a mile downstream from the rapids. The boat with the broken rudder manages to bring itself to shore a mile below the rapids. When our craft touches shore the brave soldier escort and our servants hop out and walk the next few miles but we stick to our junk and ride the rapids as our trackers with resigned countenances do their work over again. Perhaps the sprinkling of rice by our bowsman upon the boiling waters to insure a safe passage enables us to surmount the raging rapids, at least it has a morale effect upon our trackers and captain.

We walk some of the time and during one of these strolls along

swift waters the cable of the boat ahead of ours breaks with a
singing, sickening twang which we have never forgotten. Our captain by skillful maneuvers shoots out into the middle of the Min
and misses the descending boat. We miss the thrill of riding on
our boat as she loses an hour of tracking but we still hear the
maniacal shoutings of the pilot and the warring drum beats as he
dances with rage up and down on his plank throne. We enjoy the
antics of the pilot but pity the trackers who are paid by the trip.
The bamboo cables are life-lines to them.

The life and labors of the trackers is fearfully hard and monotonous. They receive two Chinese dollars (less than one in American money) and their food for this trip, which going up and down
will take ten days. For ten to fourteen hours they must pull like
horses on the bobbing cable. When pulling upstream they eat
five times a day, a meal that usually consists of rice and cabbage
made palatable with oils and peppers. Occasionally they have
horse-beans, cucumbers or greens. Pork may come once a week
depending upon the generosity of the boat-renter. We give them
three pork feeds during the six days, one for each of the major
rapids, and also extra tips at the end of the journey. Going downstream the pulling of the oars to keep the boat in the current requires less strength so the trackers eat but three times a day. Upstream they get no rest from the everlasting tracking except when
they must pile quickly into the boat and row to the opposite shore
to avoid bluffs or to seek the least dangerous channel of a rapid.
Tracking upstream they wear only a loin cloth or short pants but
when moving sedately downstream their white turbans, blue jeans
and naked brown chests are a colorful contrast as they chant while
rocking backward and forward on their oars.

Junkmen have their own deity. This patron saint is Chen
Chiang Wang Yeh or River-guarding King a deified pirate who
roamed over Tungting Lake south of Hankow in the twelfth century. He was born about 1127 and during a short life of some 35
years defied all forces sent against him boasting that he could only
be captured by air. He is reputed to have invented the paddle
wheel. Finally defeated by Gen Yo Fei he committed suicide by
jumping into Tungting Lake. When junkmen die a letter is sent,
by a ritual of burning the missive with fire, to the Lord of the

Dead who lives at the temple of Tientseshan at Fengtu which is on the Yangtze above Wanhsien. It is said that some courses of rivers are so dangerous that providing a coffin is part of the contract in the hiring of trackers.

Between Ipin and Loshan the Min river courses through rolling plains and low mountains of red sandstone with a few of granitic formation. The river has cut through many of these hills to form high bluffs reaching a height of five hundred feet above the water. In the face of many red sandstone cliffs are square caves which were improved by the ancient settlers of this region and used as tombs. These caves are carved around their openings and on their walls with figures of animals resembling bulls and with vehicles like the chariots of Egypt. The openings may be narrow but some extend back for a hundred feet broadening out into large rooms connected by narrow passages. In the rooms along the walls are niches cut out the size of a coffin in which the dead are placed. Objects were undoubtedly deposited with the corpse but during the many intervening centuries the graves have been robbed of everything including the skeletons. The present day Chinese claim they are Mantze graves but evidence indicates they were carved by sons of Han or Chinese who lived some two thousand years ago but were later exterminated and knowledge of their culture forgotten. In addition to the Mantze tombs the cliffs are the setting of carved Buddhas, especially on the third day out of Ipin, where the left face of the precipices has a long row of gaudy Buddhas whose red, yellow and white tints offer a brilliant contrast to the coarse-grained red sandstone.

At the end of the fourth day we tie up at Chukentan pounding our "stick in the mud anchor" in firmly and sparring the boat to shore (two long poles tied to boat and a stake on shore) against the current. We walk the plank ashore and stroll through a bazaar built on poles above the river. A mile inland we take a gondola across a tiny lake which is only a willow-lined arm of the Min river and debark on the opposite side amidst a multitude of salt derricks, some of which must reach seventy-five feet in height. Borings take several years and some of the wells are over two thousand feet deep. We watch the boring of a well. The jumper or long heavy drill is fastened to a bamboo rope attached to one arm of a lever; the weight of three men who step on the other arm raises the instrument; the men leap off nimbly onto a nearby narrow platform and the jumper plunges downward. A fourth man twists the rope as the jumper is lifted and the unwinding gives a rotary motion, as the jumper falls, and aids in boring through the rock.

We also investigate the pumping of the brine to the surface. Inside each derrick near the base is a wheel four feet in diameter over which a flat bamboo cable, that is attached at one end to a salt bamboo tube-bucket, leads into a nearby shed. We go inside the shed and discover that the flat cable is winding around a huge cyclinder about fifteen feet in diameter and twelve feet high. Two stolid water buffalos prodded by the stick of a small urchin are pulling the cylinder around on its axis and pulling up the salt bucket. The bamboo cable is made of flat bamboo strip one and a half inches wide and this particular one is twelve hundred feet long, others are longer according to the depth of the well. When the bucket reaches the top the buffalo are unhitched and permitted to rest while the cable descends checked by a bamboo brake. The bucket is a bamboo cylinder tube about seventy-five feet long and three inches in diameter capable of holding ten to fifteen gallons of brine. When the tube arrives above the surface a man opens a valve at the bottom and the brine flows into a trough from which bamboo tubes convey it to large iron kettles or vats. The brine is first reduced in the iron kettles by a fire of coal and then the thicker solution is evaporated to salt in clay-lined iron caldrons about six feet in diameter. Gas comes from some of the wells and this may be used in rendering the salt; burning from clay-lined bamboo tubes tipped with iron.

Besides the numerous junks being towed up the river or moving sedately downstream to the chanting of oarsmen we see a number of bamboo rafts loaded with large earthenware jars. These jars, holding fifty gallons each, are full of wine from Ipin and are being tracked as far as Yaan and Chengtu. When we cast our eyes shoreward there are lines of people on the trails some carrying loads on their backs, others have balanced baskets on each end of a shoulder pole and still others rocking sleeping people in hwagans. Once a gorgeous red sedan chair moves toward a village car-

rying a hidden bride; another time we gaze at a huge black lac-
quered coffin of hemlock wood, whose one end is decorated with a
scorpion and the other end painted with five bats in a circle.

Life on the houseboat is placid but cramped. In our middle
covered section, five feet of the length is used by our cook for
kitchen and his quarters. After we put our three cots and personal
luggage in the remaining space there is little room left, but still
more than we had on the steamer Kiafoo. We move out and sit
on the open bow which is crowded during the day in the eating
of five meals and at night as a sleeping place for the crew. At
night the bow is covered with mats supported by a hastily as-
sembled but firm bamboo framework which is quickly removed
in the morning and the mats slid over our mat roof. The stern is
the quarters for the captain and our two or three Chinese soldiers
who spend part of the day lying on their straw mats smoking
opium whose sickening fumes are usually carried downstream
from us.

For six days our motley crew clothed in scanty shorts, which
they discard when the water is deep, track up the Min river.
Every two or three hours we tie up at the bank when the crew,
crowding the forecastle, shovel in scoops of rice, flavored by sour
cabbage tidbits. Then off again we go while the bowsman washes
the utensils and rinses a new batch of rice in the river. Soon the
rice is boiling and later steaming, on the iron tripod set over a
wood fire enclosed in a large earthen jar in the forward compart-
ment, where the flooring has been removed for that purpose. We
sit serenely in the placid stretches; but strain with the crew and
share the anxiety of the captain in rough waters. We are happy
to give an extra largess in addition to the final pork feed to the
boatmen as we tie up in Loshan tanned and unrobed.

While Louise and the children John K. and Marian L. rest and
prepare in Loshan for the next stages, residing with the L. A. Lovegrens of the Baptist Mission, I make a hurried trip to Chengtu.
We had planned to buy sugar, soap and other supplies there
which could be more cheaply and conveniently bought than either
farther east or west. I buy a ticket for the bus but find at the last
minute, after waiting two days, that he local war-lord has com-
mandeered it for his soldiers. Not to be delayed I hire a ricksha at

once and set out intending to change runners when my first man
tires. To my amazement my runner, a young and strong man, insists on pulling me the first forty miles over a red clay road fairly
smooth but slightly slippery. After a night's lodging with the
China Inland Missionary family of G. Vinden I set out again. I
ride by ricksha for ten miles, ferry over a river and catch a bus
for Chengtu.

Staying on the West China Union University campus with the
Daniel Dyes I spend two hectic days buying goods and drinking
tea in varied visits with the missionaries. Chartering a small junk
to carry myself and goods down the Min river to Loshan I travel
hard for two days sleeping in my clothes on soft cypress boards
covered simply by a thin straw mat about one-half inch thick.
The mystery of a foggy night and the beauty of bamboo water
wheels, ranging from forty to seventy feet in diameter, turning,
through the force of the current, to dump troughs of water into
sluices for irrigation, are forever etched in my memory. The
creaking of these enormous water-wheels and the boiling gurgles
of whirlpools in the shallow river lightened my restless turnings to
find soft spots in the wooden deck.

On the 30th of May we take a last glance at the huge, 150
foot high sandstone Buddha of Loshan and start northwest to Yaan
or Yachow. The family are in sedan chairs and I walk, planning
to hire local hwagans, but find it impossible to hire hwagans
quickly and keep up with the chairs, so my feet support me most
of the way. We follow the Ya river, crossing it by ferry seven
times in the three-day trip. It is hot and tiring plodding through
the dust alongside rice fields, or on the narrow rocky paths lined
with bamboo whose lines are graceful but whose shade is thin.

Robber bands operate constantly at intervals between Loshan
and Yaan and the various towns are held accountable for the
safety of the road. The town fathers utilize this factor to their profit and undoubtedly are in league with the bandits when it is possible to do so with secrecy and impunity. The evening of the
second day we lodge overnight at Loba where our yamen runner
from the officials of Loshan cooperated with the local headmen of
Loba to scare and fleece us. They recite a long tale of the robbers
and how on the next day a large escort will be necessary. We

agree to take escort and pay a suitable price but the local headmen are not satisfied with a reasonable share of tea money which will come to them by an escort of ten soldiers. I state my terms and go to bed but they wrangle most of the night with my yamen runner and finally part in anger. My runner asks me if we shall wait for a larger escort. I answer, "No, we will take a chance and see what happens." We guess right and no robbers are seen.

Our third day's journey is over rougher country which has changed from the rice plains of the first day to rolling reddish hills. The river is swifter and its channel is often in narrow defiles which now and then force us to mount a thousand feet over a shoulder. We now understand why it takes rafts so long to make the upward trip in high water when the swollen river rushes with terrific speed forcing rafts to dock in harbors until the flood subsides. We are gradually mounting into the foothills of the Tibetan Plateau and by the end of the day reach an elevation of two thousand feet above sea level. We enter Yaan with the feeling that we are nearing the Land of Snow.

Figure 13
Harbour Master Buddha below Chungking

Figure 14
Our Min River junk being tracked from Ipin to Loshan. My wife and children,
John and Marian, in doorway

Chapter IV

THE TEA ROAD TO TIBET

The Tea Road to Tibet is one hundred and sixty miles of hot, red, muddy trail in summer and chilly, red, dusty track in winter. Stones, laid perhaps a thousand years ago, form a great road (in Chinese description) upon which shivering blue-clothed coolies and bony, staggering ponies tread with caution. Once the stones were packed firm and level with red earth, but now uprooted they protrude like unnumerable ant-hills, and if the unwary foot slips off, it plunges deep into a slimy sucking hole. The heavily laden tea-carrier must not slide off a stone for fear of breaking a leg or being crushed beneath a falling load.

Years ago it is reported that eight hundred coolies a day left Yaan but in 1929 careful investigation showed less than two hundred and fifty leaving the city each day. Stiffer competition from India and Yunnan and unsettled political conditions on the border must account for the reduction from the probably exaggerated previous number. In spite of this decline Yaan is still the foremost tea port of China and by its trails to Tachienlu (Kangting) the chief tea road terminal to Tibet.

Yaan is the tea collecting center for an area not less than a hundred miles in diameter. The city lies at the bottom of a bowl on a small triangular plain with the Chingchi stream on one side and the Yungching river as a curved hypotenuse, while swiftly rising hills form the third boundary. To the east the red hills are lower with gentle outlines placing Yaan at the base of a rising plateau or at the border of the foot-hills which ascend to the Tibetan plateau. The Yungching and Chingchi Rivers emerge from mountain clefts and unite to form the Ya River which disappears into a steep canyon. Thus Yaan is bottled up between high walls and one is at its gates before it is seen. The population in the 1930's was estimated at thirty thousand. The Ya here is twelve hundred feet wide in high water. The current is swift and the water deep so that it is crossed by ferry in summer and by a pontoon bridge at low water in winter. The city is supported not only by the tea trade which originates here but also by the receiving and forwarding of salt, iron ore, coal and medicinal roots. The medicines come from Tibet but the others are produced in nearby Chinese regions.

The tea plants which grow upon the hillsides surrounding Yaan for several day's distance are bushes with many shoots reaching to ten feet in height. The leaves are dark green and thick, oval-shaped and with pointed tips. The bark is light grey and smooth. The flowers about the size of a half dollar are white with large yellow centers reminding one of small magnolia blossoms as the petals are rather thick. The tea leaves are picked once a year in April and May.

We visit a tea factory covering two acres of ground within the city. Here two hundred men ferment the tea leaves in piles and mix the leaves with twigs, some from other plants which give the characteristic red or yellow color of the different brands. After firing and then steaming this mixture is baled into solid bricks with sprinklings of rice water. A long wooden shute supports a bamboo-woven case lined with paper into which the tea is compressed by an iron-shod ramrod. The process is similar to baling hay in the United States. After a slight drying over a fire the tea is ready for sale.

Each case contains four bricks separated by slips of paper. The bricks average 10x7x4 inches and weigh about five and one-half English pounds. Each bale weighs between 21 and 23 pounds and one man ordinarily carries eight to thirteen bales piled one above the other. There are said to be records of men bearing twenty-two bales but I never saw over fifteen and that number towers high above the coolie's head like a wall. The bales are strapped to a framework placed upon a waist-high base. The inner side of the frame curves like a man's back and must be properly balanced for once tipped over the bales must be unbound and retied (Photo No. 16).

The tea load for the average coolie weighs from 210 to 230 pounds in addition to the wooden framework of several pounds and the personal luggage consisting of food and an extra jacket for the cold or higher altitudes. The coolie rents a heavy blanket at night during winter as his clothing is light, only a pair of cotton shorts with a cotton jacket. In his hand is a T-shaped iron shod stick of the right length to shift the weight of his load at the frequent resting places. These iron-pointed sticks have left millions of holes in the stones on this tea road to Tibet. The carrier bears his immense burden on a diet of corn meal made into a dry cake an inch to an inch and a half in thickness and the diameter of a dinner plate. The carrier tucks one or two of these cakes amongst the thongs of his bales and plods six to ten miles a day to the next inn for a night's rest, two warm meals and fresh cakes for tomorrow's lunch.

The carriers are paid by the bale, receiving eight thousand cash, about forty-five cents American for the one hundred and fifty miles to Tachienlu. He requires fifteen to twenty days, depending upon his load and the weather, to Tachienlu, and four to eight days to return, contingent upon the short hauls of iron or coal near Yungching Hsien, or of zinc and lead from Chingchi Hsien, for all or part of the way to Yaan. The low wages which average about fifteen cents a day based on the usual time of one month for a round trip restrict the diet of tea coolies to cornmeal, the cheapest food on the border. Chair bearers fare better, receiving forty cents a day when on the road but periods of idleness may sometimes last long enough to eat up their higher wage.

Tea is a main source of internal revenue making Yaan the seat of the warlord instead of Tachienlu, the designated capital of Sikang. Liu Wen Huei has controlled this province since about 1925 when he became the Warden of the Marches following the ousting of Chen Hsia Ling. The Yaan tax of one ounce of silver per five bales nets the government over 250,000 Chinese dollars a year. This initial tax is supplemented by an export tax at every major city enroute. Whereas a bale of tea costs one Chinese dollar in Yaan, it becomes $2.40 cents or six rupees in Tachienlu. Four bricks to the bale at one and a half rupees in Tachienlu becomes three rupees to the brick in Batang and six in Lhasa. This is the price of the cheaper red tea but the yellow brand is twenty-five percent higher.

The coolie bearing ten bales can compete successfully against the small bony horses who are sometimes used between Yaan and Tachienlu. The horse carries eight bales, four on a side, but in the airless heights of Tibet the coolie yields to the yak who takes but six bales. The yak however lives off the country's grass which is free. In Tachienlu the bales are dismantled and twelve bricks are sewn into a wet yak skin which dries into a hard tight covering that will protect the tea from the blows of handling and weather indefinitely.

We hire sixty animals (small horses and mules of about six hundred pounds weight) for our loads, six carriers for my wife Louise, and four bearers for the double chair for our son John Kenneth five years old and our daughter Marian Louise two years old. The children sit opposite each other with a narrow table between them for holding toys. I am riding a staggering-gaited horse from the caravan animals, changing each morning since both the beast and I can only stand each other for one day. Horses and men cost about the same, eighty cents Chinese for a horse and one dollar for a man.

There is the usual disorder of departure with the caravan men endlessly wrangling about the weight of the loads, and the chairmen balancing their bags containing opium and tobacco now on this side of the chair and now on the other before they are satisfied it will not wear their shoulders unduly. Foreign guests are comparatively frequent in Yaan so hostesses bid us farewell at the compound gates, and hosts at the city walls. We have been hospitably entertained at our various stop-overs in this city by the Fred Smiths, the R. L. Crooks, and Miss Carrie Shurtleff. All have spent many years of Christian service in Yachow under the auspices of the American Baptist Foreign Missionary Society.

It is the tenth of June 1929 as we leave the city wall behind us to strike westward into the land of mountains. We climb up a steep stone stairway down which clatters carriers of huge iron pots called Go and baskets of hard glassy coal, loads weighing one hundred and fifty pounds brought from points forty miles to the west. At the top of the steps we turn for our last glimpse of the Red Basin and then leave Yaan out of sight below and behind us to face upward and tread the dried blood-red sandstone and clay of the tea road. Past fields of rice and corn and through grassy

pastureland of scattered shrubs and trees of horsetail pines and
Cunningham firs, we bow beneath Pailou or memorial arches of
exquisitely carved red standstone erected to long-lived widows who
did not remarry. Beyond this tiny plateau we enter winding valleys lined by fairly steep sandstone hills five hundred to fifteen
hundred feet high. In the lowest parts are rice paddies and the
higher slopes grow corn between areas of scrub, broken now and
then by clumps of wavy, graceful bamboo. Such a vista followed
us through the first day and until we crossed the first pass.

I was to make this same trip with slight variations of route for
three more times, once in November 1932, again in August 1934
and lastly in October 1935, two journeys in the monsoon and two
in the dry season. This account will combine all four trips although my companions were never the same and there was new
ground broken during the last journey. Chinese travelling is divided into regular stages but the vicissitudes of men and climate did
not always enable us to make the regular stages yet I lodged often
enough in the same towns and the same inns to find myself recognized by familiar landlords. Failure to reach the regular stage-inn
invariably retarded the caravan until we reached the proper stopping place when we would fall into the established routine. The
regulation stages are more fixed when passes are to be surmounted
and where the population is scant. Both of these factors operate
in mountainous country. Consequently four of the cities at the
bottoms of the two high passes are prosperous from nourishing caravans which have been worn out by long ascents and descents.

Our first night we rest but 37 lee (3 lee to the mile on level
ground and 5 lee on steep ascents) distant at Kuanyinpu whose
new inn has not yet become so populated by fleas and bedbugs
who must also live off the caravan trade. The end of the first
regular stage is at Malichang which is 67 lee from Yaan but is
rarely reached in the turmoil of an unavoidable late start. From
the beginning one might as well be reconciled to losing one day
but such a prospect upsets the American novice with his ideas of
railroad split-second efficiency. I soon resign myself and join the
Orient in the rut of "Go rihtze" or "getting through the day."
Spasmodic rain and deep mud do not hinder from reaching our
first day's inn before dark but five years later we are delayed

until starlight, hoisting caravan animals by the tail out of belly-deep bogs.

After twenty lee beyond Malichang on our second day we pass through the clean thriving city of Yungching Hsien whose numerous forges remind us we are in the center of the iron and coal-bearing sandstone. The blacksmiths cast iron into huge Go, the iron kettles, seen in the open windows of all inns and used twenty hours a day for frying pork, vegetables and corn cakes. Yungching is the seat of the county or Hsien and arriving on market day we can scarcely weave our way through the street vendors and buyers who use the main street for their business transactions. Everybody wants to see the golden-haired foreign devils and when we eat dinner the landlord guards the doorway to keep the surplus crowd out.

The narrow basin is broad enough here for the Yungching river to twist around so I encounter the stream flowing in the opposite direction than what I expect and only on another trip do I unravel its course and distinguish a tributary which joins it from the southwest. The river has a wide gravelly bed about two hundred feet wide with a channel of one hundred and twenty feet in width. It is shallow and fordable in the wide places except after rains. We cross it on a long iron suspension bridge.

Yungching Hsien was remembered later for an incident which revealed to us the Chinese character, and also held us up one morning for several hours. Creditors seized three animals of our head muleteer pending settlement of a twenty dollar debt which he had incurred upon a previous trip. Our muleteer satisfied the claim in some manner but tried to disguise the incident by asserting that the animals had strayed while feeding upon the mountainside. I was never sure of the truth of any part of this incident for this debt impediment threw the stage schedule back into the proper rhythm, since we had lost the customary time for the first day by the usual late start.

Our third day is a steady muddy climb following the course of the Yungching stream to where it is joined by the Tahsiang tributary from the southwest. On our third journey, some five lee beyond Shuitzepu we paid out ten dollars to thirty people for the repair of a landslide which had swept away one hundred feet of

road. The official readily consented to our request for the clearing of the road. The people ordinarily would be compelled to do it
for nothing sooner or later but we happened along at the opportune time to give them a day's wages for a few hours work.

We continue slowly upward sliding in yellow mud, drenched by
rain and switched by the wet branches of brush which had over-
grown the road. The monsoon rains are in full strength and we
resign ourselves to a wet, sloppy road. Fog envelopes us as we
ascend, hiding the dark green foliage and grey bark of slender
evergreens. We trace the Tahsiang tributary of the Yungching
river for fifty lee beyond Yungching Hsien to Hwangnipu or Yellow Mud shop which lives up to its name for the leaky roof wets
the clay earth of the partially dismantled wooden floor and we
continue to tramp in mud while breathing smoke instead of foggy
fresh air. Hwangnipu (elevation 3700 feet) is the last town below
the pass and is full of caravans. Above are only wretched one-
room shacks jammed with tea carriers and their helpers who have
been hired to carry part of the enormous burdens over this highest
pass.

On the morrow it rains all day as we ford the torrents of the
Yungching headwaters or walk foot-wide planks when the streams
are narrow and deep. We crawl anxiously around dangerous
crevasses where the earth is slowly sliding away. We ascend slippery stone stairways and rise during the day about fifty-six hundred feet in a distance of fifty lee (16 miles) to top the granitic
Tahsiang Ling (Great Minister's Range). Flurries of wet snow and
a bitter wind chills the children to tears and we hurry over the
pass 9400 feet high. I promise the family warmer weather which
we obtain by a rapid descent of fifteen lee, passing a tea shop
resting place, to reach the warmth of Chingchi Hsien.

The tea shops, especially those along the caravan trails, are a
Szechwan institution which deserves special remarks. A large
room whose front side of movable planks is entirely removed during the day, discloses a jumbled mass of square tables and chairs
(or benches in the poorer shops). For a petty cash coin the attendant drops a few tea leaves in the handleless cup and pours in
hot water, covering the liquid with a lid fitting inside the rim of
the cup. This cover keeps the tea hot and permits sipping with-

out removal of the lid which holds back the now swollen tea
leaves. The attendant moves constantly among the guests refilling
the cups but not replenishing the tea leaves unless more money
is paid, or a new customer arrives. The coolie or merchant can
sit all day smoking his pipe, gossiping, and drinking tea from one
deposit of leaves, and eating his own transported lunch without
censure. Besides being the meeting place for men in the transac-
tion of business, like the American country grocery store, it is the
rendevous of loafers and ne'er-do-wells.

Chingchi Hsien is an imposingly placed city of five thousand
population. Crowning a plateau whose three sides have been cut
down by streams into high steep bluffs which have been reinforced by walls fifteen feet high, the city, perched upon the edges
of such precipitious faces, is easily approached only from the direction of Tahsiang Ling Pass. On this side only the wall protects the
city. The city wall encloses all of the fields upon the plateau and
attains a circumference of two and one third miles. Chingchi
Hsien has been a strategic outpost for centuries against wild tribes
from the south and west some of whom, as the Lolos across the
Tung river, are still independent of Chinese control. Chungchi
Hsien however lacks the luxuriant vegetation of Yungching Hsien.
At the Tahsiang Ling Pass we left the bamboo, the yellow roses,
the columbines, the wild strawberries and a maze of other plants
to descend into a barren country of grass and scattered thorny
shrubs. From now on we have only the summer monsoon to produce vegetation, for most of the year there is no rain.

In the morning we pull out of the inn which was to shelter me
two more times; and, in a drizzle which accompanied us all day,
we descend the steep southerly sandstone bluff. Crossing a swollen torrent we round a barren range of red sticky clay and eventually turn northwest. Narrow beams, slippery with tracked lumps
of wet clay, serve as temporary bridges. When the path is not
sliding clay it is greasy round stones which are less passable on
the frequent inclines than on the level stretches. Our chairmen
fall and call the stones the sons of turtles. My horse slides and
stumbles so I keep my feet out of the stirrups.

After turning northwest, short fifteen lee of Fuchuang, we trace
a small stream to its mouth—the Liusha river, which is now an

immense flood flowing southeast to reach the Tung river, about a day's journey distant. In the dry season the Liusha is barely fifty feet wide and easily fordable but now its fills the lower part of the valley and so broad and deep that for a short time we think we have strayed into the valley of the Tung. All day for 55 lee farther we detour washouts and avalanches with only two horses killed by falling off a cliff (at least they fell and we paid for two).

We arrive at Nitou shortly before dark but our bedding and food are far behind. We eat a Chinese meal from the landlord's kitchen and doze in our clothes on straw mats. The cry is raised at midnight that our bedding has come but investigation proves that it is in an inn, a quarter of a mile away at the other end of the one long street which comprises three-fourths of Nitou. I set out and by the use of persuasion, reinforced by cash, lure the tired carrier to our inn. We bed down after midnight but I do not disturb the others' sleep by the probability that we are doomed to a day's rest in this weatherbeaten inn.

A day with a start of bad weather and a scattered caravan with men and animals worn out invariably means a day of rest. Trying to force them to live up to their contract or to go on creats exasperating delays and if one starts, something always happens, such as straying animals, sick carriers, or some of the chairmen cannot be located. If herculean efforts and extra rewards finally get part of the caravan started, only a partial stage is made, and it takes the second day to reach the end of the regular stage where those, who rested a day, join you, and you feel that you have lost face in addition to your temper. When a high pass, such as faced us, is the day's task, men and multeers will argue with you until it is too late to start.

My past experience does not deceive me so when the head muleteer comes to argue me into a day of rest, I listen patiently for half an hour and then assent without a word only stating we must leave the next day. The muleteer registers a look of astonishment at so easy a conquest, changing to admiration with my last statement that the foreigner knows them well enough not to harangue a settled question.

Our rest day is necessary for another reason. The head muleteer has a debt to settle and spends the day securing an advance

out of me so we can leave on the morrow. I chide him that it was
a good thing we had hired him else he would never have been
able to settle all of these debts and he should be very grateful that
we rich foreign devils came along at such an opportune time. The
day also has another bright spot when a former orphan of our
Batang Mission found the strain of hiding his opium smoking
from me too confining and announced his return to Yachow where
he had attached himself to me. To his disappointment I agree
with his decision and give him ample money to return. He is
scabby with a skin disease and is debilitated, so I suspect venereal
afflictions which may be the reason he has been unable to do any
work. Old China hands find great difficulty in discouraging former
workers and friends from attaching themselves to the payroll.

Our caravan (although the men are tired and demoralized
from a day's rest) leaves at a reasonable hour and wends its way
wearily up another steep incline. We take along forty country-
men to repair the road as we proceed. Around a cliff a thousand
feet of trail has skidded into several houses and dammed a small
stream to form a little lake. A bridge beside the road has to be
made passable. Where mending is not possible men will stand by
on boards placed on the deep mud to grab the caravan animals by
the tail and head and literally hoist them to firmer ground.
Where there is no mud the caravan is detoured up the mountain
through soggy fields. If necessary the load is detached and por-
tered around the break. One horse falls forty feet over the cliff
in spite of our assistance but landing in mud he is scraped and
detoured through a cornfield back to the road. My day as a labor
foreman brings the caravan to Shanchiohping, a contracted hamlet
nearer the top of the pass.

Today we should be in Tachienlu according to the regular stage
schedule but here we are in the muddy shadow of the second pass
called Feiyueh Ling. Our first task is the same as every day since
we left Yachow, getting mud in our eyes and everywhere else until
we resemble a gang of sewer excavators. Five feet of oozy mud
has spread fanwise like molten lava, creating a huge scar on the
mountainside and coming to rest where once stood three houses
and a dozen acres of corn. In another house the mud has swept
in like water to the depth of three feet and the family has de-

camped in such a hurry that a little dog is left behind. He jumps upon the high table as a raft and barks at us foolishly, since entering into the mess of his domain was the least of our thoughts, we had enough mud outside to worry us. The caravan men balk but we move through and lay planks taken out of the abandoned house. We do not fail to notice, in spite of our troubles, that here as well as elsewhere that when the local clay deities (Tuti) have disintegrated in their quaint little huts, a rudely caricatured drawing has been placed in the niche as a temporary substitute. After a long struggle with slime we ride over the pass and drop down in a long winding trail to Hualingping which is rated as one hundred and twenty lee from Nitou and supposed to be made in one long stage.

Near Hualingping (see Map No. 2) one can leave the main trail and turn up a ravine to the left where a gently graded path leads over a sloping divide into the main valley of the Yungching river. Following down this stream amidst hemlocks through very narrow blue limestone and wider red sandstone canyons one gradually comes into steep-sided, scrub-covered slopes where the brambles hide the trail and bruise the traveler. However, in time the valley widens, joins others and one enters a populous section where along the tumbling, enlarging Yungching river can be seen coal and iron mines whose product is exported to Yachow. The road traces this river until it is too large to ford, then shifts from bank to bank over iron-rod bridges which nestle amidst cultivated fields. After what seems an interminable length one reaches the junction of the Yungching with the Tahsiang Ling stream, up which we had gone some seven days ago. The junction is a short distance not over fifteen lee southwest of Yungching Hsien. This short cut is an easier (but less used road) as well as shorter by two days. However, not being fitted with regular stage inns for large numbers of travelers it is used only by small parties and by returning tea carriers who expect to pick up short porterage loads of iron and coal. By the Chinese it is called a small road in contrast to the main route which is labeled the big road. Such distinctions do not indicate size or condition of road but rather amount of usage.

The second pass of Feiyueh Ling of 9000 feet altitude brings us into the valley of the Tung river. We leave Hualingping without any delay the next morning, outside of the usual mud prospect. The town is perched upon a little plateau amidst walnut trees some five hundred feet above the stream which we have followed down from the pass of Fciyueh Ling. After a steep slippery drop to the bed of this stream we take a more northerly course. As the clouds shift after daily rains, which fall mostly during daylight but sometimes at night, away in the west is revealed a glorious panorama of snow peaks, undoubtedly those at 240° are the Boh Gongkar Peaks southwest of Tachlienlu and the least prominent toward the northwest at 255° are the Zhara group. As we go lower for twenty-five lee to turn out of the valley of our little tributary into a path along the Tung River we lose this view not to be seen again until we are upon the high Tibetan Plateau.

The dessication evident in the Tung Basin as compared to the Min is so marked that we feel as if we had stepped through a doorway into another climatic belt. It is still warm and slight rains continue but mulberry trees are replaced by tung oil trees; and grass with prickly pear covers the waste land instead of dense brush and scattered conifers. We persist in fording dangerous torrents which have carried away their bridges within a cultivated valley, until the vale contracts into a ravine and we start sliding around mountain spurs. I take along five men with hoes who aid us over our worst stretch of road since leaving Yachow. These five men hack away brush to clear a new path around breaks of sliding red standstone and slate. Every horse must be lead by head and tail through the swollen stream which we must cross seemingly countless times. The black slaty soil still slides freely (Photo No. 17) but we finally arrive at the halfway stage of Lengchi, a distance of only ten lee, in the late afternoon. It is so late that we must stay the night in a hot stuffy room over a hotter grease-burning kitchen from which the smell of burnt oils float upward to stupify us.

Our tenth day ends the mud. The next day is clear and the shaly sandstone earth which has changed from dark to red, has dried to fair stability during the night. We move rapidly for forty lee paralleling the Tung river on a hair-raising track built on the wall of a canyon until we reach Lutingchiao. Here is a famed

iron-link bridge constructed in 1705. Built of iron links ten inches
long and one inch in diameter by hand forges, the bridge seems
perfectly safe but sways sickeningly as it is between 300 and 350
feet long. Swung out from rock abutements fifty to seventy-five
feet above the water it seems more frightful than it is, for its
width is ten feet and two chains on each side support hand railings. Nine chains support the open planking broken in some
places but ordinarily close enough together to prevent falling
through. However, the swaying and rushing water seen between
the planks frighten horses and timid people who equally must be
lead across. The ends of the chains are anchored in deep pits and
tightened by enormous wooden windlasses.

We spend the night at Pempa and leave early. Part of the road
is pleasant through fields of rice, corn and beans but part is narrow
staircases around sharp-angled corners of cliffs where a miss-step
would plunge one into the foaming Tung river. The road is lined
thicker than before with wayside inns for tea-carriers whose back-
breaking loads rest on benches outside the door while the coolies
inside sip a cup of tea and buy enough cakes to bring them back
from Tachienlu where all food is expensive and corn-cakes have
to be imported from this valley.

The road is long, spurting up a hundred feet, only to drop
again alongside the river-edge. Between stones in the fences and
in the clefts of the cliffs grow prickly pears whose flat leaves,
when denuded of thorns, are food for cattle, and whose pear-
shaped yellowish fruit are very succulent for men. At the last we
climb an immense limestone cliff along a path sometimes not three
feet wide and so steep I dismounted and walked rather than over-
hang the precipice which dropped sheer to the river one hundred
to four hundred feet below. I breathe easier as we top the spur
and suddenly turn into Wassukou fifty lee from Lutingchiao and
at the mouth of the Do river descending from Tachienlu and entering the Tung. We eat lunch and turn away from the Tung to
ascend westward over a rocky trail. The long but comparatively
gentle incline winds with the tumbling tributary which leaves
but little flat land. We file through a deep-walled granite canyon
for forty lee crossing the Do river a few times by bridges, since
the waters are unfordable, being a continuous cascade which

plunges over huge boulders for three thousand feet in less than fifteen miles.

After a picturesque ride through this baby gorge we reach Tachienlu where Mr. and Mrs. Robert Cunningham and Mr. J. H. Edgar (Mrs. Edgar was absent in Chengtu with a broken arm) of the China Inland Mission meet us outside the gate. These four missionaries are intrepid evangelists who have spent twenty-five to thirty years upon the border, all that is left of the gallant C. I. M. Mission band who opened Protestant Mission work in Tachienlu at the turn of the century. They had been associated with Dr. Susie Rijnhart, Dr. and Mrs. A. L. Shelton and Mr. and Mrs. J. C. Ogden in the early days of the Tibetan Christian Mission of the Church of Christ in which my wife and I were workers for thirteen years in Batang. The Cunninghams and Edgars have greeted and entertained us so often in Tachienlu that seeing them is like the meeting of brothers and sisters. For a quarter of a century they have not only been hosts to missionaries and explorers but rendered invaluable aid in outfitting them for their interior trips. We feel that we are being escorted by royalty and can ask for no heartier welcome as they lodge us in their home.

Tachinelu is the eastern gateway to Tibet and the port of entry for most of the Chinese tea used westward to Lhasa and beyond (Photo No. 18). Sungpan with lesser points also exports tea but unfavorable terrain and wild nomads along the routes inland from these northeastern ports increase the natural advantages enjoyed by Tachienlu as the export center of tea for Tibet.

Tibetans rarely come through this eastern gateway of Tachienlu fearing the heat and diseases of lower altitudes against which they have little resistance. Except for scattered merchants, mostly Shansi traders, and the few hundred soldiers who garrison such outlying points as Batang, Gangdzi (Kanze) and lesser centers, not many Chinese go through this eastern gate westward. There is no rice and Chinese dislike tsamba. While Tachienlu is a doorway it is also a barrier. Eastward a generally gradual descent leads to the hot steaming plains of China; westward stretches upward the high, airless and cold plateau of Tibet.

Tachienlu has an altitude of about 8500 feet above sea level and a population of ten to fifteen thousand people crammed into a

narrow valley about a thousand feet wide. The city touches two
streams which unite just outside the east gate to form the river
we followed from Wassukou. Houses and shops extend for three-
quarters of a mile along the western tributary of Je, over which
are built four bridges, to the junction of the northwest stream of
Ta. The city thus clutches the handle of a forked stick lying
about fifteen degrees off a general northeast and southwest direction and inclining to the north and south points. All three valleys
have canyon walls whose upward slopes lead to snow peaks some
of which may be seen in fair weather from vantage points. Icy
winds rush down from these perpetual snow fields bringing more
rain and snow than is true of the high plateau and gives Tach-
ienlue an unfavorable climate as compared to other eastern Tibetan cities of the same height and latitude.

I analyzed the information relative to the origin and meaning of the names "Tachienlu and the Tibetan Dartsemdo." Tachienlu probably means "horse tongue junction" taken from the two
passes of Tapho La (Ta is Tibetan for horse) on the north and
Jethoh La (Je (Che) means tongue) to the west. These two
passes are sources of the two rivers bearing the same names which
unite at Tachienlu. The final syllable "lu" is the local enunciation of "la" meaning "at" which is attached to names and also
useful as an ending to names of town when speaking of them.
The name changed when the town increased in size due to the
settling there of a Tibetan merchant called Norbu Zangbo. This
merchant imported tea, and exported wool and hides in such
quantities that the Tibetans called it Dartsemdo or "ever increasing junction." The city is also known as Luchun and of late years
the Chinese have officially changed the name to Kangting but to
all Tibetans of the plateau it is known as Dartsemdo, the "do"
meaning junction.

Tachienlu is a city of Chinese shops and Tibetan traders. Not
many decades ago the population of the city was predominately
Tibetan. Chinese immigration has diluted the Tibetan blood until
less than a fifth are pure Tibetan and this element are mostly
priests from the adjoining country. Practically none of the children can speak Tibetan fluently. Very few flat Tibetan roofs exist
and even the Tibetan monastery buildings show strong Chinese

architectural influences. The Tibetan is conspicuous largely as an outside trader who quietly struts up and down eyeing the gaudy shops or sits dickering in an inner room for tea and cloth. When his purchases are completed the burly Tibetan leads his snorting horned yak through the street and quickly surmounts a 15,000-foot pass onto his beloved highlands again. Three main roads lead out of Tachienlu to Tibetan regions; one to Jyekundo which supplies the northeast and most of the territory around Lhasa and beyond; one to Batang which supplies lower Kham; and one to the southeast covering Shangchen and its contiguous tribes.

In ancient times Tachienlu was located farther up the valley but a landslide during a heavy earthquake coming from a ravine to the southeast buried part of the town and encouraged the rest to move. Earthquakes are not infrequent along the Tibetan border. North of Tachienlu in 1924 a quake destroyed many homes and killed a large part of the population in several villages. Noticeable tremors occur about once a year in Batang which was utterly destroyed in 1869. The loose timber construction of the Tibetan home with a heavy roof of clay makes the house dangerous when severe shakes take place.

During our short delay in Tachienlu the Tibetans hold their annual horse races upon a sloping plateau to the south. The once common horse races have declined in territory now occupied by the Chinese so I seize the opportunity to see a relic of former days. There is a large crowd mostly men and boys. At the crack of a gun the taut rope restraining the line of horses is dropped and the riders whip their horses to activity. They head across an open grassy plot to a line several hundred feet higher up the mountain from which they must return to the starting point. The rarefied atmosphere and the brush over most of the course, make it a race of endurance with the horses tending to follow behind each other in paths broken through the shrubs. Prizes of towels and soap are given to the first five horses. The prizes are useful and suggestive as most Tibetans take but a few baths in the hot springs which exist above the city on roads both north and west.

Tachienlu has seven separate temples of the seven different sects of Lamaism with over fifteen hundred priests. Some of the temples are very small. The two largest line the road to Batang west of the city. One is the Virtuous Path or Gelugpa and the other the Old Way or Nyingmapa. In addition the Chinese have Buddhist, Confucian and Mohammedan temples. The large number of sects arises from the city being a center of population for eastern Tibet and as the former seat of a principality known as the Kingdom of Jala (Chala).

Christian missions are represented by the China Inland Mission resident for sixty years, the Seventh Day Adventist for twenty years and the Roman Catholics for over eighty years. Church services, hospitals, schools and tract distribution are carried on extensively and have created a Christian constituency who have started the long, slow and stumbling trail toward a more perfect enlightenment.

Figure 15
Tracking our junk up the Min or Fu River

Figure 16
Tea carriers with eleven and twelve bales, over two hundred and fifty pounds
each, near Lutingchiao

Figure 17
Trail south of Lutingchiao. Landslide in left background has not been repaired, and sedan chairmen walk carefully over debris

Figure 18
Yak at north gate of Tachienlu ready to transport the bales of piled tea to Lhasa

Chapter V

WITH THE YAK ON THE GRASSLANDS

My family and I have made the high plateau trip of over two hundred and forty miles from Tachienlu to Batang (Bahthang) two different times, once in July 1929, and again in August 1932; and I made it a third time as a member of the Brooke Dolan second expedition in September and October 1934. The first two trips were in the rainy season and the last journey in the dying drops of the monsoon which were replaced by the brilliant clear skies of late fall. The description of this route will be primarily from the diary of the first trip enriched by unusual incidents of the other journeys. On our second trip Mrs. Minnie A. Ogden and Miss Grace Young, and my youngest son Robert Malcolm, then fifteen months old, were of the party in addition to our previous four members. On our first journey the party consists of my wife Kate Louise, my oldest son John Kenneth five years old and my oldest daughter Marian Louise a little over two years old. My youngest daughter Esther Jane was born in 1934 after our return to America and escaped the pleasures and hardships of this trek. Louise has a sedan chair with six Chinese men to carry her, the two children occupy a three-man double-seated inclosed chair and I ride a horse.

With the indefatigable efforts of Bob Cunningham I gather some 20,000 rupees from the Tachienlu merchants who take orders for cash in Chengtu and other cities eastward where they buy their goods for import into Tachienlu. I also buy cloth and tea for the Batang orphanage, secretly placing from 400 to 600 rupees in each halfload of cloth to make the proper weight of 60 jin (chin) or 80 pounds. Cloth and tea are bundled and sewn in wet yak-skins, which are stretched while being stitched together. The skins shrink in drying, so hard (like horn) and tight that such loads, if dumped by bucking yak (and every yak throws his load at least once each trip), bounce like rubber balls down cliffs, intact and uninjured.

We celebrate the anniversary of our country's independence by leaving Tachienlu on the fourth of July 1929. Our general direction is almost directly westward to Batang. We have a caravan of over seventy yak with more than thirty-five loads of mission cloth, tea and money. The morning is bright with just a few light clouds as we are escorted out of the city by the intrepid China Inland missionaries, Mr. J. H. Edgar and Mr. and Mrs. Robert Cunningham. The city beggars likewise do not forget us raising a racket of exploding firecrackers for which we must pay liberally before they will leave us. It is the best racket we have so far experienced in China.

Over the stone bridge spanning the western river—the Je Chu, once the boundary between China and Tibet, and past the Gelugpa and Nyingmapa monasteries sheltered behind juniper trees, we climb steadily westward and upward (Photo No. 19). At two miles is the branch road to Mili and Yunnan province leading southward. Beyond our trail narrows and steepens. At noon a violent windstorm overtakes us with such torrents of cold rain that our thinly-clad Chinese carriers seek temporary shelter under a huge rock. With the ceasing of the rain they carry the sodden chairs into Jethoh (Chedo) their own clothing soaking and their bodies quivering. We lodge in a stage house, one of the very few left from the former glory of the stern warrior Chao Erh Feng whose able but brutal administration had established stage houses with a caretaker every thirty lee (ten miles) between Tachienlu and Batang.

Scarcely are we settled before the rain again falls in such chilling onslaughts that we abandon visiting the noted hot sulphur springs whose steaming mists of over 100 degrees Fahrenheit temperature can be seen a few hundred feet up the mountain. Although Jethoh has only sixteen houses it is distinguished as a crossroads because another trail leads southwest over a pass into the Yulong Valley and eventually to Mili.

The next morning we resume our climb northwest through scattered larch and later rhododendron upon a road so full of granitic gneiss stones that we long for the monotony of grassy plains. Just above the ruins of a rest house and about a thousand feet below the summit of Jethoh we lunch amid huge boulders in a garden of yellow primroses and the pyramidal yellowish spikes of rhubarb. The Tibetans classify three varieties of rhubarb, one, with large leaves sometimes two feet wide and three feet long, is used for medicinal purposes and exported to China under the name of Da Hwang or Great Yellow Root. Everywhere the open spaces are massed with purple or golden flowers while the scattered bushes are ablaze with color.

Our caravan is an imposing procession eventually at Litang (Lithang) reaching 500 animals as tea loads sent ahead join us at various rendezvous. Officials from the rank of Mayor on down, and Chinese merchants, orginally from the province of Shansi, have seized the opportunity of traveling with us mostly for the sake of free protection from marauders as we pay the price of escort. The Shansi merchants are the true pioneers of Chinese trade in every trading city of the Tibetan border. They marry the Tibetan women, learn the language (which most Chinese disdain to do) and are the entering wedge for other Chinese elements who begin the inexorable assimilation of new territory. Their honesty and reliability is fully attested by my experience with them in oral contracts involving thousands of rupees.

At eleven o'clock after a final slippery stretch on a slate trail we reach the prayer flags of Jethoh La or Jethoh Pass. Inscribed rags protruding from the top of huge piles of stone always mark the passes of Tibet. Swirling clouds of mist in grey skies break away for a few moments to let us have a peep at immense masses of snow-covered ranges to the south. They are the famed Boh Gongkar (Menya Gongkar) which form the most extensive snow-fields we have seen upon the Tibetan Plateau.

We slip down a gentle grassy incline past the scattered black yak-hair tents encircled by thousands of yak in whose midst are a few horses and sheep. We are happy to get over the pass which is celebrated for its difficulty, evidence of this being the whitened bones which litter the roadside. This pass is the first test of weak hearts. One of our chairmen who left us two days later, because of his heart, is reported to have died at Jethoh Pass on his return toward Tachienlu.

Rain and sunshine intermingle with such frequent changes that

we are kept busy donning and shedding raincoats. We plod past
three tumble down shacks to arrive at dusk in Nahshee set amidst
a few larch in a long one-half mile wide grassy plain. Among its
thirty-five houses with tall square towers we spy the first stone
ox-heads embedded in blue slate walls. As many as a half dozen
of these heads, with now and then a white stone ball, can be seen.
These white images are placed to face the mountain in order to
scare away the spirits of the yak who have died on the range.
The people believe that these spirits, imitating their habits when
alive, have a tendency to return home, where as ghost-spirits they
would be able to harm men and animals.

Our next two days are short stages up and down sloping inclines. In these Menya valleys, at an altitude of twelve thousand
feet, grow peas, barley, oats and turnips, and in the lowest spots
an occasional field of wheat. The first day we pitch our tent
(Photo No. 20) near a place called Watse where two trails cross,
one going southwest into the Shangchen (Chyah Trenwa) country
and the other we will follow to Batang. Beside our camp rises
the manure-plastered wall of a blue stone fort testifying to an
ancient regime that has lost its identity. These towers now shelter
no more formidable enemy than blue-white pigeons who build
their nests within the crevices inside. Raising countless broods of
young their droppings have become several feet deep during the
centuries. On winter days these vast flocks of pigeons sweep over
the barren fields for food but find shelter at night within the
tower walls.

The thirty-odd houses of Watse are but little less filthy on the
inside than on the outside; on the outside surfaces hang the manure fuel for the household. At the break of day the housewives
and children go out into the fields and gather the dung in oblong
baskets. Carrying it home on their backs they mix the wet mass
with chaff and mold it into round cakes which they slap against
the stone walls. In a day or two the mixture is dry enough to
peel off and store inside. These cakes are the only fuel for perhaps a third of Tibet where forests cannot grow. All of this work
is done with the hands which are carelessly washed in cold water
before the breakfast is prepared. There is no hesitancy in the

hands alternating the flapping of light brown buckwheat pancakes on the skillet with the thrusting of dark brown yak-cakes into the fire.

A hundred feet from our camp is a fine chorten which contrary to the general rule is hollow inside. We inspect the three stories of pyramidal rooms which are crowned by a thirteen ringed column supporting a crescent moon that is embracing the sun ball. The walls are decorated with numerous figures now dampened into obscurity. The top story contains a large goddess holding the back of her clasped hands against her breasts. The first floor has three sitting figures and the fourth a standing idol with a child in its arms. All of the idols are badly battered and reduced almost to the original clay. The first story is fifteen feet high, the second five and the third ten; the second floor seems to serve largely as a connecting room. The upper stories are reached by decrepit ladders. Evidently most of the thought is for the exterior which is kept whitewashed and the outside figure resting in a niche of the third story is freshly repainted.

On the next day a half hour down the valley is the junction of two streams which uniting flow southeast to join the Yalung six or eight days distant. Here is a village called Dzonggo named for a former fort whose ancient runs are visible upon a bluff 500 feet above the houses. The outer walls of this dismantled fort inclose about five acres of a flattish grassy spur. Resuming our journey we pass twenty-eight white-capped stone prayer cairns in a connected row and beyond these we plunge immediately into a lane lined with wild cherry trees and gooseberry bushes. These undulating grassy mountains and sloping ravines in which huddle blue-stone cottages gleaming with white lines and white yak-heads seem a paradise in which to live. Yet when we draw near to the homes, muddy lanes and greasy blackened women peering out of sooty windows rob the scene of its charm. But we can regain the allurement of nature by looking behind us, for peeking above the grassy mountains is the ice-cream cone of the highest Boh Gongkar peak. Considerable interrogation revealed that Boh Gongkar (Tibetan White Glacier) is most commonly applied to what are known to the outside world as the Menya Gongkar Peaks (the white glacier peaks of Menya). They are also quite often referred to by Tibetans as the Bangyee Gongkar (high country white glacier) and in the immediate vicinity of the peaks the name Bon Gongkar (Black Hat Sect white glacier) from the former black hat priests once living in the monastery on its slope, still used but by another sect.

On these broad grassy plains the thousands of black yak are unable to consume but a fraction of the succulent grass. In years to come when marketing conditions are perfected and peaceful living is possible the number of yak can be increased until the Tibetan Tableland becomes the last great reservoir of beef to supply a crowded world. In the steep ravines especially upon the northern slopes are pines, firs, spruces and junipers of sufficient size and quantity to make the Tibetan Plateau one of the final timber reserves to be utilized.

As we strike camp on the morrow we see thin wisps of grey smoke rise from an altar on a distant eminence and hear the faint brazen blare of trumpets concealed in a tiny temple behind a hill. Nearby is a group of prayer-flagged poles waving radiantly over a corpse-cutting spot upon which rest a few vultures after a cannibal feast. We do not linger long to muse on such scenes but swing upward on to a blue-shale road leading into a forest of huge firs and glassy-leafed rhododendrons. We camp near the timber line where a tenantless former rest-shack guards a patch of potatoes and barley. We are above 13,000 feet and the growing season is short with cool nights. Over a low pass to the west is a monastery harbouring 400 monks. Red-eared snow pheasants which roam in flocks of fifteen to thirty birds gobble from the direction of the temple. I climb the range to see both pheasants and temple but a heavy thunderstorm drives me back. One of our yak-loads strays here mixing up with a large herd of grazing yak around the corner of a forest and is not found until the next day.

On the morrow, the ninth of July, we cross two passes known as the Karzhi La, the first divide being 14,650 feet high and the second 15,080 feet. There are a few hundred feet of descent so we must rise close to another thousand feet of altitude. On the higher western pass we look south and view a magnificent half-circle of snow mountains including the Boh Gongkar lying 140

degrees southeast, the Zhara at forty-five degrees and the Tachienlu snow peaks, at 90 degrees. Descending through a lane of
wild mock orange shrubs in bloom we pass many yak and four
yak-hair tents. The smooth grassy slopes soon become a narrow
plain with fields of barley. We notice our first prayer-wheels
turned by the rushing water of a small torrent. After camping
many pilgrims and travellers pause at our tent to gaze wide-eyed
and then to cry in surprise over the fairness and beauty of our
three children. They suck in their breath and exclaim, "Tse, Tse,
they are the race of the gods."

Two more short days, through a fir and spruce forest and then
the cultivated valley of Orongzhee remarkable for many wild
trees bearing a reddish crab apple-like fruit known as Dzachob,
brings us to Nyahchukha or Hokou. In the middle of Orongzhee
is the headman's house but we cannot get in since there is no one
at home and the lock is plastered with cow dung which has dried
and will reveal any tampering.

There are few real towns in eastern Tibet but Nyahchukha at
an altitude of 9000 feet above sea level is one of them. It has two
parts, the Chinese village on the left bank of the Yalung (Nyah
Chu to Tibetans) river and the Tibetan town almost directly across
the river on a high bluff. The Chinese village of forty-two houses,
is mostly Tibetan people with a few Chinese merchants and about
a hundred soldiers in residence part of the time. On the right
bank the Tibetan village of sixteen houses has most of the cultivated land, as a huge basaltic rock almost closes the mouth of the
opposite Orongzhee valley leaving the Chinese village perilously
perched on a narrow beach at the confluence. Up and down the
Yalung from its source to its mouth there are few other places as
large as Nyahchukha. Elsewhere only tiny hamlets cling to the
precipitious, bushy mountain slopes and their residents eke out a
bare living from the barren fields which are yellow clay blotches
amidst an ocean of acacia briers.

After paying the customary formal visits to the Mayor and the
Captain of the guard we are ferried over the surging river in a
wooden scow. This flat-bottomed boat utilizes the current in
going from shore to shore. About fifty feet long, eight feet wide
and three and one half feet deep the barge is divided into five

compartments for passengers, animals and baggage. First consid-
erations are given to animals and baggage, the passengers crowd
in wherever they can. The bow and stern sections are covered
over with planks as standing space for the oarsmen and steersmen.
A steering oar about twenty-five feet long is mounted in the bow
and two oars for rowing each about fifteen feet in length are in
the rear, one on a side. The crew varies with the height of the
water, this being the flood season, thirteen take us over. The
spruce planking is of two and three inch thickness. Only its
weight and broad flat bottom enable it to keep upright when it
swings broadside to the terrific current. Stout as the boat is and
heavily laden with our luggage the foaming waters toss it like a
cork and the creaking of the timbers sound ominous.

Six trips in two days are necessary to ferry us, our goods and
over 200 loads of merchandise for the merchants and the officials
who use us as a cloak to escape heavy protection fees on the road
and to lighten their ferry charges on the river. In addition to the
barge, skin boats are utilized by small groups or single travellers
such as mail runners. These egg-shaped tubs are six feet in diameter and four feet deep. The main part is one large yak skin
with other partial yak hides for the upper border. Seven sticks of
green wood as ribs extend the skins and fasten to a heavy birch
rim. A man can carry one and it is dried out after each using.

We leave Nyahchukha on July 13th and tread a stony trail
upward into firs and maples. One of the chairmen becomes ill and
at his request I treat him on my diagnosis of worms. The cramps
naturally not ceasing immediately, his companions place him on
his back and taking off his two thin cotton shirts proceed to closely
inspect the skin in the region of his stomach where he has the
pains. They find two discolorations (I could point out several more
on his unwashed hide) where the disease spirits are trying to get
out. They make three small punctures around each spot with a
needle to release these evil spirits. After a few days of walking
behind the chair he recovers and divides the credit for his recovery equally between the ancient and the modern treatments. I am
glad he recovers as his fellow-workers testify he is the only one
of the eight who does not smoke opium and if the pains had continued he might have started the habit. Opium sots rarely break

off smoking or eating opium which grips their victims with increasing power as the years pass until the individual loses all moral control and declines in physical vigor to fall an easy victim to some disease. Few opium smokers live beyond the age of fifty years and none are to be trusted when the habit is far advanced.

We pitch our tent amid magnificent trees; god-maples three feet in diameter and a hundred feet high, five-leafed poplar maples, golden oak, spruce, pines, holly oak, juniper and red firs these last being over three feet in diameter and 150 feet in the air. A few homes are tucked in open spaces among the giant trees whose quietness and mystery charmed us. It is 11,600 feet above sea level and the air is cool.

Early the next morning we slowly and painfully climb out of the forest onto grassy mountains and over Rama La 15,225 feet above the sea; then we drop 500 feet and rise 600 feet to top Dose La with an altitude of 15,325 feet; and down once more but only a hundred feet before another ascent to surmount Lachum La 15,400 feet. The Rama Passes are noted for their difficulty and the Nyah River (Yalung) for its dangers. These two factors are featured in the proverb "Try a yak on Rama Pass, Try a man on Nyah River." With this thought and another saying in mind, I always ride a horse uphill but lead him down for "It is not much of a horse which cannot carry a man uphill, It is not much of a man who will not walk down a hill." At the top of the pass the wind is cool but the day is clear. High above the dusky forested ravines in which are dancing wisps of fleecy clouds, as far as one can see in all directions, are rolling grassy plains and smoothly turfed spurs undulating like great ocean waves. To the southeast are immense snow mountains whose tips are hid in massed wool which ever changes in depth and thickness. These snow mountains are called Boh Gonkgar by the Tibetans at this place. Around us over the endless turf roam herds of antelope giving us only a fleeting glimpse before they vanish beyond the rolling summits. Spirals of foamy smoke from sheltered gullies suggest black yak-hair tent-dwellers whose shaggy herds of yak and flocks of white sheep can be seen on distant ranges.

Less desirable residents are the hordes of horse-flies (or deer-flies) which we have come to associate with every grassy vale when the sun is shining. Alas, these horse-flies do not restrict themselves to horses who spring suddenly into mad gallops when stung. Of many colors, red, yellow, gray and black they have a lunch-punch which pierces thick clothing and horsehide with equal ease. In the bright sunshine they keep us frantic but when clouds hide the sun their attacks lessen and they vanish entirely when the cold creeps over the hills with the rising of a wind, or in the rear of the setting sun.

After crossing the three Rama Passes we meander slowly down a placid incline for half an hour to where our yak caravan has settled for the night. We camp here at an altitude of not less than 15,000 feet. It is not a restful camp for the big horse-flies keep us slapping wrathfully until a fitfull cold wind blows from the southeast glaciers. Nor is the wind pleasant as it drives us to warmer clothing and cold cream. The winds blister our faces until they resemble lobsters shedding their skin. My nose is always the point of first attack causing my wife to remark that I look like a first class toper. A few bulging sheepskin clad nomads from nearby tents saunter over to gawk at our foreign equipment but we are now indifferent to such curiosity.

I breathlessly ascend a few hundred feet to the top of a mound but its low height permitted only the dreamy sight of numberless ranges which stretching away to snow-rimmed horizons leave the individual feeling like an ant on an ocean wave. Amidst an enormous crowd, among the tall buildings of a great city, or on a ship in the middle of a stormy sea gives one that same feeling—that man is merely an atom in the great scope of the universe. No life can be seen. The nomads are in sheltered gullies and on these great plains the wild animals usually see man first. The isolated nomads and their scattered unseen flocks in their quiet lives are a fitting accompaniment to such vast solitude.

The next morning we fairly tumble down a steep rocky road which succeeds the smooth incline. At the foot of the declivity we tread the placid valley of Ngoloh whose ruler belies his surroundings as he is noted for his extortions levied on traders and travellers. Every caravan, and we are not exempt, must pay one half a rupee a load for the privilege of passing through this valley. Ngoloh is the junction of the old route which makes a steep climb over a high range in a fairly straight western course to Litang and the new road which we will follow in a northwesterly half circle with less.grade and more distance.

The fir-lined Ngoloh valley with its twenty-five houses is a little less than 11,000 feet altitude at its lowest levels. Here are raised the commonest staple crops of Tibet; barley, wheat, peas and turnips. Down the valley on a high bluff is a monastery housing three hundred monks. Monasteries are generally placed on promontories or alongside a cliff where they can be easily defended. These heavily fortified strongholds are the last resort of the people when an invader swoops down upon them. Built around a spring or projecting over a stream of considerable size they can stand a prolonged siege. Their thick tamped clay walls four and five feet thick at the base can easily withstand rifle and machine-gun fire and considerable small cannon pounding. Vast quantities of grain, which are always stored in their granaries, are augmented by the hurriedly carried supplies when the people flee to the temple for refuge. The Chinese know well that all resistance to their conquest of the Tibetans are fomented within these citadel monasteries.

Leaving the old south road here we move up a narrowing valley, tracing a creek for two hours, until we arrive at the huge square castle of the headman with its neighboring satellites of twenty-two homes and six tents perched at the edge of a tall fir woodland. We part company with the stream and enter the forest through which we wind northwest and then southwest, ever ascending, until we are over Lahtse La 14,375 feet. A trivial drop and we deviate northwest to ascend another creek which is flowing southwest to finally empty into the Hor Chu or Hor River. From this·point we can see the higher pass of the old main south road with its washed tracks melting away in the southwest distance.

This tributary of the Hor Chu has fifteen gold-washer huts housing fifty gold-diggers now busy in trenches (Photo No. 21). As we are riding past them a sudden squall of rain engulfs us, and then turning to hail forces us to camp within an hour among hailstones as large as marbles. The gold miners put on their wool capes and stand moodily watching us cover up to ward off the hail. Our encampment here is at 14,000 feet altitude and the

name is Jangkarkhoh. The creek rises rapidly and we are forced
to ford the racing current at considerable risk, guided by our men
in bare feet. Tibetan boots crack when they dry out after being
wet and also the leather sewing thongs pull out easily when the
leather is damp so they never wear boots in wet weather. It
makes us shiver to see our men tramping around on the hail-
strewn ground in bare feet; yet we know that the soles of their
feet have been hardened by such exposure until they resemble
the hoofs of beasts.

During the daytime rain has fallen every day since leaving
Tachienlu except on two days and on one of these days rain fell
during the night. This is the rainy season. During most of the
year from October to June these airless plains will have only
slight snows which will not drift deep except above an altitude of
16,000 feet.

We are now in a land of shifting tents and yak chips. From
here to Batang are but two settlements. Yak dung replaces wood
for cooking and heating. We have carried along some charcoal
for our cook to use and to dry out the tent after the cold rains.
The servants will waste the charcoal and then grumble as they
gather yak chips. Tsang Wen Chin like most Chinese cooks, is
resourceful and creates an excellent meal with a large variety of
dishes out of our scanty stock of food by the heat of a miserable
yak chip fire. Yak chips keep one man busy gathering it and another man constantly working the quaint goat-skin bellows to blow
the dung into sufficient heat for cooking. These bellows are the
entire skin of a goat with three legs sewn up, leaving the fourth
one for the attachment of an iron tube whose other end is inserted into the fire. The head hole of the skin is now opened and
closed suddenly by a peculiar rotary motion of the hands which
sucks in the air and expels it with a huffing explosive sound.
There are many jeers before I learn to work it, but never as easily
as the nomad.

We need not climb high the next day to cross Kharsa La, a
series of four parallel passes with gentle valleys from 200 to 800
feet deep between them. All are over 15,000 thousand feet, the
third being the highest with an altitude of 15,700 feet. Brilliant
flowers of all colors, yellow and white predominating, among them

strawflower, pearly everlasting, buttercups and primroses have pushed their way out of the hard mossy turf in such numbers that the ranges are one vast flower-bed.

Extensive stone ruins of an ancient Bon (Black Hat) monastery have given the last of the Kharsa Passes the name of Bongo La. From it we descend to a level plain roughened by the mounds and holes of black-eyed yellowish-brown marmots the size of woodchucks. Their shrill trilling whistles warn each other of man's approach and one has difficulty arriving within shotgun range. This large marshy plain is watered by a blue-black stream winding through the center past a tall white chorten from whose decaying eaves hang small bells that tinkle with every breeze. After the destruction of the Bon Monastery the Gelugpa sect built this chorten which gives the locality the name of White Chorten Plain. We pitch our tent at the farther end of his plateau. All day we have been travelling mostly west with a slight inclination to the northwest.

Our coolie Aki takes his foreign fishhook to the nearby stream and soon returns with speckled trout about six inches in length. He has twenty beauties taken from the stream which is only a foot deep and about three feet wide. The Tibetans consider it sinful to eat fish, so after the cook selects our needs, our caravan leader Drale Gonchoh carefully carries the remainder back to liberty and life. Fish have no voice to protest their slaughter and it is more sinful to kill them than other animals. Gods of the region might become angry and create a flooded, unfordable river to detain us, or send a destructive hail to injure the stock.

It is the seventeenth of July the following morning as we mount westward over a low pass called Jeri lying 14,625 feet above the sea. It seems low because our elevation is already high, probably 14,000 feet. The pass is an elongated saddle for the ranges present long parallel sides rather than the usual ridgedip slope. The Jeri La is the boundary between the two tribes of Washi (Washee) and just beyond beside the Hor river are 102 tents of the Othoh tribe with whom we have been travelling under the sponsorship of Drale Gonchoh, our escort guide, who now rides to beseech the priests with two rupees to cast lots and hold back rain until we arrive in Litang.

Like immense black spiders at rest the yak-hair tents almost fill the long valley of the Hor Chu which has a grassy plain running north and south for three miles before it enters a gorge. The altitude is 14,000 feet and like all of the high plains is covered with mossy or wirelike short-stemmed grass on which graze several thousand head of yak. Every householder also owns horses and many have flocks of sheep sprinkled with a few goats. As the yak frequently wander up to 17,000 feet it is no easy tasks to herd them. Merely walking on level ground is tiring.

Nomadic life on the Tibetan Plateau would be almost impossible without the yak (Photo No. 22). Every necessity of their life is provided by the yak except tea and the very poorest nomads have little of that. Shelter in the form of a tent comes from yak-hair cloth, food is produced by the milk and flesh of the beast and fuel by the dung when dried. At home boiled or roasted yak steaks and cottage cheese are washed down with yak-butter tea. On the road dried raw yak beef and hardened squares of yak-cheese demand only a small fire to heat the reddish leaf tea spiced with yak-butter to make a perfect ration. Yak-hair cloth-cloaks clothe the poor, yak-hair ropes tie yak-hair cloth bags on top of a yak-hair saddle pad loaded onto a yak. Yak bones make glue, the shoulder blades are useful for the writing of prayers to be placed on a prayer-stone pile, and even the bones are ground up for their marrow and for soup stock. The yak horn makes a splendid snuff box, or powder horn or even a whiskey flask. The yak skin is converted into all uses possible for leather from boots to bedding, from thongs to thimbles, snow-goggles to milk-strainers, and sacks to slings. Yak-tails adorn the gay rider's horse and lay low the persistent horse-fly. Certain glands are used medicinally. Other uses are too numerous to mention.

The grassland nomads have only a perfunctory interest in stationary monasteries as compared to their movable religious structures which follow the wanderings of the tribe. In the midst of the Othoh tribe settlement where we are camped is a large black yak-hair tent ninety by forty feet able to seat 180 monks in six long rows (Photo No. 23). At the far end brass idols gaze placidly down upon vessels of grain and water set before them. Near the large tent crowded groups of red-robed priests peer out beneath the flaps of four smaller tents. This movable monastery has all the equipment for the conducting of ceremonies from exorcising of demons, which cause sickness and rain, to invoking aid of benevolent deities for the welfare of the tribe. The Gelugpa sects are theoretically presumed to have advanced beyond the use of exorcism in combating devils but actually their ceremonies are cluttered with ritual for the expelling of evil spirits. Such ritual has been inherited from the older sects of Lamaism (the Red Hats and the Black Hats) by the nomadic Yellow Hat or Gelugpa.

Our tent is pitched beside that of our caravan guide, Drale Gonchoh. His wife, a beautiful but dirty-faced woman, whose silver head plaques and tinkling silver chatelaines hanging down her back contrast oddly with her greasy braided hair and blackened clothing, comes out to meet us. So did his aged parents around seventy years of age, rather unusual for a couple as the average life is very short in these high altitudes especially for men. The nomad women carry their heavy gold and silver ornaments all day long whether milking their Dzo (female yak) or gathering yak chips. Seen by an outsider not wearing these signs of wealth would abash them more than if found stripped to the waist on a hot day. Of course, there are very poor women who have no such array of ornaments and are compelled to be content with a few miserable rings on their fingers or a pair of earrings. Those who have the full panoply of jewelery, usually handed down as heirlooms, are expected to wear it as part of their daily costume.

We go into the tent of our hosts later in the day, soon after a light drizzle, in which a rainbow circles the sun (Photo No. 24). Such brilliant halos and three rainbows one above the other are quite common in these clear skies after a rain. We present them a red silk scarf and also the customary white gauze scarf or khatah. They reciprocate with a chunk of butter in a sheep's stomach. The tent which measures thirty by fifteen feet is cluttered with their complete household equipment. The stove of dried clay occupies the center with sitting and sleeping spaces on each side. Boxes and bags containing food and clothing encircle the edge of the tent keeping out the wind with the aid of yak dung piled around outside the tent bottom. The back end is a shrine with

brass idols and pictures of deities fronted by a row of bowl offerings. Stomachs of butter share the supporting poles with bamboo
tea strainers, dippers and a sheaf-shaped offering of field and
animal products. The tent-top is in two halves with a line of par-
tition in the center open a foot wide, and being directly above the
stove, serves as an effective chimney and skylight. In one corner
the aged couple lie beneath sheepskin blankets and in another
corner rest a couple of lambs. The utensils stacked around or on
top of the stove include a dipper or two of copper, a clay teapot,
a brass kettle, a wooden churn of birch for tea mixing, a pine
meat cutting board and a granite stone hand mill. Life is hard
but the people are happy. As a rule they have plenty of meat,
cheese and tea, this last being the principal article bought in
trade. Coins are little used except for the making of ornaments
or utensils. We chat and drink a cup of buttered tea. When we
depart our hostess holds back the huge lunging mastiff with black
shaggy coat and tan-coloured legs, whitish throat and yellow
dotted eyes. He is an effective watchdog which every nomad keeps
to guard his tent and herd.

Later we visit and photograph the immense tent and jeweled
inmates of the Prince known as Othohbon or Prince of the Othoh
tribe (Photos Nos. 25 and 26). His kitchen is 60 x 30 x 12 feet
and his sleeping tent, where guests are received, is 40 x 20 x 12
feet. His dress is somber as contrasted to the females of the family. His wife and mother vie with each other in the gorgeousness
of their costumes. Each wears six dinner-plate-sized, jewel-adorned
gold plaques, the gold in each worth 600 rupees. A plaque is worn
on each side of the head, one at the back of the head and three
triangularly on the back below the shoulders. With jeweled silver
chatelaines, gold earrings, rings and other accessories as flint case,
toilet case, charm boxes, snuff box and knife with chopsticks in a
scabbard, each princess carries her fortune on her back. It is said
that orginally every gold or silver plaque indicated a lover.

In milking the nanny goats and ewes the nomadic wife takes a
low wooden bucket flaked with cheese and dirt and places it under
the udder. Then straddling the animal at the shoulders with her
face on the rump she embraces the middle of the beast and milks
both sides at once. Yak are usually milked from the animal's

right side with the milk falling into a large wooden pail whose top is partially covered with a yak-hair strainer. As the utensils are not washed acid remnants almost instantly sour the fresh milk. I was never able to get a drink of sweet milk even when taking it immediately after milking. Milk is either made into butter or cheese; very little whole milk is drunk.

To the products of his herds the nomad adds barley to his diet when he is able to exchange butter or cheese for it with the valley dwellers. Dried turnips is the chief vegetable with now and then a few dried peas. In the lean springs among the very poor and those who have been robbed of their grain, dried turnips is often the only food for two or three months. Times are very hard indeed when dried turnips are not to be had.

We strenuously resist the urging that we stay here for another day to await the collection of our various loads scattered in many caravans of this valley. We know from experience that we can best press our further advance from Litang by being in the city. The carrying of loads and the furnishing of escort will be done by the Yonru or the other branch of the Washee. Breaking camp the following day we circle first southwest and then west fording the Hor river which is often a serious obstacle. It is raining slightly at times which causes me to remark to Drale Gonchoh, "I thought that you paid the priests two rupees to hold back the rain so the river would not be swollen." "It won't rain very much, they are keeping most of the rain away," is his ready reply. From the state of the sky I thought he might be mistaken but the sky soon clears giving us fair although slightly cloudy weather the rest of the day. The river is not high for we are near its source and the heavy rain of last night has ceased in time for the stream to fall a foot and the slight rain of this morning is not enough to make the crossing dangerous. It is only stirrup or shoulder high, the limit for safe fording of rivers.

Beyond in the Hor valley are seventy nomad tents whose curling yak chip fires make cheerful the gloomy, misty air. As we go up a side branch we pass the sandy mounds of abandoned gold diggings. The crude method of panning gold must leave the greater part of the metal in the ground. The inability of the miners to dig more than a few feet soon exhaust the possibilities. I get a

slight touch of gold fever as I think of the ease in following the
stream a few miles to its source to discover if possible the lode
which the stream must tap.

About noon we cross Tsasha Pass 14,800 feet and before us
spreads out a vast plain bounded by high ranges. On the other
side of this marshy tableland twists the Litang river, its ends lost
in distant mountain ranges. At the foot of the spur which we are
descending the town of Litang lies snug and cosy. Abuting above
the town is the monastery whose huge white buildings almost ob-
scure the dirty one-story hovels which line the streets.

Glancing to the south I can almost see the range in the Molashe
country where I surprised a lynx in a cut-over woodland during a
hunting trip six years later. A nail in my boot had caused me to
lay my gun down and sit upon a nearby stump while I took off my
boot to remove the offender. My servant moved to one side with
my horse and up jumped a lynx, who leaping through the tall
grass made for the forest. He was among the trees by the time I
could grab my gun and take a long chance at a spasmodically seen
figure. I missed the lynx but pulled the nail out of my boot.

We circle around the monastery and enter the south gate to
pass through the one long street to its farther end where we lodge
at the northwest corner of the alley in a building, once a school,
but now deserted and dilapidated.

Figure 19
Past the Gelugpa and Nyingmapa Monasteries of Tachienlu our tiny caravan
moves westward to the grasslands of Tibet

Figure 20
Our tents at Watse in the Menya valley at 12,000 feet altitude

Figure 21
Washing gold along tributary of Hor Chu

Figure 22
The yak, ready for our loads, is indispensable to Tibet

Figure 23
Lamas in tent monastery resting during exorcising-prosperity-ritual

Figure 24
Inside Drale Gonchoh's tent

Figure 25
Tent of Prince of the Othoh—small tent contains sick man, with a lamb beside
him to receive disease demon

Figure 26
Othoh nomad moves by first taking down tent which man in left rear is folding

Chapter VI

TEA CARAVANS OF THE WASHI-GOLOH

The houses of Litang are dungy on the outside and dingy on the inside. The familiar nut-brown cakes dot every housewall; they repose in piles by each clay-stove, and their acrid smoke in the low dark houses produces multitudes of sore eyes. The ground floor of the houses on the lower slope are several feet below the level of the street which is the official Chinese and business section of the town. In these 100 houses live also the artisans, the workers for the monastery, traders, and carriers of wood and water. The eighty-five houses of the pure Tibetan population lie out on the plain a short distance south of the Chinese village. In the Tibetan quarters stands the scarred walls of the old Prince's palace. In one of the huts clinging to these historic grounds with forlorn hope dwells his daughter Gezong-Lhamo the former queen of Batang. Phantom reverence, as compared to the past, is paid to her because of her previous glory. She proudly shows the pictures of herself holding the severed head of her husband's murderer, the bloody Chao Erh Feng, who was decapitated by the revolutionists in 1912. In viewing pictures the Tibetans clasp their fingers to the palm forming a hollow tube and gaze through this tunnel.

The Litang river hugs the southwest side of the Litang Plain which runs in a general northwest and southeast direction; going westward toward Batang it contracts from six miles in width opposite Litang to one fourth mile within twenty miles; for the next twelve miles it varies from 100 feet to one fourth mile; after this it changes to a miniature canyon for five miles only to quickly broaden into a swamp about ten miles long and three miles wide; this swamp is the confluence for all the source streams which tumble down from nearby glaciers. Easterly downstream the Litang River leaves the broad Litang plain through a short expanded canyon but soon its course is not known in detail as only a few men have crossed it at various ferries and have not traced it for any great distance. On the right bank toward the west are rugged, barren limestone mountains where the protective spirits of Litang reside but toward the east are undulating grassy shale ranges where white elk roam. Wherever the Litang Plain approaches flatness it becomes a marsh with the river branching and curving from one side of the plain to the other. It is one of the world's highest inhabited plateaus lying on the average 14,000 feet above sea level. The city lies in the northeasterly corner surrounded on three sides by rolling hills smooth with wire-like grass, and millions of flowers such as blue gentians in late summer. Northward these undulating hills extend as far as the eye can see from the top of the range back of Litang, at least thirty to fifty miles toward Gangdzi.

Previously nothing would mature on the plain except a few miserable turnips until some few years ago I sent in some seeds including potatoes at the request of the Mayor named Wang who had known us in Batang where he served a term as the army commander. Other vegetables were added by experimentation and lettuce, radishes, spinach, beans, mustard and Osun, a Chinese vegetable resembling white radishes, besides potatoes grow to maturity in the short hot summer. Potatoes three inches in diameter were produced in the rich black soil. Rapid growing barley is being tried but when the frost is too early it does not mature, only furnishing fodder for stock. In time grains will be acclimated to ripen in the short plateau season and then thousands of acres now just above the crop line will yield bounteous harvests. At present superstition and transportation difficulties prohibit the development of vast agricultural and mineral resources which with water power, timber and beef will be the chief future sources of wealth in Tibet. Banditry and lack of capital also are leaving idle vast acreages which might be cultivated.

Deposits of soda and sulphur are found on the surface of the Litang plain but their exploitation awaits a wider market. Walking one day over the valley carpeted with yellow buttercups, strawflowers and pearly everlasting we discover by the side of the brook many little black square pebbles whose weight is much above that of ordinary stones of equal size. The Tibetans call them Oshudoshu and claim that these stones indicate the presence of gold. We gather a small bag of them.

The Litang monastery is located in the northeast corner at the widest expanse of the plain (Photos No. 27, 28, 29, 30). It is one of the largest lamaseries in eastern Tibet. The present registration of 3700 priests represent eight different tribes including the two branches of the Washi and the Shangchen. Probably there are less than 500 lamas at any one time resident within the walls except at the New Year Festivals when all monks try to be present. In addition to the two main temple buildings there are smaller temples for each tribe, and two hermitages a few hundred feet up the hillside. Another huge building houses the printing establishment. Other structures, to the number of 120, house the monks, supplies and smaller shrines.

One main temple is dedicated to the God of Love (Jyampa Shampa) the Coming Buddha and the other principal structure is the idol residence of Tsongkhapa (Lozang Drapa), the Precious Lord (Photo No. 31). Before these idols stand seven huge cauldrons of butter where tiny wicks are kept perpetually burning. We are warned not to breathe upon the feeble flames lest they go out. We then enter the kitchen where four great dark bronze kettles six feet in diameter will provide tea for 4000 monks at a time. We thoughtfully observe worshippers prostrating themselves in depressions worn in the human shape as much as four inches deep in the wooden floor. We wonder how many years and how many millions of prostrations were needed to groove the floor to that depth.

In the main temple resides the abbot who holds office for two years when he is succeeded by the elected representative of another tribe. He may, or may not, be an incarnation but this system rotates the tremendous power in his hands to the same tribe every sixteen years. The present abbot is not an incarnation but his successor who takes office in 1930 will be. The abbot is a tall man, handsome and affable, and about forty years of age. An able practical man he has distinguished his administration by building a new residence at the south end of the town for the Mayor so as to remove the unholy Chinese officialdom from the holy monastery buildings. We also met the abbot-elect who is of a pious mystical turn of mind much sought after for divination advice.

While taking a picture of the abbot-elect a few days later a nomad interrupts us, presents the monk with half a rupee and inquires the whereabouts of his cow which has either strayed or been stolen. The wily lama asks several questions and then calls for his dice. He shakes the dice in one hand and then blows upon them muttering at intervals some low jumbled words which the rest of us cannot understand; fiinally he casts the dice in a bowl.

"Your cow has been stolen and taken in a southern direction," comments the priest.

"Precious Incarnation, will I be able to recover my cow," asks the bowing nomad humbly.

The lama repeats his dice-throwing act, but the return seems unsatisfactory and he repeats but the results are not favorable so he tries a third time.

"The forecast is unfavorable to your finding your animal. Your enemy of the Shangchen tribe has stolen the beast and you will not get it back," replies the lama.

The nomad is not as crestfallen as I expect him to be. He either has surmised where his cow has gone and will try to even matters when the time is favorable, or being of the fatalistic mind, now certain that his chances of recovering his cow are slim, he is accepting the verdict calmly. The uncertainity of his mind has been dispelled and the anxiety of his face has been replaced by resignation and peace so he has obtained his money's worth in spending a half rupee for the loss of a thirty rupee cow.

We visit the print shop, a substantial structure sixty feet by 100 feet in size and filled to its fifteen foot ceiling with the heavy blocks used to print the Kahgyur or Buddhist Scriptures. Here lie thousands of hand-carved boards probably never to be used again since wood and paper have become so expensive in Litang that it is cheaper to buy the scriptures in Dege, and transport them 200 miles. At the present time one of the Washi chiefs called Aden is absent on a trip to Dege, a journey of fifteen days, for the purpose of buying a set of the Kahgyur which includes 108 volumes, each so heavy that eight volumes make a load. The set will cost 2000 rupees but by using their own animals the cost of transportation will be less than a hundred rupees.

The printing blocks are boards one and a half inches thick, nine inches wide and about four feet long. The letters are carved by hand which demands a high degree of accuracy and an immense amount of labor. The carved boards are piled on shelves in cases four feet long, twelve feet high and two and one half feet wide. Eleven cases make a section across the room which has ten such sections. Many scarves of silk are suspended from the center of the ceiling and in their midst three hideous masks and stuffed wild animal skins peer down upon us. The scarves are largely ceremonial but the masks and animals are to repel evil spirits.

The whole process of printing is done by hand. The work of rubbing the rough bark-like paper, after it has been produced by boiling from bark, into smoothness is a big task. Preparation of the ink is laborious. Keeping the printing blocks from becoming mixed is no small chore and I notice the attendant is careful to see that I place blocks back in the same niche from which I have removed them. Many monks are busy several months printing one copy of the Kahgyur yet the cost is comparatively cheap, about 400 dollars in American money. The monks work for a mere pittance, just a little more than their food and clothing.

A few days before we arrived in Litang we learn that three men who owed the monastery considerable sums of money, which they could not repay, had been expelled from the vicinity. The lamas had threatened to cut off their right hands but finally decided that it would prove more creditable to Buddhistic tenets and more humane to punish the bankrupts by stamping a seal on their foreheads which proclaimed that they were ordure; and then stretching each of the debtor's arms wide with wooden crosspieces they were cast out from the south gate. No longer able to reside in Litang they will probably seek refuge in the Shangchen country and may wind up as members of a robber band.

The Litang Monastery with its white-washed walls, its red and black painted timbers is quite pleasing but the adjoining dirty clay shacks where the laymen live are repulsive. Houses must be one-story as one may not live above or look down upon the gods in the temples. The city trends northeast and southwest with the monastery on the northeast and the new Chinse official residence or yamen and the school on the southwest. The flat clay roofs of the shacks are still gay with the tops of little fir trees attached to the four corners. The firs are decorated with prayer flags and tufts of wool all of which were placed on the third day of the sixth lunar month or in July for the pleasing of the local deities. White stones clustered around the base of the firs while holding them in place likewise hint that white stone ritual has a place in the festivities which are marked by horse races upon the plain. When incense fires, set by easterly facing devotees from the cone-shaped altars on the eastern house corners of the roofs, curl sky-ward in the frosty mornings, we think of smoking chimneys from pioneer woodland settlements in our homeland.

To the south the traces of an ancient city said by the Tibetans to have been built by the Jyong show a remarkable orientation. They were only two degrees off from a perfect north and south line. Their city had a width of 500 feet east and west, and 1500 feet north and south.

Litang is the trading center for a large but scantily settled region. Its seventy Chinese families are merchants who eke out a meager living selling tea, blue cotton cloth and a few miscellane-ous articles. The 125 Tibetan families live by their flocks or by serving the lamas and Chinese officials. Commerce in the Tibetan articles of salt, wool, woollen cloth and musk are brought in by Tibetan caravans who deal directly with the Tibetan population except for the musk which is sold to Chinese exporters.

Litang is not wholly under the control of the Chinese. The turbulent monks backed by the nomad population cause much trouble and often refuse to obey the Chinese officials who have come in as conquerors. The people are adept at evasion and mal-ingering. Prior to 1905 a native prince with a second royal family ruled the district but Manchu despotism under the conqueror Chao Erh Feng, in order to further limit the local autonomy of the independent mountaineers, caused the extinction of the royal fam-ilies, the chief prince being beheaded and the second prince dying in prison. About 1915 an abortive outburst to regain their local autonomy resulted in the burning of the two palaces leaving nothing but ruins of the former princely splendor.

Our long stay here of eight days taxes my medical resources. 111 patients have come for treatments. My success with ringworm, worms, wounds and pulling of teeth have procured many hearty invitations to come again and stay longer. A butcher accidentally cut his palm halfway through the hand and for the first time I find my suture clips of great value. On a later trip I set a boy's broken femur sustained from falling off a second story roof. He was brought to me within fifteen minutes and, by careful padding of the splints taken from boxes with daily releasing of the bandages for a period, and with other careful attention the lad suffered no infection and recoverd completely with very little deformation. The boy's family was poor and could give nothing but the butcher rewarded me with a quarter of beef. Several serious operative cases are offered to me but I refer them to the hospital at Batang where a physician is available. A hospital would do an untold amount of good in this area.

The Washi are reluctant to start before the new Chinese Mayor for Batang arrives from Tachienlu. We paid 100 rupees to the Othoh tribe for protection through their territory from Tachienlu to Litang and we must pay another hundred from Litang to Batang to the Yonru tribe. The Chinese always travel with a large escort of soldiers and we consider it safer to travel with them and they reciprocate that idea. Only twenty of the Chinese soldiers will be armed out of the 100 going in as replacements at Batang. The Yonru of the Washi furnish fifteen armed men. The raiding tribes of Shangchen and Kemo sometimes number from fifty to 100 but hesitate to attack large armed groups as it results in too great a possible loss of life. We set out on the twenty-second of July taking the old main road westward which we had left three days out of Hokou. This old route dipping up and down gives greater comfort at night due to reaching lower altitudes where most settlements abound.

Our first bit of scenery is the hill to the west where black and white vultures stalk clumsily after a hearty meal of corpse eaten at the break of day, the mortal remains of a dead lama which had been cut up and thrown to them. As we file past, the gory-headed birds run uphill, wheel and take off in flight downhill as it is difficult for them to do so on level ground and impossible on an up-slope.

In three hours travel we reach the fork of the road where the main road turns left and crosses the Litang river over a rickety bridge, but we continue straight on the north side of the stream.

The main and former post-road after crossing the Litang river climbs over a gap in the grey granite ridge and daily with strenuous descents and ascents of mountain passes goes in a great southwest half circle before we see it again two days east of Batang. Another hour's journey up the river and we camp among the homes of our Washi caravan. We are on the high level plateau and northern route to Batang never below 14,000 feet above sea level until the last night before reaching the city. Only two passes, and but one considered difficult, mar this more direct route. The greater altitude gives a colder road which is very trying to those without a strong heart. Water and fuel are plentiful upon both routes but our northern one is more dependent upon yak chips for boiling tea and partially cooking the yak-beef.

During our first day's journey we have passed numerous hot springs of sulphurous origin. The nomads believe the odoriferous waters are efficacious in keeping their flocks healthy so once a year, at least, the animals are pastured in the vicinity for a few days. We encourage our servants to obtain some of the same tonic effect by long soaking in the baths.

The next three days we follow the Litang river in a general northwesterly direction. The black shale hills are strewn with flowers and the streams in the intervening valleys are lined with piles of gravel thrown up by gold-diggers who live in miserable sod huts and supplement their meager earning with the produce from small flocks of sheep and a few yak. The miners divert a portion of a river into a side stream and over turf in a long trough which washes away the fine soil. The stones are thrown out and the residue shaken over other slabs of turf as water rushes over it. These second slabs of turf are beat over a pan to cause the heavy flakes of gold to drop out which is cleansed by panning. A rupee's worth of gold a day is possible, one half of which goes to the prince. Sometimes the top soil is thrown out by shovels and only the gravelly soil underneath washed for gold. The final flakes of gold are carried in a skin bag.

Near the end of the second day the dark slaty earth gives way to a narrow granite canyon which soon spreads out into a wide marshy plain not less than two miles wide. At the beginning of this plain we ford the Litang river which here divides into five

branches. The recent rains have increased the waters so that the
swift current runs three feet deep at the shallowest places wetting
our loads and menacing our chair carriers. The five streams with
their smaller tributaries wind in gigantic S curves through the
marsh. Of the two biggest branches the largest continues northward rising in the snow mountains which can be seen peeping
over a range of low hills. The second most important branch is
the one we follow upward in a westward course. After fording
the streams we ascend a little mound to encamp near a sulphurous
pond upon which floats a single quacking sheldrake. Too hot to
bear the hand at its point of issue the springs which feed the pond
must be at least 115 degree Fahrenheit. The masses of white plan-
tain flowers have given the marsh the name of White Grass Plain.

Beginning with the lower end of this plain and extending up
the river for the next thirty-five miles are the assembly grounds,
every autumn about the middle of October, for the Washi tribes
who in full force number 615 counted tents and an estimated 3000
individuals. The black spider-resembling tents thickly dot the
plain seeming to crawl amidst thousands of yak, tens of thousands
of sheep and hundreds of horses. In this great gathering of the
nomadic clans the guns are counted, the stock estimated and the
people enumerated. Horse racing, archery and rifle shooting con-
tests intermingled with feasting and drinking bouts enliven the pro-
ceedings. Disasters are discussed such as raids upon stock and
ambushing of men, plans of revenge are laid and relations with
the Chinese are surveyed. It is also a time of lover's trysts and
marriage arrangements.

The lamas have left their settled monastic temples and followed
the tribes to their annual convocation. A huge black yak hair tent
is erected and here a hundred monks hold exorcising ceremonies
before their tribual deity called Gonbo praying for prosperity and
chanting against calamity. Tea is boiled in four huge kettles as
the lamas groan out texts to the boom of four big drums, the
clash of cymbals and the weird honk of conch shells. The chief
priest sits on the right at the front upon a high seat while solid
walls of religious scrolls adorn the other three sides of the tent.
After a long recital the ceremony pauses for the serving of tea to
each monk whose bowl has been resting upon the ground before

his feet. Although tea and tsamba are their principal diet, yet they will also feast with their lay relatives on wheat crullers boiled in butter and eaten with whipped cheese. Hot noodles topped with grated beef is a favorite dish and hunks of boiled mutton are gorged daily.

Mythology clothes the encircling mountains. On the north side of the valley in the high snow peaks reside the Zhidah or protective deities of the Washi. Once a lion lived in these ranges and when he was killed his intestines and urine flowed out to create the many earthen bumps at the base of the slopes. Wild animals are held sacred here and anger is aroused among the devout when the antelope are slain by the cynical.

This enlarged river plain is a vast horse-rhubarb plantation. Thousands of tall yellow candles spring from a center of small plaintain-like serrated leaves, rising to a height of one to two and a half feet. The leaves line the stem for the first foot and then the small lemon-yellow flowers continue to the tip in a tall imposing spike. The horse rhubarb is found only above 14,000 feet altitude and along streams or in marshy ground. Its stalk is chewed but is not as palatable as another variety uprooted for its roots which are valuable for medicinal purposes, forming one of the exports from Tibet to other lands. The medicinal rhubarb is found on drier ground growing down as low as ten to twelve thousand feet in altitude. It is a tall dock-like plant with long green spikes rising sometimes eight feet above a clustered nest of heavy, indented leaves, and more closely resembles the American domesticated rhubarb. Both plants may be found close together, one by the stream and the other above on the drier slope. Children buy the medicinal plant stalks as refreshment sticks at the festivals and annual tribal fairs.

During the remainder of the year the Washi tribes live in the numerous ravines leading from our route pitching their tents in sheltered coves. The Washi comprise two tribes, the Othoh and Yonru, and claim that they are Goloh (Golog) asserting the sameness of their dialect with the Goloh around the headwaters of the Yellow River. My men confirm this common origin and affirm the Tibetan dialects of the Goloh and the Washi are identical.

The Goloh women wear four to six huge silver plaques upon their backs from their waists over the buttocks, and down to the feet. The Washi women (Photo No. 32) array themselves in like manner except higher up and with some platters upon the head. It is not easy for the settled Tibetans to understand the Goloh and the Washi dialects. The Washi and Goloh men are both more hairy than the village Tibetans. Perhaps the Goloh are the original Tibetan nomads and the progenitor of all Tibetan nomadic tribes. The nomads roam over vast territories which are limited to definite boundaries, each tribe having alloted grounds. Infringements of these boundaries cause bloody feuds which may last until one tribe is too weak to continue the struggle.

As we wade through the purple heather of the plains we startle the mountain lark who, as he rises, trills a joyous musical song from a white yellowish colored throat encircled by a black ringlet. We find them scattered over the undulating grassy mountains up to 15,000 feet. As we quietly round mountain spurs inky-black ravens croak from jutting rocks warily flying off long before we come close. Once one had white feathers in both wings, a rare variation. A few times blackheaded cranes with black-tipped wings and tails propel their ungainly white frames, a weaving white bag of bones, across the moors.

After leaving the gold diggers on the third day out of Litang we see no other people for five days except one camping caravan and one group of medicine hunters. This isolation does not bother us since our own caravan is large enough for a good-sized Tibetan village. Our 500 animals (400 yak and 100 horses) travel in groups of fifteen to fifty. At a distance as the yaks stream over the immense plain they resemble black marching cavalry. Incidentally constant counting of large herds revealed that out of twenty yak seventeen will be black, two will be yellow and one white. One out of ten is a mulley or hornless. For the pack animals there are forty Tibetan drivers. Deaths and desertions enroute from Tachienlu have thinned the original 100 soldiers to 75. Merchants, officials and camp followers swell our company to over 150 persons. Up to Litang our small group with only one gun was worried when two armed hunters appeared upon a distant hill. Now the appearance of twenty armed horsemen riding in a nearby ravine cause us little concern as we count up to fifty guns although all are careful to keep within protection of the caravan.

The big shaggy yak moving sedately in a close group seem submissive until one is frightened by an unusual noise or is galled under the heaviness of his burden then he will start on a rampage which may stampede the whole herd. Snorting and with erect tail the beast will plunge and buck until the load slides under his belly. Now begins a kicking and stamping on the boxes to loosen or break the thongs of the monster holding him around the middle. Only our yak-hide can withstand such rough treatment. Several animals go on the rampage every day so we considered ourselves lucky that we suffered only one serious loss. Toward the end of the journey the bamboo basket of iron utensils used daily by the cook was reduced to iron debris and hashed vegetables. Our iron firepan which our cook had cherished from Chungking was shattered to bits, the handle of the skillet broken and divers utensils smashed into junk. We had cautioned the cook to pack all utensils in skin boxes and now his disobedience forces him to use utensils which burn his fingers for the rest of the trip. I listen carefully as he daily consigns the yak to both the hot and cold hells in which Buddhists believe sinners will suffer. One or two tins of coal-oil are leaking and doubtless will be empty when we arrive. The Washi offer to pay for such damages but I purchase good will by saying such losses must be expected and are due to forces beyond their control.

On the fourth day we turn southwest leaving the wide plain at its northwest corner and follow the next largest source branch of the Litang river. Sometimes we must stick close to the beaten path lest we mire in the rain-sodden bogs near the stream. We top a little incline as the river cuts through a small canyon and emerge on another plain one eighth to a half mile wide and two miles long; in its midst the river carves a gigantic S. To the north and west are a few snow peaks which must be 19,000 to 20,000 feet high as the line of perpetual snow is around 18,000 feet at this latitude. We shift south and southwest for short spaces until we reach the end of the plain, ascend another spur and camp in another swampy bulge. Here are a few blue and white cotton tents where rhubarb and aconite hunters are residing for a few days. When the opportunity offers such temporary sojourners rob small caravans or mail-runners.

During the night rain and snow soak through our fifteen cloth tents placed over the loads but the Tibetan yak-drivers huddled on the leeside of the boxes in heavy sheepskins do not mind the moisture. These cloth flaps are light, easily dried and drain most of any rain which falls. The caravan leader has attached strings of prayer flags on the ropes of his shelter for the wind to flap out prayers for the welfare of men and beasts. At dusk when we are camped in lonely spots a few shots are fired to warn thieves that we are ready for them.

The next morning which is the thirty-first of July we curve in and out with the river trending westward for three hours until its source goes south up a canyon to issue as a tumbling torrent from glaciers a few miles distant. We have followed the Litang river and its tributaries for four and a half days rising from 13,800 to 14,800 feet above sea level which indicates the comparative placidity of the river-bed. We now ford the river whose grassy plain slopes from a cave capable of holding a dozen men and adjoining a hot spring which provides mail runners between Batang and Litang with room and bath. Beyond the stream we begin the steep climb up grassy Shari La or Deer Mountain Pass.

Upward and westward we breathlessly crawl between granite outcrops in whose crevices bloom blue poppies and on whose flat spaces grow whorls of juniper. We climb until noon when we eat lunch by the roadside to save time and give us strength to climb some more. With panting stops we reach the top to rest by a turquoise lake a quarter of an acre in extent (Photo No. 33). To some of the soldiers I give heart stimulants from my drug box so they can surmount the 16,200 foot pass of Shari. One man ahead of us lies limp like a sack, having died because his heart was not strong enough to endure the continuous high elevations. A robber trail from this pass can be seen winding into the Lingkashi country and brooding over that tribal land are the Tsirashi Peaks which are the Seven Sisters seen from the western heights of the Batang Valley.

After our rest on the summit we descend to a rocky camp for 750 feet, where water comes out of a rocky ravine to start a stream.

The day is far spent and it is necessary for the animals to have a little grass. I limber up my joints in a stroll and finding some claw-marks I am told by a Tibetan that this flat scratched spot, pawed out by the leopard, shows that the beast is casting lots as to where he will find game.

On the morrow we stumble down a granite-bouldered ravine recrossing the constantly increasing stream six times, each time more dangerous and with greater soaking of the loads. Moving through juniper and rhododendron and then at lower altitudes through fir forests we enjoy our first trees in eight days travel. We are riding happily in the midst of the forested valley when men upon the far mountain side fire two shots at our caravan as some of the animals are crossing an open glade. We halt in the shelter of the woods and watch our Washi escort return the fire from be-hind rocks and trees. It may have been a party of hunters, ready to rob us if we are weak and panic stricken, or only conscienceless in the use of their firearms. At any rate the attackers flee at our fusilade and we continue to travel westward. Each time as we ford a stream we watch in dismay the burly yak seeking the deep water in which to swim (Photo No. 34). They love the coolness of icy water against their sweating heaving flanks, but we think of the arduous task of drying out clothing and the large quantities of cloth we are bringing in as cash to meet the running expenses of the Mission work. Snow peaks loom far to the east as we camp by the river at an altitude of 14,400 feet (Photo No. 35). For the sec-ond time we dry our bedding, which in spite of being tightly wrapped in oil sheets and then waterproof canvas with a final outer covering of yak skin, has soaked too long in the fording process.

We spend part of the next morning tracing the river and then, letting the stream continue south, we abruptly turn up a spur which runs down in front of an immense cathedral of granite. The absolutely barren jagged points of this peak are thrust upward above 17,000 feet altitude, but the spires are too steep to arrest snowflakes. Back of the ridge is reputed to be a good-sized lake, and in front we see a small pond fed partially by a mass of ice which probably disappears before the end of the summer. Through the needle-pointed saw-toothed backbone of this granite mass are two immense holes and one small one. Legend affirms that a great warrior, King Gesar, made these holes by shooting arrows at the cliff face. His heroic exploits are found in a book called Dragyi.

We climb rapidly by way of a forest-lined depression between two spurs of the range. Here in 1927 200 Shangchen Tibetans ambushed 100 Chinese soldiers and slaughtered over twenty of them. Today just above this ill-fated battlefield a platoon of Chinese soldiers from Batang meet us. Crossing over two shoulders we plunge along a narrow rocky road bordered by juniper and fir. In time we creep past granite cliffs to stay for the night on a moraine above 15,750 feet high above the sea. This is our highest camp between Tachienlu and Batang (Photo No. 36). We have very little desire to walk about, an act of the will being necessary to inspire one to physical effort. The children are less active than usual. Of course the camping site is not level nor smooth, consisting of a granitic graveled plain with fitful tufts of grass which give the yak a scanty supper. The mountain masses and valleys seem to have been glaciated and what resembles glacial striae are seen upon some of the rocks. There is other evidence of glaciation such as receding lakes and amphitheatrical valleys.

To the southeast beyond the narrow gorge up which we have just come are the Nehmdah (or Dajola) snow capped mountains, projecting like a rough silver wall and blocking further view. Near by and all around us rise a medley of bare, jagged granite tips 17,000 to 18,000 feet high. The highest is on the northeast and is called the Tshongponale or the Merchant Ale's Peak, which gives the pass its name. This peak is a seemingly unclimbable mass of granite boulders. It is related that a merchant, whose name is Ale, boasted that he could climb this peak. His companions wagered two yak that he could not. The merchant arrived at the top before the surprised eyes of his friends and then started to descend but was soon lost to view. No one dared to ascend for the purpose of ascertaining what had become of him. Although never heard of again the pass was named in honor of his exploit.

Snow fell during the night and is still falling as we shake the white flakes off the tents and packing the heavy canvas upon the yak begin the painful grind to the top. We have only a little more than 500 feet to attain but the wet snow makes the going slow and treacherous. We course southwestward for one and a half hours passing three turquoise lakes sheltered along caverned walls. The two upper lakes undoubtedly overflow slightly at times as they are fresh and water-marks indicate higher waters, and from the lowest lake is fed a stream through whose carved passage we are reaching the pass. It is the third of August. We can mentally picture the sizzling heat of Shanghai and Washington as we surmount the pass in a blinding snow storm which follows us down on the other side for several hundred feet of descent (Photo No. 37). At the top of the pass stands two whitened piles waving ghostly ragged arms. They are the usual stone cairns topped by fluttering prayer-banners. Very few have the enthusiasm to honor the spirit of the pass with the votive offering of stone and to cry "Oh-la-so-la." The caravan is almost as quiet as the softly falling snow.

In the descent we reach juniper trees around 14,000 feet and fir a few hundred feet lower. The path winds in a narrow course so that the grey, yellow and black drooping streamers of "old man's beard" which hang from the fir branches caress us with drops of water. After going down for one and a half hours we join the main road from Litang and can look up it almost to the point where it crosses this same range farther south over a pass equally high called Daso by the Chinese and Charaka by the Tibetans. After twisting about in a westerly direction through a thick fir forest we camp in an open glade at Bongtramo, a deserted village that once boasted eight houses. We have been on the road for five hours.

During the afternoon one of our Chinese escort eats some poisonous mushrooms and I am able to save his life by hypodermic injections of strychnine and apomorphine. The next morning as we break camp he shows his appreciation by prostrating himself flat upon the ground before me to my outward embarrassment but yet to my secret satisfaction that he is treating me with proper Oriental courtesy and gratitude.

Another day westward over a rocky trail by a foaming river and we arrive in Batang. The Washi dump their tea at Meliting where donkeys and bulls meet the yak and carry the loads the final ten miles to Batang. The yak, relieved of their burdens, scatter over the hillside and quickly become great black lumps against the green foliage (Photo No. 38). The Washi rightly fear the heat and the lack of grass on the Batang plain, which has an altitude of 8,500 feet. They refuse to weaken their yak by this two day's trip from the safe height of 12,000 feet at Meliting. The yak are kept only over night at Meliting, as the loads to go out to Litang have already arrived and are stored in the houses of the village. Tomorrow the shaggy beasts will be started on their upward climb, to move slowly and to pasture upon the uplands, while the leaders of the caravan transact the necessary business with us and the export merchants in Batang before catching up with their main caravan of yak.

On this last day, shortly after breaking camp, Dr. N. H. Bare with a large party of Batang Tibetans meet us. From this time on we greet groups of delighted people including Mrs. Bare, Mr. and Mrs. Raymond Peterson and the children of both foreign families. Members of the church, Chinese and Tibetan officials, lamas, friends and the curious, delay our progress with greetings and feasting upon noodles at the hot springs; not forgetting sips from five bowls of milk, each with three pats of butter forming the corners of a triangle upon the edge. We walk the last two miles until we enter the familiar Mission compound after an absence of a little over two years. Everything is homelike. Some faces which we had hoped to see are absent, having passed to another land. We are saddened by their going but glad to be back to help the living in their great spiritual quests of Life.

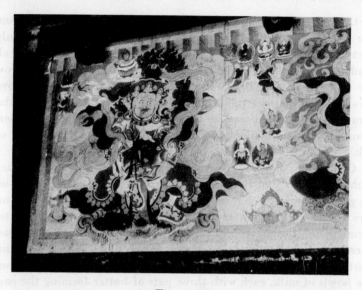

Figure 27
Yellow King of the North and God of Wealth symbolized by cat in left hand.
Litang Monastery.

Figure 28
Green King of the south.   Litang Monastery.

Figure 29
White Guardian King of the east on left holding mandolin; and Red Guardian
King of West on right. Litang Monastery.

Figure 30
Wheel of Life. Litang Monastery.

Figure 31
Tsongkhapa, Founder of the Yellow Hat Sect. Litang Monastery.

Figure 32
Three Washi Women display their heirlooms and wealth.

Figure 33

My wife and two children beside sedan chair resting on Shari Pass, 16,200 feet above sea level.

Figure 34

Fording the river between Shari and Tshongpon passes; spruce and fir forests form background.

Figure 35
Our tea caravan camped below and west of Shari La amid flowers, grass and evergreens.

Figure 36
My wife, John and Marian in our tent at altitude of 15,750 feet near top of Tshongpon La.

Figure 37
My wife in chair topping Tshongpon Pass in blizzard at 16,500 feet on
August 3rd.

Figure 38
Tea caravan of the Washi-Goloh at Meliting, one day's journey east of Batang.

Chapter VII

THROUGH A SIDE DOOR INTO INNER TIBET

With the fall of the Manchu Dynasty in 1911 desultory but bloody fighting broke out between China and Tibet. The peace treaty of 1918 arranged between the representatives of China, Tibet and Great Britain permitted travellers to come and go freely in China and Tibet. The then Chinese official government at Peking refused to ratify this treaty which may account for the refusal of the Tibetan Government to permit any Chinese citizens within her borders. This ban was not lifted until the death of the thirteenth Dalai Lama in 1933. As we were living under Chinese sovereignty east of the de facto Sino-Tibetan border it was not easy for Americans to obtain permission to visit within the Tibetan-governed areas.

It so happened that a high Tibetan military official in Gartok, the capital of Lower Kham, was suffering from an annoying skin disease. Hearing of Dr. N. H. Bare's medical prowess in Batang he invited the able physician to visit Gartok. Dr. Bare responded gladly and was so successful that the way was open for me to experience the same journey, one of a hundred miles, and three days inside free Tibet.

In reply to my letter to the Dahpon (Daben) or military governor regarding my visiting in Gartok the answer is in accordance with Tibetan custom and diplomacy. My request is not granted in the written answer, accompanied by a Khata or ceremonial scarf, which is for the official records. The runner by word of mouth informs me that I will be welcome. Upon this easily evaded responsibility for my entrance into a closed land I prepare to go.

The Chinese saying that a thousand days at home are equivalent to one day on the road properly evaluates travel in the Orient as contrasted to the Occident. In the wild lands of the Tibetan Plateau this is exceptionally true. From narrow precarious roads animals now and then plunge into foaming rivers. The accommodations but not the comforts of a hotel must be transported. Cloth

tents during thunderstorms and blizzards at high altitudes demand
personal attention lest one's quarters fly away. The principal food
procurable on the road is tsamba (parched barley flour), stale buttered tea and goat steak. However, appetites are not fastidious
after rugged mule riding up airless passes and scrambling down
stony trails.

We take a full month's supply of food but dispense with the
tent as the dry season is near at hand; when no house is available
we will sleep in caves or out in the open. Nomad tents are a last
resort but too often they are not pitched in the right place for an
inn, usually over a high range in another valley, and when found
too full of home folks for a large party.

The worst obstacle are the bandits. Rarely does the frequent
traveller in these parts escape being stripped clean of clothing and
food and having his beasts driven away. Clothing, being so essential in such a frigid climate, is peeled off only at the insistence of
a pointing gun. Sometimes the owner of the gun gets too nervous
with the trigger (the profession of highwayman is hard on the
nerves in this land where cutting off the head is the penalty when
caught) and a dead merchant is added to the other losses.

Travelling being a matter of life and death a propitious day
must be found. Astrological books and the stars are carefully
scanned to discover a lucky day. We have no faith in the stars pro-
phetic voice but as it is the 29th of the Tibetan month, the day
(our October 10th, 1931) is easily arranged. Journeys are not
undertaken except on certain (usually the uneven) days of the
month and on the days which are auspicious for that direction.

We hire mules from the chief priest of Batang since bandits are
less prone to attack the caravan of a high ranking lama. Robbers
fear the power of his charms and evil prayers which are said to
cause sickness, ill-luck and even death to an offender; such charms
being projected through the air from the residence of the priest to
the home of an enemy—perhaps the first wireless messages. The
priesthood of Tibet is a religious guild in which, if one member is
robbed, a representative is sent to the home of the robber to argue
the brigand into giving back the goods, if necessary using the bandit's own personal priest as a mediator. Lamas know that it is to

the welfare of the monastery for all men to be in deadly fear of their power.

As usual our mulemen want to delay a day at the last minute but an ultimatum that it is now or never is conclusive. The high hire I pay is too good to lose but their customary promised arrival at sunrise (in these high mountains about seven) is converted, as I expected, into a departure about noon. Friends escort us down the road for a half mile or more as is the custom in Tibet when one takes an extended trip. Our departure is under auspicious circumstances for outside the gate we meet a woman with a full barrel of water,—an empty cask would have been an ill-omen.

Coursing down with the Batang River we climb over the 9,500 foot shoulder pass of Khuyee formed by a mountain spur through which the Batang River is compelled to cut a deep defile in order to reach the Yangtze River which here is about 8,400 feet above sea level, perhaps a hundred feet lower than Batang. This pass is a favorite rendevous for brigands and its soil is tainted with the blood of many men, including Dr. A. L. Shelton who was assassinated from ambush near the top in 1922. Like all passersby we gaze intently into the bushes scattered amidst countless bowl shaped resurrection plants, for all know that Tibetan robbers keep themselves well hidden before firing suddenly from behind rocks; either killing, or intimidating travellers, before revealing themselves. We are unarmed but the chief priest has sent along two guns which he thinks are enough to risk losing because guns are valuable.

We go prepared to lose everything at the hands of robbers and figure on the law of averages to retain our lives. Our party is hardened to such eventualities. Brigands had attacked us in 1927 generously leaving the clothes we wore.* My Tibetan teacher Atring had lost his father by beheading at the hands of Chao Erh Feng because he was one of the late Prince's chief stewards; in addition his older brother, some five years previously, had been killed by bandits and his caravan pillaged a half day's journey below the pass we are now crossing. The medical assistant, Shao Pin Sen, is the most nervous as he had only helped my party once put on a bold front to keep us from being attacked by nomads two days west

* See my book "The Mountain of Silver Snow"

of here in 1925 when we visited a Red Cap shrine at Dorjetroleh. Our guide Jitsen is a hardened old sinner who has been trading on this road for many years, losing money to both officials and thieves so that he has to keep on trading to make a living. Last of all our cook Chohdrah has been chased by robbers and had his animals stolen, besides being a thief who filched from a former foreign resident of Batang and survived a period in an Oriental jail after having been beaten a thousand strokes on the thighs.

Arriving at Li (Leh) we set the talk in motion for the use of the ferryboat down to Druwalung. We have wisely secured a Chinese official travel pass telling all headmen not to delay us on the road by refusing to grant Oolah or forced transportation. We have animals to carry our goods but desire to send them empty to Druwalung and avoid the possibility of being held up by robbers at their favorite assaulting place halfway down. Furthermore the boat ride will be quicker and easier and a new experience for me. The boatmen wish naturally to avoid the arduous labor of pulling the boat back against the Yangtze current unless they are paid more than the usual small rate.

"How much will the master give us," is their opening question as they gather in a group around our teapot over the open fire at the temple.

"You know the custom and this is part of your taxes," is my answer, knowing full well they wish to hold me up for an exorbitant price.

"If you give us twenty rupees we will take the teacher down," is their opening offer, settling down for the long harangue.

"You know that the official rate is five rupees and sometimes with officials you do not get that. This is an official pass, and you don't want to ignore that, do you?" I return.

"What will the master give us; it is a long hard trip and you as a teacher of religion should have mercy upon us," they reply, knowing the weak points of my position.

"Well, I will not state what I will give you but you know that I have always been generous and no foreigner has ever given you less than twice the official rate," I state, and in spite of their pressure I will not promise what I will give, preferring to let the force of authority rule rather than the force of cash. They have no work to do and whatever they get will be a bonus. So in time they assent to ride us down in the boat the next morning.

Li is built a little above the Yangtze high water mark, upon one of the numerous alluvial plains formed by a small mountain stream. The Yangtze in this region rises above twenty-five feet in summer and does not expand much beyond its usual width of about three hundred to nine hundred feet. The houses of Li are built of masonry and plastered with soot inside. The inhabitants, human, quadruped and insect, with the last not the least prominent, dwell in lively companionship. However if one has to wrest a living as do these people, from tiny fields, oppressed by robbers, religionists, and rulers, one can understand their poverty and dirt.

The Yangtze is in mid-flood at least fifteen feet above low-water level. Fifteen days previously it was some seven feet higher for the dirty line can be seen on the white yellow sands. September had unusually heavy rains which has piled immense tracts of sand into miniature mountain ranges along the banks. So vast are these sand banks and containing so much gold that the Chinese have named the Yangtze within the Tibetan borderlands the "River of Golden Sands." Above this point the Yangtze is better known as the Dri Chu or Female Wild Yak River because of its legendary origin.

The sands are not always beautiful. When the dry season sets in, the steady southwest winds of winter stir up the tiny pellets and hurl them relentlessly upon the unwary traveller. The tightest cases are useless, even those of watches, while the faint-hearted along with the courageous must swallow grit to strengthen them.

Early on the eleventh of October we embark with all our goods on the wooden ferry barge which is preferred to the skin coracles in use in most places (Photos Nos. 39 and 40). At the coracle ferries animals must swim and the weaker ones are sometimes lost in the swift currents. Our craft is wide, flat-bottomed and heavy. Its length is about sixty feet, its width seven feet and seven compartments divide the hold. The previous one burnt by the Ranalama in 1923 was fifty-one feet long, nine feet wide and the same number of compartments. At the stern is a steering oar twenty-five feet long. On each side are two rowing oars each twenty feet long and manned by three men apiece. Every trip about ten animals and their loads can be carried. The actual crossing is a matter of three minutes but an hour is required for the round trip. The boat must be pulled by hand upstream, for the current in each crossing sweeps the craft down several hundred feet. The Yangtze in this stretch is from two hundred and fifty to three hundred and fifty yards wide.

We sit in the boat enjoying the varied scenery of brushed mountain spurs and alluvial plains created during the ages by the raging torrents from mountain tips. Scarred houses remind us of the Ranalama's raid in 1923 when he led his monastic band to within ten miles below Batang, looting and killing. Later chased back to his monastery three days below us, his own subjects chopped off his head with an axe one dark night, notwithstanding his sanctity as an incarnated saint popularly called a Living Buddha. His killers were men from a rival monastery whose monks he had mistreated and whose relations he had slaughtered. In one and a half hours we arrive in Druwalung but our animals take four hours on the trail.

At Druwalung we board a slightly larger ferry barge to cross the river and then, to continue downstream on that side past the mouth of a tributary river, the Sheh Chu, entering from the west with rain-swollen waters too deep for fording without wetting the loads. This river, whose headwaters we crossed on our return farther north, has carried away the flimsy wooden bridge, which is rebuilt every winter and washed into the Yangtze every summer.

We go ashore and mount our mules, entering a canyon where the fierce rapids, filled with huge boulders, prohibit navigation. Gazing upward on the western range one can see where an immense landslide has carried away half of the mountain into the river, compressing the channel into barely three hundred feet wide. The rains every year wash down great fields of mud and stones which must tax the angry waters to carry it away before the next rainy season.

Most of the Yangtze tributaries are from the east, small torrents formed and fed by springs. The maintenance of streams throughout the year is through numerous powerful springs rather than through the melting of snow. The rainfall of twenty-two to forty-five inches falls mostly during the summer while winter and spring are the dry seasons with scarcely an inch of overall precipitation.

In Batang and along the Mekong and Yangtze rivers the altitude is low enough for two crops a year. The first crop is wheat or barley and after this is cut in July, buckwheat or millet are sown, and harvested in October. One variety of millet called Tri is pulled up by the roots instead of being cut off. Millet and buckwheat are never grown at the higher altitudes, above ten thousand five hundred feet, as buckwheat especially does not stand frosts; furthermore when only one crop can be grown barley and wheat are more valuable.

On our third day we leave the Yangtze to turn south over a high cliff, whose eroded soil, of variegated colors, is said by the Chinese to indicate deposits of gold. The Yangtze yearly eats out great chunks of this rainbow cliff, carrying the gold for deposit in sands farther down where some of it is panned out by washing. From our turning point the mighty river goes southeast into a still more formidable canyon, most of it untrod by men. Savage rapids must tear at the rocks for the altitude here of 8,200 feet drops a half mile during the next one hundred and fifty miles of the river's course.

We rapidly ascend the bed of a small stream leaving behind us the grey limestone and granite regions of the last three days to enter a country of red clay and sandstone where the grassy plains are endless. Our observation is that spruce and firs prefer a limestone country, pines growing rather in sandstone areas; perhaps a matter of soil composition and retaining of moisture. Likewise a red soil, perhaps because of its heat absorbing qualities, seems to make crops possible at a higher altitude than other ground.

Through a fir forest we mount over a low pass and enter the Pamothang valley, whose population of a hundred homes is scattered across a grassy plain ten miles in length and one mile in width which makes it one of the most populous valleys in Tibet. It is harvest time. Turnips are being pulled up and carried to the homes on the backs of people and donkeys. Often in Tibet a man as a carrier is worth half a donkey because he can carry only half the load of a donkey. The barley and wheat had been cut some ten days ago and now make small round cones on the roofs of the houses.

While resting in the home of the Pumteh headman at the upper end of the Pamothang valley our landlord relates how robber priests from a monastery near Romee about two days away on the east side of the Yangtze had attacked one of the nomad tents in the valley, killed a man and driven away sixty head of cattle and a large flock of sheep. The vows of priests prohibit the taking of life but some of the worst atrocities are committed by bands of lamas in feudal and religious wars. Some monks are trained for war and most lamas do not take the higher vows of priesthood until they are about fifty years old when supposedly the desires of the flesh are no longer irresistible. In 1923 after the marauding forces of the Ranalama from Chungtsa five days to the south were driven back, baskets containing twenty monk's heads were brought into Batang. The heads were kicked around the military headquarters for several days. A short time later the two shaved heads of priests were hung up to public gaze by cords attached to the ears. Heads of laymen are suspended by means of their long braided hair.

After two hours ride over hard grassy turf toward the southwest we cross over the Pang Pass which divides China and Tibet. It is October 14th. Brilliant skies and sky-blue flowers, poppies and primroses, have charmed our daily rides on plains and in rocky ravines. We are amazed at the greenness of foliage on these high turfed plateaus whose smoothness is sometimes broken by millions of little holes in which live mouse-hares or Ochotona who scamper too fast for us or for our dogs but not for the yellow-furred weasels which are occasionally seen darting from hole to hole. Seeing a weasel when one is setting out on a hunting trip is considered good luck.

The Pang La boundary stone was once engraven with characters, but being of soft sandstone, weathering has now effaced them, although in 1924 when I first saw the stone traces of them could still be seen (Photo No. 41). The most distinguishing mark now is the ragged flag-tipped stone cairn built up by every traveler as he crosses the pass. With a shout of O Lha Soh O (Oh God I beg) the Tibetan grabs a stone, and rumbling a string of prayer phrases casts a stone upon the heaped up stones confident that he has appeased the spirit of the pass.

We put up at the village of Palungda near Lhandee. At Lhandee we visit one of the most revered figures in all Tibet known as Rang Jon (Rang jyung) which means self-evolved. High priests come from all parts of Eastern Tibet on pilgrimages to prostrate at this shrine. The figure is reported to have sprung up miraculously about the time of Songtsangampo, who was Tibet's most famous king, ruling about 640 A.D. Near Yenchin (Tsakhalo) three days southwest of here are three self-evolved figures hidden in a rock cavern near the road. These three images are reputed to be Songtsangampo and his two foreign wives, one the Chinese princess and the other the Nepalese princess.

Legend is rife about the Chinese princess who was escorted from Peking to Lhasa by Gar, one of the two famous ministers of Songtsangampo. Gar and the Princess passed through Eastern Tibet on the Batang road. Gar was susceptible to the charms of the Chinese maiden for she bore him a child near Tsongi (Dzongngon) five days south of Batang. The child did not live long and was buried at Dzongngon where a black chorden or relic pagoda, erected over its remains, exists to this day. To cover up their amour the child was declared to be the offspring of a demon and as such would be buried beneath a black chorden to hold it down.

Housed in a fair-sized temple the Rangjyung main figure is flanked by eight others, four on a side, which are also said to be self-evolved but of lesser holiness. The principal Rangjyung is said to be an effigy of Nambanongtseh (Vairocana in India) who is the chief of the five Dhyani Buddhas and presides over the uppermost paradise situated in the zenith of the terrestrial skies. Nambanongtseh is reported to have arisen out of a lake where dwell the subterranean spirits called Lu. The base of the image is said to be four carved lions, with a frog beneath as a center, from which Nambanongtseh rises as a sitting Buddha figure about eight feet high.

The holiness and power of this image is such that, when the Chinese in a time of war tore off the clothing and nicked the arms with swords, they were not able to do any serious injury. The faithful prostrate themselves three times before it and then circle to the right, stopping to touch their foreheads to stone hips left bare for the use of the devout. I neither rest my forehead nor prostrate before it but as I circle I try to scratch the hips with my fingernail but the dark grey rock is so hard that I cannot make any impression. From its texture and hardness it appears to be a granite batholith left after the overlapping soft red stanstone was eroded away. In the course of centuries it became worn into the semblance of a human figure; whereupon monks accompanying the first settlers of this region, awed by its uncanny appearance, claimed it to be supernatural.

The face has been remolded into the common yellow-painted Buddha features; the legs and the hands carved into Buddhistic positions by the lamas, troubled lest the eyes of common humanity would not be able to detect the hand of divinity in the crude outlines of the rock. Butter lamps are kept perpetually burning before it. I am refused permission to photograph and so holy is the figure that the offer of money does not change the refusal.

Lhandee, altitude 11,000, is located in a valley running southeast and northwest drained by a branch of the Dzong river, which is a tributary of the Yangtze. The drainage system of the Mekong is very narrow compared to the Yangtze, probably because it is constricted between the Salween and the Yangtze river valleys. Eastern Tibet is truly the land of parallel rivers, for not less than seven great streams course almost north and south through its mountain ranges, beginning with the Yalung in the east, followed to the west by the Litang, the Yangtze, the Mekong, the Salween, the Irawadi and the middle Brahmaputra. The first two, although tributaries of the Yangtze, are large rivers which probably had their own outlets to the sea through Kwangtung until captured by the Yangtze when this mightiest of China's rivers was deflected or cut through to the east ages ago at Likiang. Others such as the Tung in the extreme east might well be included.

We hire animals for Gartok as it is more satisfactory than Oolah since we could make short cuts when we desired and there would not be the delays of exchange at villages. Hiring is difficult until we visit the captain in command of the local garrison and he speaks a potent word for us. The captain had heard that foreigners liked to drink milk (Tibetans, although using much cheese in their diet, do not often drink milk) so he plies me with highly sweetened hot milk which to my discomfort was pressed upon me from this time on, by all of the high Tibetan officials I meet. It is hardly preferable to their buttered tea, which is always made with strong butter, the stronger the better, the butter being kept in sheep stomach's for months until green mold forms in it.

Leaving the next morning for Gartok (Garthoh) we ride up the cultivated valley northwest through an evergreen forest and over Sherepetse Pass, 14,000 feet above sea level, and down into Pangda Plain, stopping after a four hour jaunt to eat Gokway by a small stream. Gokway is Chinese unleavened wheat cakes the shape and size of dinner plates and nearly two inches thick, in texture and hardness reminding one of the hardtack biscuits served in World war I. We season the Gokway with lengths of cold tough yak beef, each mouthful is sliced off with a knife while held by the teeth. Our hard ride in the rare air of Tibet gives us a voracious appetite which rapidly reduces pioneer rations.

Continuing northwest we pass over a grass plain and surmount another pass called Phu La, 14,000 feet, and down through another spruce and fir forest to Phula village in a three hour ride. Some of the ranges here being composed of harder intervening sandstone have been compressed into anticlinal folds with decomposed red soil in between the folds, fashioning the whole surface into red corrugated roofs with countless gables. From the passes we can see the immense rugged massif across the Mekong. All of the higher peaks are bathed in perpetual snows, some of them reaching up to twenty-two thousand feet. The most famous of them—Khawakarpo,—the Mountain of Silver Snow, is too far south to be seen from our comparatively low heights.

We are now in the main Dzong river valley which we follow over grassy turf for four hours in a northwest direction to Gartok. Most of the plain is covered with the hard needle-like grass checkered by spasmodic patches under cultivation. Millions of mouse hares squeak in alarm as they dive into their holes but such is their curiosity they reappear soon for a look which their enemies utilize. Grey and brown mountain larks which are said to live in marmot holes greet us with flight and song.

Gartok lies secluded behind a mountain spur so that one is almost upon it before it is seen. It is a village of sixty one-story houses besides a large square fort containing a force of Lhasa troops. Only two homes of high ranking officials have a second story in this town, one of the dirtiest and most miserable upon earth. People must not look down upon deities which caused the religious authorities to forbid the building of second stories to houses.

After dispatching ceremonial scarfs with gifts of cloth, I call

upon the Dahpon or Military Governor and his two Majors (Photos
Nos. 42, 43, and 44). The Civil Governor or Tiji of Markham has
gone to Chambdo, distant ten days journey to the northwest. There
is much rivalry and conflict between the two rulers over control
and jurisdiction in this province of Markham which occupies an
important strategic position relative to China.

The higher offices in both civil and military affairs in Tibet can
be held only by members of the Lhasa nobility and appointed by
the Dalai Lama. Indication of their rank is in the little rolled top-
not of hair on the head. In Tibet all ranks have certain signs of
attire to indicate their social and political status. Men of ordinary
clay can but rarely rise above the rank of Major in the army or
chief assistant to the Governor of a province.

The Dahpon is a young man of thirty-two, handsome of figure
but vain of position and knowledge. His two Majors are much
older, nearly fifty, having come up from the ranks of a common
soldier. When I visit them they feel compelled to hunt up high
Chinese chairs and tables although I would be much better pleased
to sit on the rugs spread on low platforms which they use. My pro-
testations are rated as politeness. I am thus placed higher than the
Dahpon, whose rug is slightly higher than that of anyone else.
People of rank lower than the Majors are not permitted to sit in
the presence of the Dahpon and his Majors on divans; they sit on
rugs spread on the floor or on the floor itself.

When people of low rank come into the presence of the Governor they unwind their hair and hold their hat with both hands
against their breast; likewise sticking out their tongue and sometimes scratching their head with their right hand. When they
speak they use the honorific language sucking in their breath at
the end of each sentence as they wind up their words with Lhaso.
When the official speaks they punctuate each of his sentences with
one of these sucking noises which sound the same as the sound
we make when afflicted with sudden pain. To us such actions indicate the most abject humility but the Dahpon would also perform
in this manner when in the presence of his highest superior, the
Dalai Lama. Equals address each other in the polite language but
use the vulgar tongue with inferiors. As I am rather weak in my
knowledge of some of the honorific terms, I am afraid the Daben

is secretly horrified at times by my familiarity, but if he is, he does not show it. Sometimes the situation is saved by my teacher, Gegen Atring, who takes my colloquial and dresses it up into the high honorific so that the delicately bred ears may not be offended. I am always much amused when, after a prolonged conference with the Dahpon, who treats me as equal, we go home and Gegen Atring will "Lhare" and "Lhaso" me with sucking breath before we can get back to our former intimate conversational customs.

We lodge in the best two-story house in town owned by an official and allotted to us by the Governor's favor. On our arrival the Governor presents us with parched barley flour, eggs, butter, wheat flour, vegetables and whole sheep carcasses which are placed standing upon their stiff legs as if they were alive. We are continually receiving accessions to this supply by those who come for medicine. The supply of food is greater than our needs and we will sell or give away the surplus when we leave.

In a room next to ours are an abbot and other high ranking monks of the Lhora monastery, one day distant to the northeast of Gartok. They are here for the purpose of gathering money to pay a blood ransom. This monastery had a quarrel with another monastery and a steward of the Tiji was sent to arbitrate the dispute. The Lhora Abbot claimed the steward ate too much of the goods received in the settlement and started to quarrel with him which resulted in a fight that led to the killing of a monk and the loss of the steward's life. The murder of the monk made no difference to the rapacious officials who demanded indemnity for the death of the steward.

The abbot and I became very friendly and I ask him about his troubles.

"The steward got drunk and threatening, and because the lama would not give him all he wanted he started beating him and in the fight the monk was shot and then the other monks beat the steward to death. It is a very sad affair but we have to pay the bill," sorrowfully bewails the abbot.

"How much will you have to pay?" I asked politely.

"We do not know exactly but we have already given four thousand rupees. I have sent some monks to Chambdo to discuss the final amount with the Tiji and his superior the Galon Lama. It is not like the old days when the lamas had more power. Now we must submit to the civil and military governors and the army use any pretext to get more money out of us," and the abbot gloomily shakes his head as he thought of the new forces at work.

"Four thousand rupees is a pretty good sum which will keep the family of the steward in comfort the rest of their days," I venture to obtain his reaction as to where the money goes.

"Yes, it is lots of money but the family will get only a small part of it. Each official will take a share beginning with the highest down to the one who hands the widow the final amount. She will only get a few hundred rupees. If we could have settled with the widow directly it would not have cost us so much," stated the abbot, revealing a disposition similar to that of the officials.

We have arrived in the midst of the wheat and barley harvest delayed ten days this year by rains. We watch a layman upon the roof of our landlord make the customary thank offering for the crop (Photo No. 45). Oddly a layman may be used instead of a monk. Tohma (Dorma) or molded figures of barley flour some shaped like a cone with a dab or two of butter to resemble an idol, one shaped like a bird and another like an animal are set upon a box whose top has been sprinkled with barley grain. These figures have been daubed with a brush of goat's hair dipped in a red dye made from a tree root boiled in water. Three vessels of water and two of barley grain are placed before these figures. On the clay ground of the roof before the box, rests a large bowl of barley flour adorned with three stalks of wheat stuck in it and dabs of butter on the edge of the bowl. There are also a copper bowl of tea, two of milk and one of beer.

In front of the offerings hangs a drum from a three-pronged frame. On one side is a pair of cymbals and on the other side a board encased book of prayers. The shaggy-haired layman sits himself between the cymbals and prayer book. He reads from the prayer book mingling rapid recitations with groanings and rumblings. At intervals he clangs the cymbals or pounds the drum. Now and then he sprinkles water on some barley flour which he casts into a small fire of juniper branches glowing nearby. Later he thrusts upright a fir branch with a red rag into the clay roof near the parapet. The ceremony lasts most of the day its length varying ordinarily from one half to a day depending upon the amount of money presented by the householder. At the end of the ceremony all of the offerings will be technically consumed but actually a small part is placed on the family altar and the remainder given to beggars for the gaining of merit.

Men are seen tanning hides and engraving prayer stones; women spinning and weaving both yak hair and sheep wool cloth. Silversmiths are watched as they ply their goat-skin bellows in the melting of silver for lining tsamba bowls. Certain areas are famous for the manufacture of articles such as Derge for saddles and teapots, Batang for boots, and Shangchen for pottery and locks, but Gartok has no specific product or distinction, unless it be the making of paper. All official centers must make their paper locally, if possible, because of its cost.

There is not a single shop in Gartok. Officials and priests do desultory trading but brigands take all of the profit for an ordinary trader. Lhasa governed Tibet is freer from robber bands than Chinese governed Tibet but, in both areas, caravans need an escort of soldiers or a large armed party to escape raiding. The ordinary merchant can not pay such a high cost. Then the government officials by using low-priced Oolah or forced official transport can undersell the lay trader.

Personal liberty from an Occidental viewpoint is much restricted in Tibet. The use of tobacco except in the form of snuff is forbidden and the killing of wild animals banned although these laws are clandestinely evaded. Around Gartok the people are not allowed to pasture their own animals on the grass lining the edge of the fields after the harvest is removed but must herd their stock on the mountain side; the fields are for the horses of the official and military classes. However, the law against any stock invading growing fields is very severe, each step is one fourth of a rupee. Moreover soldiers are not permitted to live in the homes of the civilians and they must forego whiskey. Soldiers every evening gather in groups on their drill ground and rumble off a string of prayers before retiring to their barracks at sundown.

The belief that one who has a picture of an enemy may end his life by enticing his soul to dwell in the picture makes photography difficult at first, but as their ideas change I am besieged by demands for photos. There is great reluctance in permitting me to photo dedicated idols but I am asked to take pictures of idols before dedication. The monks fear that photos may later be desecrated by trampling or discarded as waste paper by careless foreigners. The rush for American postcards and sheets out of travel magazines is so great that I discontinue giving them away and sell them, especially to priests, who use them as charms, or to adorn their private chapels as offerings pleasing to the deities. During the New Year Devil Dances in Batang pictures of the Dalai Lama and the Panchen Lama presented by us to the Batang monastery are carried in procession along with ever-present idols and banners.

Gartok is about 12,350 feet altitude and near the limit of cultivation in this latitude. When crossing a pass from one valley into another I note the aneroid height of the highest fields as I descend and also compare known heights on the map and the presence or absence of cultivation in these places. By careful calculation in these two respects it seems that the limit of cultivation in this red clay-sandstone soil is 12,500 to 12,700 feet. However, this is the grain ripening altitude, barley for fodder being grown upward another five hundred feet. Up to 10,500 feet by use of irrigation to supplement rainfall, two crops a year are grown.

Our ten day stay in Gartok is marked by brilliant weather and when near the end of October clouds begin to cast snow whirls around the distant peaks I know that it is time to seek a lower, warmer clime. By the gracious permission of the Dahpon we are provided with Oolah in order to take a shorter and more northern route which is not on the maps of Tibet. Animals cannot be hired over this route as it passes through several tribal areas where the tribes do not trust one another; and then, the people being self-sustaining money gained by hiring animals has little meaning to them in their barter trade. Self-sufficient economy and distrust of neighbors were the original causes in the creation of Oolah which serves for long distant transport.

Opposite to the direction by which we entered Gartok we go northeast, escorted by a sergeant, over two low spur-passes of 14,700 and 14,000 feet in four hours and then downwards touching only one forest, most of the way being undulating grassy plain. The evergreen forest is located in the one stretch of limestone formation while the plains are the old familiar red-clay sandstone. Every little valley has several homes and the larger have several tens of homes. Five large flocks of the big snow pheasants, the cocks gobbling, the hens chirping and all running uphill make us wish for shotguns and an open hunting season.

At noon we are at 12,700 feet above sea level and only ascend the rest of the day. In the afternoon we follow up a branch stream northeast for one hour to the junction of two smaller branches. Here is located Lhora Monastery whose abbot was my neighbor at Gartok. We do not stop as we must reach the end of the stage which we accomplish by a two hours ride up the northeast branch. The other stream comes down from the northwest draining similar rolling hills of grass.

At night we sleep in the log cabin second floor of a Chunohnong village house. Where timber is near part of the sun-dried brick walls for the second story are replaced by notched logs which are not as airtight as mud walls and yet ideal for the storage of grain. They are nice and clean as compared to the usual sooty kitchen with clay brick stoves; consequently, as a queer foreigner I always seek for them.

The hills in this region are so low and rolling that fields extend almost to their tips. On a walking survey of them, a pack of the black Tibetan mastiffs almost as big as small donkeys charge me but a vigorous use of stones ward them off. The villagers rush to my aid and laugh when I tell them that I am not afraid as long as they keep such a plentiful supply of stones. In some places rocks are so numerous that they are piled as fences along the field boundaries.

All next day we continue northeast, first crossing a grass pass 13,500 feet high and then plunging into dense fir forest which shut out the sun but reward us with magnificent flocks of the red-legged, purple-tailed white snow pheasants who gobble protestingly as our dog chases them into trees. As we wind in and out, up and down, we pass the black tents of four nomadic families. A multitude of ropes pushed up taut by stakes, like our tightening of clothes lines, keep the heavty tent sides from sagging inward. At the tent doors are the huge dogs with lolling red tongues and evil eyes, lunging and barking until we are out of sight. The burly black yak, the

black-belted white sheep, and the black curly-haired goats brows-
ing quietly among the prickly oak bushes, with the stillness of the
forest nearby, entice us into the land of enchantment and dreams.

We cross three more passes clothed to their tops with juniper
and fir. The passes range from 13,900 to 15,450 feet above sea-
level. Just before crossing the last one we see in the distance the
curling smoke-spires of Dorjetroleh which my wife, John Kenneth and I were the first and only white people to visit. In 1926
we made a special trip to this shrine sacred because of three self-
evolved figures which sprang up between two conical mountain
peaks a few hundred feet apart. Around these two peaks is a
pilgrim road on which pilgrims circle every year and on which
local devotees encircle every day for there is both a monastery
and a nunnery nearby. The pilgrims are much more numerous in
certain years which are exceptionally sacred to one shrine such as
the Tiger Year (the last one in 1926) for Dorjetroleh and the
sheep year for Khawakarpo the Mountain of Silver Snow. This
is the sheep year and today a number of pilgrims returning from
circumambulating Khawakarpo have joined us for protection from
bandits. Dorjetroleh is also noted for hermitages in which priests
incarcerate themselves for a period of time, some for months, some
for years and others for life. In a walled up mud hut, without
heat or light, and holding intercourse with no one they sit praying endlessly; falling asleep from exhaustion, and upon awaken-
ing, starting again to count their prayers with their rosary as they
mumble, "Om Mani Padme Hum" in the hope that they may
escape from the eternal round of rebirths and be able to dwell
forever with the gods in the western paradise.

Fir forests usually stop at about 15,000 feet altitude and then
juniper with rhodendron take up the ascent for another thousand
feet when grass continues to cloth the ground until stopped by
glaciers and perpetual snow around eighteen thousand feet above
sea level. Scarcely a flower is now seen at the mid-levels and they
were so plentiful just two weeks ago. Women are out digging the
donkey-ear flower, so called from the leaves resembling that
humble animal's ears. These roots and others are sold to the
Chinese for medicine.

Just before we drop down a stairway road to Dzongshee we pass out of the scarlet sandstone into a limestone area which will be with us to Batang. We descend to an altitude of ten thousand feet where a wide valley has made possible considerable population. After a long trip over high barren and uninhabited ranges above the clouds it is like coming back to earth when we reach the homes of men again.

Dzongshee is at the junction of two streams which unite to form the Sheh Chu, here running south but its southeast turning can be seen three miles below us where it continues through a deep canyon for about two day's journey southeast to enter the Yangtze below Druwalung where we saw it on our way to Gartok. There are about a hundred homes up and down these streams within a few miles of Dzongshee but still farther up and down even the paths are too wicked for popular use.

A former soldier of the Indian army but now a lieutenant in the Tibetan service aids us in hiring animals across the Chinese border distant one day's journey. He has married a Tibetan woman and is now a citizen of Tibet. Fluent in Tibetan, English and Hindustani he hopes some day to send his two boys to our school in Batang. His friendship was very valuable to us now and in the later wars around Batang. The next two days will be through a desert and past robber caves used by brigands as a rendezvous for forays upon caravans and nearby villages. The authority of the Dahpon has weakened the farther we are from Gartok and we can no longer drive Oolah. Hiring animals, however, requires a liberal use of presents to the local headmen and several hours wrangling coupled with a generous use of money for the drivers of the pack caravan.

The next morning when the first horse arrives I have my saddle thrown upon its back and immediately ride off down the valley. This vigorous action gets us off at nine o'clock, arouses the headmen to more prompt requisition of pack animals and forestalls their hinted demands for more money. Four soldiers of the Dahpon escort us southeast through a dense forest over a pass 15,500 feet above sea level and out upon vast grassy plains. The turf of these smooth plains is so hard that one can barely nick it with a pick which may be one reason why evergreen forests in conjunction with constant close grazing have such difficulty establishing a foothold in some valleys.

Shortly before reaching the pass, as we are passing above a cliff, one of the straps to our food box gives way and the box goes crashing down a hundred and fifty feet, one drop being a sheer fifty feet. Rattle and bang the box comes to rest with clouds of flour shooting out of the cracks. The utensils are badly battered and some of the food hashed but our luck is good as any other box would have damaged valuable stuff. My men wanted me to fine the muleman heavily as is the custom, but I merely have him carry the box on his back, back up to the road and furnish a thong to tie the box in lieu of a broken lock.

On the rolling plateau we keep a sharp lookout for robbers for only one day to the north is the country of Sangenwa or Bad Lands whose people are of the antagonistic sect of Nyingmapa and live mostly by plunder, which neither the Tibetan nor the Chinese authorities are able to stop.

Immediately below the pass, above 15,000 feet altitude, are six small lakes maintained by springs fed from melting snows on the nearby peaks which are just below the perpetual snow line. We drop down to 14,500 feet in elevation to a small cave called Kundee Dropuh or the "Cave where robbers assemble." The cave is damp so we camp outside under the stars which at this height resemble wells of fire. A full moon arises making the night almost as bright as day, at least I could read large print. With seven hours of travel behind us we eat heartily and drowse by the yak-chip fire.

We have no tent. I sleep on the bare ground with my cot as a barricade against the cold wind. The men are bivouacked around the blaze. The temperature drops to ten degrees above zero Fahrenheit according to my maximum-minimum thermometer. The ground is hard and thoughts of brigands whose favorite operating season is at this time awaken us all at two o'clock in the morning. It is Oct. 31st. I rout out the force who are cold although fully clothed and after a cup of hot buttered tea we scramble up a rocky pass full of granite boulders. It is over 15,000 feet.

Down an avalanching slope we lead our horses toward the east.

Our line of horses resemble whitened frozen ghosts moving through yellow moonlight. Mounting over another pass, a little lower than the other one, we go silently. Most of us are too cold to enjoy talking and the others are scared of robbers. Soon the moon begins to turn white under the unseen glare of the approaching sun. Across the Yangtze the peaks are little round acorns atop a huge sprawling shadow. With the lightening of the sky they roughen until they lose their mystery with the rising of the morning sun which escorts us after a bitter ride of five and a half hours into the hamlet of Shisonggong. Here we can see our home in the distant Batang valley twelve miles away.

Shisonggong is situated near a saucer-like hollow three thousand and five hundred feet above the Yangtze. The trail to the water is so steep that one imagines a running jump will plunge one into its yellow waters. The next day we wait impatiently here for the ferry boat which had taken Chinese soldiers and baggage down to Druwalung the afternoon before. I climb out to a point and spy the barge as a long black worm crawling along near the bank. I predict its arrival at three o'clock and announce I will walk alone if I can not get animals for the baggage, for as usual, no one wants to hire their beasts. By giving the landlord no rest from my tongue we make it to the bank and cross the river to wrangle some more for Oolah transport to Batang the same day. Another four hours and we ride into our courtyard at Batang as the moon is tinting the mountain tips with sombre silver.

Figure 39
Our Ferry Boat crossing the Yangtze River at Druwalung

Figure 40
Skin-boat on Yangtze at Druwalung used for crossing by mail runners and
small parties

Figure 41
Left to right: Sheao Pin Sen, medical assistant; Chodrah, cook; Atring, my
teacher; and Jitsen, guide, at badly eroded Sino-Tibetan boundary stone

Figure 42
The Dahpon or military governor of Gartok, my host

Figure 43
Honoring me with a parade of Tibetan regular army troops at Gartok

Figure 44
Wife of a high Tibetan official at Gartok

Chapter VIII

BATTLES OF BATANG

The distant sounds of scattered shots arouse my wife, Louise, and I from deep slumber shortly after midnight on the infant day of February 28, 1932.

"Some outlying houses are being robbed by country Tibetans, or maybe the ever-late Chinese soldiers are arriving and firing off a few shots in order to claim they drove the brigands away," I remark yawningly to Louise.

"Yes, I suppose it's another gang of robbers and I hope they don't come our way," she replies a little tensely.

Both of us were thinking of a night the previous winter when a gang of Deshohdunpa tribesmen invaded our compound and were leading away our cows when our two armed guards carrying shotguns and swords discovered them. The ensuing fusilade punctured with the high pitched Tibetan war cries and the muffled scurryings of men sounded like a battle. The melee cost me twenty-five shot-gun shells but saved our cows who had bolted at the first shots. One Tibetan was reported wounded slightly. Since the firing is continuing, I now glance to see if my rifle is in the corner, where I take the precaution to keep it every night.

Our house is about a quarter of a mile from the city upon the side of a bluff about fifty feet high overlooking Batang on the south and separated from the city by the little Batang river which is fordable except after heavy rains (Photo No. 46). This bluff is known locally as Japoding and contains the major portion of the Mission properties used in our Christian work. After climbing the bluff beyond the river one comes first to the hospital, then the school, followed by the home of the doctor occupied now by the family of Dr. N. H. Bare, and then our home. Still farther out a short distance beyond us is the orphanage. These buildings are scattered in a compound of about eight acres in extent and surrounded by a pounded clay wall ranging from four to eight feet in height. Surrounding this compound are farms with dispersed

farmhouses. East of the compound the land slopes steeply to a
hill about five hundred feet high topped by a fort, and backed by
a long spur of land rolling upward, with one dip, to a mountain
range. The fort is garrisoned by a platoon of Chinese soldiers
numbering between twenty and thirty men. The city lies northwest of the hill almost in the east to west middle of the main
plain, but on its southern border. Northward the plain stretches
about a mile to the large Batang river, which circles westward to
the western side of the valley, and flows southward to be joined
by the little Batang river at the southwestern extremity of the
plain. The united streams speed southward through a narrow
valley plain, never over a quarter of a mile wide, to the Yangtze.
West of Batang alongside of the big Batang river near its junction
with the little Batang river is the big monastery with some thirty
buildings, enclosed by a clay wall twenty feet high and five feet
thick. East of the city in the southeast corner of the plain is the
small monastery where about fifty monks live as contrasted to the
750 in the big lamasery. The small lamasery faces the northeast
corner of the hill and commands the road which leads southeastward to Tachienlu.

Occasional shots, some quite faint, continue to ring out but not
until morning do we know the cause. Our servants rush in to relate the sudden overthrow of the local government by Whang
Tien Hwa or Gezong Tsering. They declare terms are now being
discussed for the transfer of power. However, other shots are
heard and we walk over to the hospital to obtain a better view.
From its top floor we watch troops scale the hill to attack the fort
from the southeast and also notice men scurrying around the south
gate of the city. Firing soon ceases but we stay within the compound until assured that the truce is in effect. Late in the afternoon a messenger arrives from Gezong Tsering (who was once one
of our schoolboys) that we are not to worry and that the city is
safe. In this dramatic change of government one man is killed
and two men wounded who are now brought to the hospital for
treatment by Dr. Bare. The old regime under the control of Liu
Wen Huei, a Szechwan warlord, is now replaced by a representative of Chiang Kai Shek. The new ruler, Gezong Tsering, assumes
power as Ge Siling.

Ge Siling is a Sino-Tibetan from a wealthy Batang family. He had been in my first class of physical training in 1922. In 1927 he had gone down to Nanking and attracted the attention of Chiang Kai Shek in a spectacular manner. When Chiang approached Peking, Gezong Tsering, who had gone ahead, used his knowledge of Tibetan language and custom in persuading the Lama Temple of Peking to parade their monks in a colorful procession to meet the Generalissimo. Gezong Tsering at their head, of course, utilized his position to become known to the General and in time persuaded Chiang to support him in seizing Sikang province for the Nationalist Government. Gezong Tsering came through Yunnanfu province gathering troops and equipment and securing the support of Tibetan tribes as he approached Batang from the south. Leading one hundred Yunnan soldiers, and supported by tribes without the city and by relatives inside Gezong Tsering entered Batang without resistance. The Chinese troops were weak and poorly led with the exception of the local Batang company under Captain Yang Chao Tsung who revolted to Gezong Tsering and assisted in the subjection of the Chinese regulars in last night's battle.

The previous Szechwan rulers of this area, Hwang Tuanchang and Wang Yinchang, have no alternative but to accept unconditional surrender terms and after two weeks they are forced to lead their ragged unarmed soldiers southward. Dejected and with only allowances of food they start on a long southern circular route through Yunnan province to Szechwan. Most of them undoubtedly will enlist as soldiers or bandits with Yunnan leaders and the remainder will arrive home jobless and in disgrace.

Probably the present turmoil of the Tibetan Border has seemed propitious to both Chiang Kai Shek and Gezong Tsering for the wresting of Sikang province from the feeble grasp of Liu Wen Huei. Fighting has been going on for two years between the Chinese and the Tibetans. It had its earliest foundations in the actions of Szechwan rulers when Chao Erh Feng in 1905 used the money intended for the building of a Szechwan railway to conquer the territory previously held by native princes who had been granted seals of office by the Manchu Emperors, Kanghsi and Chienlung, in the early eighteenth century.

Known as the Butcher because of his severe, although rated as fairly just, rule which caused hundreds of Chinese and Tibetan heads to roll off the shoulders of their owners, Chao Erh Feng carved out thirty-three districts, six never existing except on paper, until the Chinese revolution sent the head of the able general to join those of his victims. His death caused the Tibetans to revolt and the Chinese conquests were halted.

Desultory fighting after the fall of the Chinese power in Tibet, culminated in a war during 1917 when Lhasa troops seized the western half of eastern Tibet; but English intervention and Chinese diplomacy saved the eastern half, a vast region extending from Tachienlu and the Tung river to the Yangtze-Mekong divide, and from Yunnan province to north of Batang, with Dege going to Tibet; then the boundary crossed northeast to Gangdzï (Kanze) and then north to where it met Tsinghai province.

The 1918 peace signed by the Tibetan Galon Lama for Tibet, by General Liu Tsan Ting for China and by Consul Eric Teichman for England was from the beginning of an unstable nature; the Chinese government did not ratify the treaty and Tibet was unsatisfied because she naturally desired to control all Tibetan-speaking territory. However, both countries abided by the terms of the treaty insofar as the boundary was concerned with only minor trespassing until 1929. In that year a dispute occurred between two lamaistic monasteries on the Gangdzi borderland.

One monastery, Darjyeh of the yellow sect, being within the Tibetan border and the other, Guluh of the Red Hats, within Chinese jurisdiction, it was natural that the officials of each country were soon implicated in the controversy. Both countries concentrated troops upon the border to see that their subjects secured justice. Chinese troops under Col. Ma Chen Lung first achieved some success driving back the invading forces of the monastery in Tibet. Later, when the Chinese soldiers were merry-making during the New Year feasting, the reinforced Tibetans crept up in the night, surrounded and utterly routed the Celestial soldiers, killing a hundred and taking two hundred prisoners. The defeated soldiers did not stop in their flight until they were fifty miles distant in the district of Luho. Tibetan forces now captured Nyarong once under the direct control of Lhasa but which they had not governed since the days of Chao Erh Feng.

This 1929-32 war had been confined to the Gangdzi area and did not seem likely to break out farther south in the Batang region until Gezong Tsering assumed the title of chief commander, or Siling, and organized a local army. The previous Szechwanese Chinese officers did not have the troops nor the supplies for an offensive and the Tibetans are awaiting a favorable moment.

Gezong Tsering with his Tibetan affiliations soon secures the cooperation of all the surrounding tribes. His Batang friends among the nobility are commissioned as officers and the commoners are enlisted in the ranks, all keeping their Tibetan costume. The Batang Tibetans constitute one force, and the Yunnanese with the former regular army unit of Batang men under Yang Chao Tsung comprise another body which Gezong Tsering organizes into a small army. On April 24th he assumes command of his army in a brilliant review upon the parade grounds of the big monastery to the west, and at the same time proclaims the establishment of Sikang as a new province, under the control of the Nationalist Government at Nanking (Photo No. 47).

Men are sent toward Tachienlu but lacking local support are not able to accomplish anything. The Washi tribes between Batang and Tachienlu stay neutral. Tachienlu remains in the hands of the Szechwan warlord, Liu Wen Huei, who is too weak to attempt the recovery of Batang. Gezong Tsering has the support of all tribes and monasteries within the Batang general region for fifty to one hundred miles except the Gongkha Lama at Dzongon. This Yellow Cap priest, although once under the sovereignity of the Batang princes, seizes Yenchin for Gezong Tsering but then will not yield it to the Batang leader, preferring to keep the rich salt tax revenues for himself. The salt tax is collected at Yenchin, a short two days' journey southwest of Dzongon and only a half-day's journey from the Tibetan borders to the west and the north. The salt revenue of Yenchin since the Lhasa Government became independent have been coveted by Tibet and at various times they have seized the locality when the Chinese were weak, only to yield it up again under negotiations, but always retiring with the salt taxes which they had collected for a period of a week to three months.

When Gezong Tsering insists that Gongkha lama surrender the rifles and control of Yenchin the Gongkha Lama sends a messen-

ger secretly to his old Szechwan master, Liu Wen Huei, offering
to fight against Gezong Tsering. The messenger is captured by
tribesmen faithful to Gezong Tsering, who was so angered by this
act of treachery that, in accordance with Oriental custom, he has
the messenger executed. Then he dispatches a force of one hundred and fifty men under Yang Chao Tsung on May 12th to Dzongon to capture the Gongkha Lama and give him the same treatment. Tibetan troops meanwhile are mobilized along their own
border near the historic boundary stone a mile from Pamothang.

In the battle about the 19th of May north of Dzongon near
Pamothang the forces of the Gongkha Lama are beaten. His envoy
immediately contacts the Tibetan commander for help who attacks the Batang forces on the flank and defeats them. The defeat
is turned into a rout and the Tibetan forces follow the fleeing
Batang troops so closely that the ferry boats at Li and Druwalung
cannot be destroyed. The Batang remnants reach the city on May
20 and 21 reporting a loss of ten men killed and eight taken
prisoners. Soon after daybreak on the 22nd of May the Tibetan
force of two hundred men assault the city expecting to capture
it before the people can recover their morale.

Batang is almost captured. The day previous Gezong Tsering
had stationed fifteen men in the hospital and fifteen in the school.
We stay in our homes and cower in the basement to escape bullets
from both sides. The Tibetans advance under cover of walls and
graves and behind our houses and pour such a hot fire into the
hospital and school that a charge of forces from the city is ordered
about three o'clock in the afternoon to relieve the almost over-
whelmed garrisons. The Batang boys advance in several lines
from the city and fort on the hill to the east toward the Mission
compound. The Tibetans have almost exhausted their ammunition and slowly retreat leaving their seriously wounded behind
who are decapitated by the pursuing Chinese who also sever the
right hand for a second grewsome trophy. The Chinese lose four
killed and ten wounded but the Tibetans contribute ten heads for
display. I go over later and recognize one of the bravest Tibetan
leaders, a young lieutenant whom I had met in Gartok seven
months ago. He fell in the middle of the day as his men neared
the city in a charge.

These Chinese dare not pursue the retreating Tibetans more than a mile as fortified nests of soldiers cover their flight. However, that evening rumours of pursuit cause the nervous Tibetans to overcrowd one of the ferry boats at Li, ten miles south of us. which sank in midstream with the loss of eighty men. The captain, whom we knew in Gartok, tries to control them and commits suicide on the bank when he sees his company is being swept away in the swift, merciless Yangtze.

What are we doing all this time? Information regarding the advancing Tibetans, who came up so swiftly that they brought no reserve ammunition and food, has been so vague, and relying on the friendship developed by my trip to Gartok last October, we missionaries decide to rely on our neutrality. We barricade the house, and Louise with the three children sleep in the basement. I join them when the firing becomes hot. With the two hundred regular Tibetan troops are about two hundred militia of the Gongkha Lama. When the militia approach our home the Indian lieutenant whom I had met at Tsongshe last October arrives in time to chase the Gongkha Lama rabble out of the orphanage which they were looting, and stationing himself outside our back door, orders them toward the front. He does not attempt to recover the loot and I watch one of them carrying a stolen bedchamber in one hand and a rifle in the other as he moves stealthily alongside terraces toward the hospital. Rolls of cloth and bundles of thread are recovered from corpses and returned after the battle to the orphanage by the Batang soldiers.

The 14th company captain, a tall handsome Tibetan, comes to our back porch door on the second floor. I hasten to open the door and go outside to greet him. He asks for whiskey but I tell him as a religious man there is not a drop in the house and offer him tea. He refuses the tea and declines to come in for fear it will remove his protective taboo. He with all Tibetan soldiers carries a charm box which has been blessed before the battle by high ranking Lamas and Living Buddhas and will ward off bullets as long as he does not touch women, or objects handled by women, and blood. Thanking me for my offers, the captain moves with a few men toward the hospital. He is later wounded in the hand which is dressed by Mrs. Minnie Ogden and Miss Grace Young who occupy the house halfway between us and the hospital and about four hundred feet from it. All day long soldiers come to our house where we feed them tea and tsamba in the outbuildings and on the back porch, having laid in a supply of these articles for that purpose knowing the invaders would be hungry. Most of them had no food since yesterday having started away early with no time to eat. They had followed the retreating Chinese by forced marches and seemed gaunt, tired and nervous. Some of them are the Gongkha Lama's militia, among them men who had robbed us on Tsaleh Pass in July of 1927, events told in the book— "Mountain of Silver Snow." We keep our doors closed except when passing out the food, and although our lieutenant has gone, none attempt to enter by force, all being under the strain of fatigue and death. When the Chinese sortie occurs the hasty retreat of these frightened, bulletless men as they flatten themselves against walls and dart from our house corner to the wall gate is an unforgetable memory. Nor is the sight of four corpses in our gardens, and of Namjyeh, one of the Mission gardeners, holding up the head and right hand of one of them, eraseable.

After the retreat of the Tibetans, Chin Shin Fu, our shoemaker, and also now a captain in the new army, stops at our home and while eating asks for the army rifle and cartridges which I have hidden in separate places to thwart sudden seizure and use. I willingly hand them to him but am disconcerted to have him tell me that some have said they have heard the crack of this rifle in the battle. The cleanness of the gun and the time it takes me to find the cartridges as well as the statements of our four servants, who have courageously stayed with us, soon dispel such false suspicions. Incidentally the rifle is used by the Chinese in the siege of Batang and I recover only the gun, minus the one hundred and fifty cartridges, the cost of these however, being paid to the church pastor after our departure.

The next day, however, we survey our losses. The orphanage has lost some cloth, thread and pots by the Tibetan pillaging, besides suffering considerable fright. Two of our farm houses are burned. Books in the school and minor items in the hospital are damaged by looting on the Chinese side. We are not pleased with our location as the walls near the house were used as firing points and the yard back of the houses as a passageway for assault troops. One bullet has pierced a window and others have chipped off chunks of whitewash from the walls. We decide if the Tibetans return, and reasoning is soon confirmed by fact, that we will move over to the Chushozhing mission house which lies in a deep valley between the city and the present Mission compound.

The Tibetans, after retreating across the Yangtze, hold the west bank where they recuperate and reform for another attack upon Batang. This time they are moving up supplies of food and ammunition, lack of which had defeated them in their first sharp attack.

The Chinese, unable to attack the Tibetans, strengthen their position, converting the school and hospital into fortresses by bricking up the windows. They burn the three outlying mission buildings upon the orphanage farm and make paths protected by terrain and brush to the three main forts upon which they intend to rely in defending the town. If the Chinese had known that the Tibetans would have the nerve to occupy our mission homes and the orphanage just a few hundred yards away from the two main forts, that is the hospital and school, they would probably have burned them also.

The Dahpon, the commander of the besieging forces whom I had visited in Gartok sent a letter to us, announcing that we could stay in our homes and that "not a hair of our heads would be touched." However much we might trust in such a statement we do not relish living in the midst of an invading force in such an exposed position. Gezong Tsering, the commander of the Chinese, suggests, as an old friend, that we move over to the city. On May the thirty-first we decide to move to Chushozhing which we accomplish by calling in all the people we know and giving each a piece of furniture or a box of goods, my wife or one of the trusted servants and teachers accompanying the more valuable loads. The confusion is indescribable and a number of pieces are lost, some of which are recovered either by the tattling of envious neighbors or by my own recollection of mission articles received from my hand. We give some stuff away and find it almost as good as a fire to get rid of white elephant material.

A letter also comes to Gezong Tsering from the Dahpon offering to arbitrate naming the chief abbot of the Batang Monastery known as Ba Lama and myself as arbitrators. However, I find the Chinese adamant about giving up the lush salt revenues of Yenchin and demanding the Tibetans retreat back to Gartok, terms to which I well know the Tibetans will not listen. The least the Tibetans will do is foregoing the attack on Batang and withdrawing to the other side of the Yangtze. Permitting the Yangtze to be the boundary (Tibetan ruled Dege was exchanged for Chinese Yenchin) was the final result of all the fighting, and the de-facto border has been the Yangtze river until 1951. The useless bloodshed but deciding battle of Batang had to be, because each side wanted the same thing; only slaughter and fire finally changed their minds.

The feud between China and Tibet is of long standing. China never had more than a conqueror's right to any of the Tibetan plateau. Shadowy temporary acknowledgment of sovereignty in the Mongol and Ming dynasties became more permanent and official after the Emperor Kangshi of the Manchu Dynasty sent an army to Lhasa about 1706 as aid to one element in an internal dispute. This finally resulted in the sending of Ambans to exercise general supervision and handle foreign relations leaving to the Tibetans local autonomy. At least half of the time this supervision was very weak and finally under the thirteenth Dalai Lama, Ngawang Lobzang Tobtan Gyatso, was entirely overthrown at the time of the Chinese Revolt against the Manchus. From 1912 until the death of the Dalai Lama in 1933 no Chinese were permitted even to reside within Tibet, that is west of the Yangtze-Mekong divide. Since then with Tibet ruled by a regent, both China and England have kept representatives in Lhasa but the British seem to have more success influencing foreign relations.

Back to the Battles of Batang. The Tibetans cross the Yangtze without opposition upon the 28th of May and advance leisurely toward Batang arriving in the valley five miles to the south on the 13th of June. The Batang males are mobilized, even my old gardener, Aku Tseden, is drafted and compelled to find a gun which he accomplishes by borrowing an old muzzle-loading flint-firing home-made affair, largely valuable for noise. A force of Chinese soldiers and Batang militia move south with a cannon and attempt to halt the Tibetan advance. However, bravely as they fight, the same result from the same cause is often repeated during the siege. The Tibetan forces with their Enfield rifles and British-made ammunition are so much superior in accuracy and range that the Chinese fighters are killed before they can come close enough to hit the Tibetans. The German Mausers and heavy lead bullets of the Chinese-loaded shells of the defending forces are slow in speed and short in range. The Batang boys retire within the city carrying ten dead men and some wounded, but the Tibetans have only a few men wounded.

A second sortie by the Chinese to prevent the attackers from besieging the city fails on the 15th of June. Under the cover of darkness early on the 16th of June the Tibetans occupy our two mission homes and the orphanage upon Japoding while the Chinese wait tensely in the hospital and school and the hill fort. The Tibetans throw out small parties who dig trenches and construct rude shelters at strategic points commanding all roads and the approaches to the fort on the eastern hill. On the western side of the valley across the big Batang river the attackers seize Pakhalo which the Chinese have abandoned planning to hold the big monastery opposite Pakhalo and nearer the city. The monastery is garrisoned by armed monks who are encouraged in their efforts by Gezong Tsering's aged uncle, a high ranking priest.

After the Tibetans have consolidated their positions both sides settle down into the siege routine of a surrounded town, the attackers firing upon all who venture within sight and the besieged replying toward the supposed source of the bullets. On June 20th a desperate surprise attack is staged by the Chinese whose daring lieutenant leaders are either killed or wounded by the hot firing from Tibetans hidden within the fortified buildings of our Mission. Nothing is accomplished except a loss of ten Chinese soldiers killed and probably less upon the other side. We find it difficult to ascertain the loss of either force since, as is customary, the loss of the enemy is magnified and of one's own forces minimized. One of our Christian young men, Song Chuen Shi, a former orphan and once assistant to our cook, is killed. His body disappeared although it may have been one of the decayed corpses found lying upon our Mission compound after the raising of the siege.

June 21st. The Tibetan forces burn five houses in the main

part of the valley and its eastern spur as an interdiction of their use by the Chinese. Other houses are burnt from time to time. It is reported that the Tibetans cremate their dead in some of these houses. Chinese killed in the various sorties are in some cases left lying where they fall but in others removed and mutilated, as we found a decayed hand and a part of a head in our cow barn after the siege.

June 22nd. Up to date, including civilians, thirty-five of the Batang besieged have been killed. Twelve wounded soldiers are now being treated in the hospital including one wounded Tibetan soldier left behind at Sashe after the first attack and captured by the Chinese before the second Tibetan advance. Gezong Tsering ordered him brought in alive and as a publicity feature extends mercy towards him although the poor fellow daily expects to be executed. (Although severely wounded he recovered to be liberated.) Many wounded die of gangrene and invariable those suffering broken limbs by timbers falling after shell fire develop gangrene and succumb.

The Tibetans shell the city and one cannon shot lands inside the church where the orphans are lodged. The shell bounces harmlessly off the concrete floor and does not explode and no one is hit but Lozong Pintso dies of a heart attack. This orphan lad had suffered from dropsy and cyanosis for more than two years due to an enlarged defective heart. His condition was constantly deteriorating and Dr. Bare had prophesied his early death especially if he were subjected to acute excitement.

June 25th. The new Chinese Mayor for Batang sent in by Liu Wen Huei creeps in during darkness. He had travelled rapidly with the powerful Washi tribe to Meliting a day's journey from Batang and then walking a steep precipitous trail over the mountains and leading directly above the small monastery avoids the scattered Tibetan guards who have closed all of the main roads but do not have enough men to block this goat trail.

The ring of Tibetan guards draws tighter daily and continues more closely to envelop the city. All of the valley fields except the huge bulge surrounding the city, an area enclosed by the two rivers and the small monastery, are outside the besieger's lines. The bulge comprising two thirds of the total crop area is under long range fire, some of it within three hundred yards of the entrenched Tibetans. As the grain becomes dead ripe, women and children venture out to cut and carry the harvest to their homes. The Tibetan sharpshooters fire upon them with such accuracy that one or two are slain each day. In the sum total of those killed among the defenders, it was these women and children who constituted the heaviest loss. I unwisely walk out one day north of the city but retire when a bullet strikes near me. Although the people harvest their wheat and barley at the cost of blood they are not able to sow the usual second crop of buckwheat or millet from lack of water. The summer proves to be one of the most arid in years and the entrance channels of the irrigation ditches are under the control of the Tibetan forces. The richer landowners hire the poor, who in their necessity risk their lives to cut what grain is grown in the bulge. Thus this conflict, like many wars, lays most heavily upon the least guilty.

July 8th. The Tibetans have placed cannon in the basement of the mission home nearest the hospital and are bombarding this former building of mercy now occupied by Chinese soldiers. So heavy is the shelling that the front wall which is four feet of tamped clay threatens to fall. The Chinese during the night send over a swarm of men and women who fill bags of dirt and build a new wall behind it which is further strengthened by braced timbers. Gezong Tsering directs them and the next morning walks calmly across the little river bridge but draws scant fire since the sharpshooters are probably at breakfast, or taken by surprise. Our gardens and orphanage farm produce are reported drying up for lack of water and all of the surviving vegetables are being consumed by the Tibetan forces.

July 12th. Thirty days ago the Tibetans began the siege. The Chinese have tried no more sorties all of which ended disastrously with heavy losses to them and practically none to the Tibetans. The Chinese are strictly upon the defensive. The Tibetan soldiers frequently attack the hospital and school at night attempting to set fire through the windows but the Chinese light pitch-flares which they hurl out of the upper windows. The flares are so strong that the attackers are clearly revealed and they flee from the heavy cross-firing.

We missionaries are kept fairly close within our bricked windows and thick clay walls. We go into the city to care for the wounded and to hold our usual church services. I call on the officials and in the homes of the people who have resigned themselves to a long siege with an unknown future in loss of life and property. Mankind soon becomes inured to danger and callous of suffering when it is ever present but uncertain. As neutrals our home is not a usual target so at times we take short walks upon the roof or outside in the yard. Rifles at a long range can reach us. Our home is about two hundred yards through the air from the school which is a Chinese fort shielding us from the Tibetan fire coming from the two mission homes upon Japoding.

"This walking upon the roof is too hard upon my nerves and it is an unnecessary exposure," I remark one day to Miss Young as we are strolling upon the roof. I go inside and she soon follows. Later that day as we are standing with my wife Louise, and our son, John Kenneth, in the third story doorway watching a sharp exchange of gunfire, a bullet whizzes by. It is apparently aimed at our son who stands exposed in front of us all. John extracts the bullet from a bureau in an adjoining room and the angle of entrance indicates it was fired at him by a rifleman entrenched southwest of us where a swivel cannon is located.

We have a large American flag spread upon the roof and few shots are fired at us intentionally. Our house is in the deep trench of the little Batang river valley and the roof of our third story is but little lower than the main valley floor and the street level of the city. The houses and walls of Batang rise above us and since it is at these the Tibetans are firing it is inevitable that some shots should hit our home, especially when widespread firing is exchanged. After the siege I picked out many slugs and counted thirty chipped bullet holes in the snowwhite surface of our limed house-walls. Two cannon shells were found buried in the earth, one twenty feet and the other fifty feet to the west. They had been aimed at the hospital but went high. As some of the shells were explosive I have them dug out carefully to make sure they are duds. Rifle bullets only make a dent, one or two inches thick, in the pounded earthen walls of our house, which are three feet thick at the bottom tapering to one foot at the third story. During the siege we observe that packed clay walls three feet thick just halt a three inch shell and drop it dead inside. Fortunately neither side have cannon larger than three inch caliber.

Firing is continuous day and night except on some days there is a respite just before dawn. The singing of high speed bullets as they hit the mud walls with a "da dung," the crack of the explosive shells and the dull roar of the three inch cannon keep us awake all day and permit only broken sleep at night. Regularly at about four o'clock in the morning as the light begins to overcome the darkness a swivel cannon shot screams past our house coming from a thick-walled house to the southwest, and going towards the big fortress-like house at the eastern south gate. This shot calls in the patrols who are hidden near the city and have kept up intermittent fire against open windows all night. From this time until dawn few shots are fired and we catch an hour's restful sleep.

The siege is not devoid of its lighter elements. Above our home in a well-fortified house are a squad of local Tibetan militia. Each night after dark a Tibetan with a stentorian voice stands on the roof of this building and hurls filthy epithets against the Lhasa Tibetans who may answer with shots or similar shouts. Our Tibetan ally calls his enemy "hares" with untranslatable obscenity and dares them to come out of their holes and fight. The Lhasa Tibetans among other filth return epithets such as "Chinese yellow buttocks."

I call on Gezong Tsering occassionally to discuss military strategy to break the siege for I am convinced the war is a stalemate. At my suggestion he sends a force of the Tibetan militia under his brother, a former monk, southeast up the mountains to Retreh and threaten the rear of the besiegers. However, this band of about two hundred merely feint and do not attempt to fall upon the scattered Tibetan outposts.

July 17th. I discover that the Chinese have been almost out of ammunition for several days and have been concealing their shortage by firing occasionally, using the old handmade Tibetan muzzle-loading rifles charged only with powder. In the hospital (Photo No. 49) is a Chinese cannon which replies to the Tibetan cannon in the Mission house (Photo No. 48) about a hundred

yards away. Although they tear holes in each other's walls their
firing is not accurate nor are the shells plentiful, so neither side
is able to topple the other's clay walls. In the school the Chinese
take an old piece of an iron pipe from a printing press, charge it
with powder and apply a fuse from a distance. Laid in a hole in
the clay wall the explosion not only makes a noise sufficient for
a cannon but drives the iron pipe backwards with terrific force.
Twice one of the servers barely escaped being hit in this backfire.

In the evening darkness of this day ten Chinese soldiers arrive over the steep monastery road with nine coolie loads of ammunition which brings renewed hope to the sorely distressed Batang forces. Better news is the report that Ma Chen Lung, former
commander of Batang is in Litang. Gezong Tsering, as Siling or
commander of this area appointed by Nanking has been forced
to appeal for help from the warlord of Sikang, Liu Wen Huei, at
Yachow who has sent in Ma Chen Lung to be Siling and supersede
Gezong Tsering. Although Gezong Tsering has been offered very
advantageous terms with official position by the Lhasa Tibetans
he has chosen to surrender to the Chinese warlords rather than
to the Tibetan religious hierarchy of Lhasa.

Heavy fighting is rumored to be still in progress around
Gangdzi with the results indecisive. Ma Chen Lung had been
leading the troops in that area, but gaining only minor advantages, has been displaced. His successor is merely able to hold his
positions waiting for heavy reinforcements which later arrive forcing the Tibetans to abandon Dege and Nyahrong and retreat
across the Yangtze.

July 27th. Four hundred to a thousand Chinese soldiers are
said to be on their way in from Litang. Fierce shelling of the
hospital is again followed by a half-hearted assault which fails with
little loss to the Tibetans and less to the Chinese. Dun San Pao,
one of our orphan boys stationed in the hospital, has his right
eye blown out by a rifle bullet which comes through his own
rifle hole as he is shooting. He is recovering under careful hospital treatment.

July 30th to August 1st. The fiftieth day of the siege and Ma
Chen Lung comes over the hill-road in the early dawn with 250
soldiers. The Tibetans greet his column with long range machine-

gun fire but wound only two of them. This re-enforcement and
the supplies of ammunition which they carry encourage the besieged and all hope for an early end of the struggle. Ma Chen
Lung and Gezong Tsering outwardly greet each other with great
cordiality. None doubt but what Ma Chen Lung has orders to
sieze and execute Gezong Tsering when the Tibetans are driven
back but Gezong Tsering is too strong and wary to be taken. I
take their pictures together after a feast but I read the facts in
their faces.

August 4th. Gezong Tsering definitely turns the command over
to Ma Chen Lung and leaves the city with the remnants of his
Yunnan soldiers who have suffered heavy losses in the fighting.
Accompanying him are a few Batang followers and a considerable
number of tribal auxiliaries, in all about two hundred men. They
climb the hill-road eastward and will go south from Tshongpon
Pass toward Romee in order to threaten the Tibetan army's line
of supplies. With the departure of Gezong Tsering the new Sikang Province collapses for the second time. The first set-up was
under Chao Erh Feng which really reached only the Memorial to
the Manchu Throne stage and collapsed with the almost immediate outbreak of the Chinese Revolution in 1911. Gezong Tsering's
encircling movement undoubtedly was a factor in the early Tibetan
withdrawal.

August 5th. After the preliminary shelling of the hospital and
fort upon the hill to the east, the Tibetans fiercely assault the
school and hospital. Their cannonading is very accurate. They
are shooting one gun from a low hill about a quarter of a mile
away. They put eight shells out of eighteen into the small but
higher up hill fort collapsing part of the roof. They strike the
larger but lower down hospital fourteen out of eighteen shots and
have the defenders in jitters. Remarkably no one is hit in the
hospital and only one man in the fort. It is at this time that two
shells strike near our home.

Led by a Colonel the Tibetan assault almost captures the hospital. As the Tibetans are advancing with scaling ladders it is
the timely use of hand grenades, dropped over the side at the
base of the ladders as they are being placed against the walls,
wounding and killing the leaders of the assaulting party which

causes the rest to flee, leaving their five dead but assisting their wounded to safety. The hill-fort is also assaulted at the same time and barely manages to repel the attackers who have three killed and others wounded. Part of the time I am in the city sitting in the company of Ma Chen Lung and watching him direct the sending of re-enforcements to the hill-fort and to the hospital. Sweating and anxious yet confident he tells some incidents of his many battles and sieges which he has participated in during his thirty years upon the Tibetan Border, coming in first as a lieutenant under Chao Erh Feng. The remainder of the time we missionaries watch the battles from the windows and roof of our home taking care to stay out of sight. Although neutral we hate to run the risk in a sacking of the city if the Chinese defenses should fail. However, this assault proved to be the last desperate attempt to take the city.

August 7th. Steady firing all day after a lull on the sixth. The day following attacks have always been quiet during this siege, both sides burying or burning their dead, succoring their wounded and recovering from the shocks of fear and death. Our chief fear all summer has been the threat of a night assault as the river in the unusual drought is easily fordable most of the time. The few heavy rains are welcomed since they raise the little Batang river into a devastating torrent which no one dare attempt to wade for at least two days afterward. We wonder if the Tibetans will attempt a night attack as a last desperate resort and we know that if they do the city will probably be burned and captured. In our own defenceless position we can only hope that the well-disciplined Lhasa troops approach on our side rather than wild Tibetan tribesmen.

August 8th. The Tibetans were evidently covering their withdrawal by their steady firing yesterday as they fire a final salvo from their swivel cannon about four in the morning and withdraw down the valley. The Chinese dare not follow. The Tibetans retreat to the west side of the Yangtze which becomes the new Sino-Tibetan Boundary. When we see swarms of people going over to the hospital about seven o'clock I join the procession and later take over the whole family to inspect the damage.

The relief felt by all is undescribable after fifty-seven days of siege. The confinement has been especially trying for the children who have not dared to venture out except in the close protection of the eight foot walls around the yard. John Kenneth, eight years old, and Marian Louise, five years old, have been playing inside and they will never forget the horror of these days. Robert Malcolm, slightly over a year old, is still thin and fretful after recovering from a severe attack of malaria during the fore part of the siege. The women, Mrs. Ogden, Miss Grace Young and my wife Louise, are worn and thin. I myself probably look as bad as they do. We have lived mostly on the second floor of which we have three rooms and they have one room with a kitchen on the first floor. A mutual study is shared on the second floor. Miss Young sleeps on the third floor exposed to stray bullets from one direction. Surplus goods and medicine are stored in the basement as we have cleaned out all valuables from Japoding.

In a few days my family and I take a survey trip over the battlefield. Upon the hill-fort mountain spur is the bloated corpse of a Tibetan soldier of fortune, his head swathed in his cloak and his body exposed to the vultures. He was a floater as the dead with friends or relatives were not unceremoniously dumped but buried or burned. Beyond the corpse at the neck of the range are the wooden remnants of rude huts which sheltered the outpost of probably fifteen men who besieged the hill-fort. We circle southwest to Dora viewing the burnt and gutted houses. In going over the straw-littered floor of one courtyard, John Kenneth and I pick up an army of fleas. John being shorter has so many that we retreat outside where we strip the lad while he jumps several feet to one side to get rid of them. We come back through the mission farms and compound. All tenant houses are mere piles of clay. The orphanage is in the best shape with some doors and windows gone and floors intact but black and filthy. The Tibetan Commander had used the orphanage for his quarters and thereby saved it from spoilage. The two mission homes, the school and the hospital, having served as forts, are wrecked clay shells. Holes in the roofs, floors all or partly gone, partitions broken down, windows and window frames removed and clay walls punctured by cannon shot present a scene of utter devastation. They are no longer livable even by Tibetans, until repaired, which may never be (Photo No. 50).

A year previous, orders had come from the homeland to close

our mission work and leave. With wrecked buildings, no money,
no doctor, and a shortage of medicines, we feel helpless (Photo
No. 51). Dispirited by the death of many friends (Photo No.
52), we view the devastated country side and the shortage of food
for the coming year with overwhelming sorrow. We had con-
templated staying until fall and perhaps through another winter
but now unable to be of much help and knowing our absence will
mean less people to feed we prepare to leave. We create a self-
perpetuating Board of Trustees and place in their hands all of
the Mission property and give them complete authority to continue the missionary work, which had first opened in Tachienlu
in 1903 and transferred to Batang in 1908.

We send word to the Washi leaders, Ngen Druh and Aden,
and make arrangements to leave. The Washi come in and we, Mrs.
Minnie Ogden, Miss Grace Young, my wife, Louise and I with our
three children, John Kenneth age 8, Marian L. age 5, and Robert
M. age 1½ years, leave Batang on August 22nd amidst a huge
crowd of sorrowing people who line the road for miles. We feel
as if we are running away from our duty as we bid farewell to
the faithful pillars of the church and mission after a noodle feast
at the "hot springs."

Thirty-two days of high-plateaus and passes, with rain for
thirty days, brings us to Tachienlu upon Sept. 23rd. A cholera
epidemic, stopped as if by a wall east of Wassukou forty li below
us, holds us at Bob Cunningham's for six weeks. In this period I
travel ten days with J. Huston Edgar upon the trip described in
Chapter XIII. With the coming of cold weather in mid-November
when cholera is no longer to be feared, we leave the Tibetan
Plateau, some of us forever.

Figure 45
Layman conducting a religious Thanksgiving offering at Gartok

Figure 46
Batang from the northwest during wheat seeding time. Corner of large Monastery at right edge

Figure 47
Ba Lama flanked on his left by Gesiling at inauguration of Hsikang Province
March, 1932. Dr. Bare with his son Edgar and my son John are in front row

Figure 48
Mission House (100 yds. from hospital) occupied by Tibetan troops, scarred
by cannon and bullet shots

Figure 49
The hospital occupied by the Chinese troops showing cannon and bullet marks which came mostly from Mission house 100 yards away (See picture No. 48)

Figure 50
My wife, three children and our maid Gwayin in front of our Japoding home, after the siege

Figure 51
Our family and servants after the Battles of Batang. My old hunting dog Jack
is held by Gezang Tsering who was with me on my Rong trip, as told in
Chapter XIII

Figure 52
The final scene in Battles of Batang. Tibetan water burial

Chapter IX

WITH ROBBER TRIBES OF TIBET

The road northward from Batang tracing the large Batang river is always dangerous. Directly north are the Deshohdunpa or Seven Tribes who have close blood relationship with Batang citizens, but, in their mountain homes, are so independent of Chinese control that half of the taxes are not collected and the other half are squeezed out by display of armed force. Those who pay taxes attempt, by robbery of Chinese protected caravans, to reimburse themselves.

It so happens that when we three, Brooke Dolan II, financier and leader of his second Natural History Expedition, Ernst Shafer, zoologist, and I as interpreter, liason officer with Tibetan and Chinese officialdom and caravan commander plan to go northward from Batang to Dege, some 186 miles distant, the Seven Tribes are on the warpath. With a permanent force of eight Tibetans— Gezang Tsering (Gegen Atring), Tringleh his son, Dendru, Dingtzin, Namjyeh and Drashi, of Batang, Wang and Jurmeh, of Tachienlu, and three Chinese—Lee, Tsi, and Tsang Wen Chin, our former cook from Chungking, all armed with guns, it is not necessary for us to fear petty thieves or ordinary robber bands. Moreover our Tibetan carvan leader, Gegen Atring, has relations and is well known to the Seven Tribes. A final measure of safety exists in our caravan animals, all mules, which belong to the living Buddha of Batang-Ba Lama who has religious jurisdiction over the Seven Tribes.

However, all this carefully built-up protection perishes overnight. A number of young braves from the Seven Tribes are winter raiding as usual and attack a caravan going eastward on the Litang road not knowing that a stronger party of soldiers (Draya Tibetans in Chinese pay) returning westward, are not far away, hidden by forests and a projecting mountain spur. The noise of shots and yells bring the soldiers who, with the aid of the attacked caravan, killed one and captured four of the Tibetans. One captive escapes during the night but the other three are led into Batang and given a summary trial.

My men inform me of the captured robbers' possible fate and that they might be executed at once. Such a procedure they reason (to which I agree) will so anger the Seven Tribes that travel will not be possible northward through that territory. I hurry with them over to the military yamen or official quarters of the commander, Colonel Fu, in order to delay the execution a few days until we are clear of the Seven Tribes jurisdiction. I am too late. As I enter the gate the three men stripped naked, hands bound behind them and forced to their knees, show faces of ashen gray as the Colonel is seated at a table signing the death warrant. He finishes the warrant and in answer to my plea says it is too late as the crime and its punishment have already been proclaimed publicly but if I had arrived a little sooner he would gladly have granted my request for a delay of execution.

At my suggestion we postpone our departure a day to reform our plans. The priestly astrologers inform our men that tomorrow is also a lucky day to go northeast so we decide to go first east and then north through the Lingkharshee country. Gegen Atring whose father was a noble and managed the estates of the late deposed Prince of Batang has kinsmen and friends among this tribe. Thus in the midst of winter we are compelled to go not only over higher and colder mountains but also to spend several days longer on our northern thrust.

It is a gloomy and depressing day as we mount our riding beasts in the orphanage compound which has been our quarters for two months. In the disorder of departure we leave at different times and I am the last foreigner to go. The entire Christian group of believers and adherents with crowds of others including merchants, officials and lamas bid us farewell. The church under the leadership of Lee Kuei Kuang the pastor feeds us with noodles and meat at the Hot Springs, distant five li or about two miles from Batang. I part from them in mutual expressions of sorrow and tears. Most sorrowful of all was bidding goodbye to Mrs. Minnie Ogden whose courage and devotion to preach the Christ alone, two hundred miles from the nearest outpost, can scarcely be surpassed in the annals of missionary enterprise. However, I am somewhat disgusted with non-Christian friends who get Namjyeh so drunk he is unable to walk and I must hire two men to support him to our first day's camp. Although others had taken a few swallows he is the only one drunk with the wine of departure.

As we ride through the east gate on Jan. 20th, 1935, my men tell me the Seven Tribes are out for vengeance upon the Chinese and those who accept their protection. Halfway between the city and the little monastery we file past the grotesque, naked bodies of the three Seven Tribes men, their heads half cut off and the stones of the road spattered with dried blood. I have a twinge of sadness for the tragic end of these Tibetan young men for a crime bred in hatred of their conquerors, the Chinese, and fired with uncontrolled energy and the spirit of freedom ever deep in the people of the mountains.

We follow up the course of the little Batang river, threading the limestone canyon over sheets of ice to snow-covered Tshongpon Pass. As we cross we look east to see the three snow peaks of Nehmdah (Dajola) south of Shari La (Deer Mountain Pass). Beyond the pass we drop down into another canyon on a river of ice cutting our way with axes except over long smooth stretches where we slide down upon our seats. In a short time we reach a grassy valley where the entire Kemo tribe are wintering, pitching their forty tents up and down the valley for two miles. This tribe supplement their income by robbery, and outlaws from this tribe are credited with the killing of Dr. A. L. Shelton in February of 1922 during a highway holdup such as had been attempted by the three executed Seven Tribe's boys.

The Kemo have been impoverished in raids by the more powerful Chyah Trenwa (Shangchen) tribe during the last twenty years and they are now a small and wretched, but defiant group. They suggest that we hire four of their warriors for a hundred rupees as escort to Samar through the Lingkharshee country whose young warriors are not adverse to robbing a passing caravan. We finally accept this suggestion, first to buy their favor so they may not attempt to steal our horses or goods at night and secondly to increase our own strength for the dubious risks ahead. With the Ba Lama's muleteers who also carry rifles we leave the Kemo encampment the next morning with twenty-six guns and trace the main Lamaya stream through a fir and spruce forest to its source and surmount the divide of Shari La.

We are now in the Litang river system and we track the tributary course of its second largest source stream. This tumbling torrent pours out of a wild limestone gorge from the Lamaya ranges of perpetual snow about ten to fifteen miles slightly to the southwest. These few peaks called Nehmdah have one to three thousand feet of everlasting snow and the highest must be close to twenty thousand feet above sea level. I judge the snowline at this latitude to be between seventeen and eighteen thousand feet. A small trail leads along this cascading stream, the Shari Chu, to Lamaya and Rathi, two days' journey to the south, and these places mark the southern borders of the Kemo tribal area. North of here beyond the Tshongpon La begins the Lingkharshee grazing grounds and east of them is the Dezhungpa.

With tall scrub juniper upon our left we reach the mouth of the tributary torrent and cross the Shari Chu which is ice-cold and dangerously swift. Upon the far side we camp amidst tall dried grass where we had camped three times previously. We employ a lone Lingkharshee traveller as an additional guide through his home country.

The next morning after breaking camp a party of horsemen across the river view us with suspicion which we reciprocate. Both sides halt and in accordance with custom two men from each party ride to meet halfway. We send Tringleh and Dendru. The four horsemen make themselves known and satisfy each other that both sides are peaceful. The other party are Washi going from one of their camps to visit another encampment. We ford our Litang fork again, climb a low narrow saddle and find ourselves paralleling the one half mile length of a deep bluish lake about one fourth of a mile wide. The surface is a smooth crust of plate glass ice at least a foot thick and so clear, fish resembling carp and catfish can be seen in it. Just beyond we pitch our tents upon a heavy spongy carpet of dry yak dung, a foot thick, left by years of nomadic encampment.

We soon regret the location of our camp which we at first had thought ideal because of an inexhaustible supply of fuel. When the evening breezes arise we are sprinkled with fine yak-dung dust which penetrates our tent, covers our clothes and flavors our food. As to the fuel the yak dung itself is afire, but not aflame, smoldering with a stifling smoke when we uncover the top layer. We try to extinguish the fire but there is only yak-dung covering the bottom of the little valley and when we use it to cover parts that are burning we find we are merely spreading the fire. It must burn itself out like an inflamed peat bog or coal mine, probably having caught afire during the last huge encampment in October and if it does not burn out will be quenched by next summer's rains. We make sure that our tents are some distance from the hidden fire. To generate sufficient heat for cooking, yak dung must be stimulated by blowing when it bursts into a slightly bluish flame, and gives off acrid fumes with a little smoke. Human blowing soon exhausts one so a goatskin bellows is used continuously by one of our men.

The night is cold, four degrees below zero Fahrenheit, and marked by wolves attacking our horses leaving one badly gashed, before the dogs and our movements drive them off. We rise at daybreak and after a hasty brown breakfast start northward across the great upper bowl-shaped plain of the Litang river. General G. Pereira and Dr. H. G. Thompson had continued east from this point and then surmounted a pass in front of us to go north to Gangdzi in 1923. We, however, leave their route and follow northeast, the main source of the Litang river, until it turns northwest when we ford the stream and proceed along a tributary north almost to its source, and in a bitter wind, under a cloudy sky, camp on yak-dung again. Gazing northwest we can see the beginnings of the Litang main stream amidst the glaciers of a great snow peak twenty to twenty-one thousand feet above the sea known as Chungtsang Mehya and regarded as their "Zhidah" or guardian peak by the Lingkharshee tribe (Photo No. 53).

After another sub-zero night we start upon a stiff climb leaving the small branched plain to go north and northeast over a barren pass, Chungstsang La, about 15,500 feet above sea level. Beyond the pass a flock of blue sheep entice Dolan and while he stalks them we turn northwest and circle over a saddle. On our right is a long grass valley which leads into the Dezhungpa country and eventually to Gangdzi. We slide down into a rounded valley with grassy slopes pursuing a stream downward for a few miles in a general northerly course. Now and then our little stream is joined by other brooks from similar valleys. Finally we begin to arrive into a flattish area covered with small barberry bushes and thorny shrubs. At our end is another valley leading east whose stream joins ours. Beyond us the enclosing range on the east circles about a thousand feet north and seems to meet the western range but I know the stream must go through a defile. Across our creek, we are on the right bank, is a stony alluvial fan covered with high shrubs growing amidst huge boulders. It is an ideal location for an ambush.

As our caravan noisily winds its way into this apparent dead-end plateau shots begin to ring out and whistle nearer than we like. The men and I try to discover their source without making any effort to return the fire. We continue to move slowly forward at my order, whereupon more shots are fired, then I command the caravan to halt. I consult with Tringleh and Dendru who are near me as to the source of the firing. We do not have to wait long to discover the origin. With diabolical yells several men (later we learn there were six) jump from behind rocks on the left bank about two hundred and fifty yards west of us. These men leap into the saddles of horses hidden by the tall brush and come racing towards us.

"You and I will ride forward to meet them," I say to Tringleh and Dendru.

"No, they may harm you as you are a foreigner. I know some of the tribe and I will meet them," Tringleh speaks up quickly.

"If you think that is best go ahead," I answer. At these words Tringleh and Dendru with a Kemo guide whip their horses and race to meet the oncoming Tibetans.

The opposing parties meet on this side of the stream, all leaping from their horses but our two men merely wait calmly while the others advance with yells and flourishes of their swords.

"They will kill our men. I can pick them off," excitedly speaks up Schafer who has dismounted and kneels to fire.

"No, you must not, they will not hurt our men, that is their custom. I know what I am doing. Besides there must be others and they will fire then at us." I speak sharply, whereupon Schafer rises and waits, assured by my calmness and confidence.

Tringleh and Dendru afterwards relate how the Lingkharshee, for the attackers are of that tribe, threaten and beat them with the flat of their swords a time or two, but desisted when our men declare their identity. Tringleh is also recognized by two of the Lingkharshee who had been to Batang. Tringleh and Dendru quickly explain the nature of our caravan. Whereupon the six Lingkharshee come back to us with our men, all laughing and talking. At this time Dolan rides up at a gallop having missed the excitement but upon hearing the shooting has hastened to us, abandoning his futile chase after the blue sheep.

The six Lingkharshee as guides begin to conduct our caravan down the valley, one on foot leading his horse. This footman pulls up a naked knife blade about six inches long which had been sunk into the middle of the foot wide path leaving a sharp point, about an inch long, protruding above the ground.

"Why was that knife placed there" I curiously inquire of Tringleh.

"Teacher, knives have been placed in the middle of all paths in this area to injure the enemy whose bare feet or thin leather shoe sole will be penetrated by the blade. Infection will set in and give a bad wound or perhaps kill the person by gangrene. The Lingkharshee and the Dezhungpa are now feuding over the right to pasture their herds in this valley. They raid each other and these knives are to protect the trails. The Lingkharshee thought we were a group of raiders from the Dezhungpa tribe and that is why they ambushed and fired upon us," answers Tringleh whose courage had been proven in the Batang siege two and one half years ago when he was second in command at the hospital. He had been one of my school boys from his early youth and his faithfulness is beyond question. I had heard of these knife booby traps but this was the first one I had seen.

Before Tringleh finishes speaking men begin to rise up from behind rocks and bushes on our right and in front of us as we curve around to the left to follow the creek through a narrow defile. We had ridden into a death trap and some forty men had us covered when the six men farthest away had fired upon us. We are astonished to see that some are not over one hundred and fifty to two hundred yards from where we had halted. I ponder upon the narrow escape from probable annihilation as well as the devilishness of the sunken knife which could injure a shepherd boy or kill an innocent person since the remedy for a wound in the foot is soaking in fresh yak dung.

We make a strange procession as our own varied guards and caravan are escorted by the Lingkharshee through the defile about a hundred yards long into a long wide plain. Herds of yak line the undulating hills from which lookouts keep constant watch for the approach of unknown persons. They thus have ample time to lay as clever and formidable an ambush as any modern general could contrive. This is my second ambush and this time it turned out more luckily than the one on July 10th, 1927, when we were robbed of our entire caravan upon Tsaleh Pass as told in my first book, the "Mountain of Silver Snow."

We camp about three hundred yards from the fifty odd black tents at the foot of the ranges to our left. Our own tents are pitched at the edge of our enlarged creek which is the chief source of the big Batang River. The nomadic element of the Lingkharshee are represented by these black yak-hair tents, the remainder, some two hundred fifty families, live in houses to the westward in areas drained by the big Batang River and its tributaries. Our ambushers retire to their tents leaving us to pass a cold and somewhat anxious night setting guards every two hours to avoid surprise and to thwart thieves.

We sleep fitfully in the subzero temperature and rise at dawn. After consultation with Gegen Atring I spread the word that everything possible should be packed away, and that everyone should hold on to every object they do not wish to lose, and each one must be alert against surprise keeping his gun unobtrusively handy.

"I am glad they missed us yesterday and since bullets cost money here are ten rupees to give the Lingkharshee for the shots they wasted. This will also pay for a camping place and for a guide to take us through their country. We certainly are lucky no one was hit and we did not fire back," I remark to Tringleh. To my words Tringleh fervently agrees and gives them the rupees without any comment.

Our early rising is wise and our precautions are necessary. As we are loading the animals the Lingkharshee gather in front of their tents with their German Mausers on their backs, mount their horses and charge towards our camp. We wait calmly and as my Tibetans and I expect, about one hundred yards off, they wheel and dismount. They come up to us laughing and swarm through our camp picking up any loose object. We say nothing about these trifles but Schafer carelessly lays his notebook down and before he is aware the book is lost within the cloak of a burly nomad. Schafer is worried but I tell him we likely can get it back. Tringleh and I linger behind the others and walking to one side I give Tringleh ten rupees to recover the book. Tringleh soons joins me after I mount and ride away. He returns five rupees and triumphantly waves the book.

"Its redemption price was only five rupees. One of the Lingkharshee had slipped it into his cloak, and in accordance with custom, lost articles have to be paid for. That thief obtained five days' wages for his work," informs Tringleh, as I gladly grab the valuable notebook and carry it in my own saddlebag.

It is our bitterest day with a northwest wind that cuts to the skin where one is not protected by fur-skin garments. We continue down this treeless grassy valley following our stream of yesterday and watching it constantly enlarge through tributaries until it is joined by another creek almost as large. The united waters, forming a small raging river known as the Ba Chu or big Batang River, cuts through a straight walled canyon, where it leaps and boils to vanish around a bend. Later this canyon widens out into narrow valleys where tiny villages abound and amidst them is seen the princely seat of the Lingkharshee.

We now begin to trace upward the other main fork of the Ba Chu and after a few miles ford it to follow a tributary. We pass some hot springs but no one suggests a bath. For seven and a half seemingly endless hours facing the chilling wind we go northwest and as the sun is setting we turn at right angles and mount southwest for a half hour. We pitch our tents at 15,500 feet altitude in a small cedar forest as the partly clouded sun plays with golden steps upon the glacier-studded mountain on our right and to the northeast. It is a snow peak perhaps 19,000 feet high. The glaciers come down to 16,000 feet and I do not remember ever seeing any-

thing quite so cold as this frowning mass of ice about a half mile
off. To our left the snow fields had receded behind a rocky barren
range which reflected coldness. Only the nearby cedars comforted
us but their creaking coolness in the engulfing twilight foretold
a chilly night.

The temperature dropped to seventeen degrees below zero
Fahrenheit. Sensing such a drop I sleep in most of my clothes
and barely keep warm. I welcome in the dusky dawn the warmth
of the crackling evergreen fire which the men kept up all night.
Barring precipitation the Tibetans prefer to sleep in the open
rather than put up a big tent. They are wearing either lambskin-
lined gowns or cloaks made from seven sheep skins which will
last from two to five years of constant use. Sleeping beside fires
they bake on one side and shiver on the other, that is on nights
as cold as this one.

It is the 29th of January as we leave what proved to be our
coldest camp. Our course is southwest and upward but we turn
west in the final stretch over the 16,500 foot pass of Manlung
whose dark red limestone walls give way to a granite range upon
the other side. The cedar grove which sheltered us during the
night grows to within five hundred feet of the summit which is
flanked by two lakes, one on the eastern side and the other on
the western face. From the top of this beflagged stone-piled pass
a magnificent field of snow peaks spread east bounding the Lingkharshee country on the northeast. We had seen these peaks the
last two days but not so closely. They are known as the Drang-
chen Lhari Dukar and are the guardian diety of the Dezhungpa
tribe. The highest, perhaps 21,000 feet high, has three to four
thousand feet of snow. The Manlung La is the border of the
Lingkharshee tribal grounds while to the northeast is the Trang-
tha tribe which has one thousand families.

We descend westerly and steeply over granite boulders turning to look at the panoramas around us, noting the snow peaks
southward which lie near Batang and attempting to discern the
break to the west which will outline the Yangtze river but the
ranges and forests are many and we are not sure which dip encloses the mighty stream. As we go down past an immense cedar
forest on our right we marvel at their size. Some are three to four

feet in diameter and a hundred feet high. The cedar is replaced by spruce and fir as we reach lower altitudes.

We continue north led by a Samar nomad from one of three nomadic tents which we pass. He displaces our returning guides, one Kemo and one Lingkharshee whom we have insisted should fulfill their contract although they wished to turn back at the Manlung Pass. We circle in a tremendous curve along the forested mountain slope to camp by the Posheekhoh or Deneh stream whose course we can follow as it runs northwest and then north, describing a large arc before it is joined by another stream and the united waters called Gumdah Chu flow into the Yangtze river.

The night is much warmer and we enjoy the next day's ride moving generally northward. First southwest and then northwest we trace the curves of the range over the blue and yellow limestone pass of Lamar, 16,500 feet. We descend once more, but lower, a total of about two thousand feet in a long mountainside ride, cross Tama La, 14,500 feet altitude, and finally drop deeply to enter Samar. Fifty scattered houses comprise this village which is one-half of the strength of the Samar tribe including fifteen to twenty tent dwellers (Photo No. 54). We lodge in our first house within ten days, a castle-like home of four stories and each floor with high ceilings, the third floor being reached by a log ladder with seventeen steps.

After an unusually late start at 10:45 A.M. we proceed north, travelling but a short day of three and one quarter hours. Our trail leads through a red limestone canyon lined precipitously by walls from five hundred to seven hundred and fifty feet high. Sandthorn shrubs with yellow berries gladden our hearts for such bushes grow in the Batang valley and we feel more at home. We reach the Deneh river, beside which we had camped day before yesterday, and follow it to our camp at Zhosothang on the last day of January.

Another day and we meander north down the torrential Deneh now about ten yards wide and pass within an hour enormous springs pouring out at least six thousand gallons a minute starting a good-sized stream which we cross on a wooden bridge. After moving through forests of fir, oak and maple we arrive at the first

monastery since leaving Batang, one of fifty lamas belonging to the
Samar tribe. After a trip of twelve miles we stop at some hot
springs for the night.

During the day our men under the influence of comparative
warmth break out into song and jest. Azong, one of Ba Lama's
muleteers, and Drashi chant love rhymes. Drashi, who is unusually
clever in composition, surpassed Azong who goes by the nickname of "crow" because he will eat anything regardless of its
state of decay. He naturally does not like his scurrilous title.
Azong piqued by his defeat remarked that "not having a goat
head he could not quote poetry." A goat is considered clever but
also tricky and evil-minded.

February 2nd. Fourteen years ago today Louise and I were
married and this is the first and I hope the last anniversary we
will be separated. For an hour we move in a northerly direction
descending with the Deneh River, whose drainage basin we have
been in for several days, until it is joined by the Gatse to make
the Gumdah River which goes southwest and then south into the
Yangtze. We ascend with the Gatse River past the headman's

PLACARD ON TIBETAN GRAVE

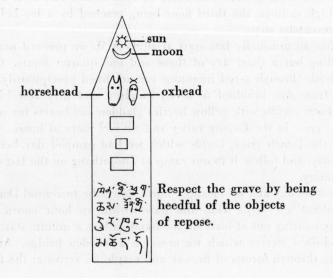

sun
moon
horsehead
oxhead

Respect the grave by being
heedful of the objects
of repose.

castle and the sixty monk monastery of Khamzhung. From a northwestern course we turn northeast to enter a magnificent hemlock forest with trees four and one half feet in diameter and one hundred and sixty feet high. In addition large fir, spruce, a golden prickly oak, and maple are interspersed with the hemlock. Flurries of snow greet us as we pitch our camp in a chilling wind.

Northward we climb over the grassy 15,500 foot Man Pass in a stiff wind which we gladly escape by a steep drop into wooded valleys where no less than ten flocks of snow pheasants, with twenty to thirty in each group, gobbled against our intrusion. My horse falls on the ice several times but does not succeed in breaking my saddlebag stuff nor myself as I hop nimbly off each time when he goes down. From Samar on we recognize we are in a different tribal region by the jewelry of the women who wear a large round yellow amber egg with a red coral cherry in the center, placing this flowerlike piece in the middle of the forehead.

Tringleh, Dendru and I ride ahead of the main caravan down a wooded valley, mostly northward for about fourteen miles on the fourth of February to arrive at Pehyee (Beyu) where we secure quarters in a school for the caravan. Since this is an important agricultural and commercial center we desire good guarters for the day's stay to replenish our tsamba for the men and our chopped grain and straw for the horses. However, we have a two days' delay due to the inadequate facilities for buying, parching and grinding our barley for tsamba (Photo No. 55).

Pehyee is the magistracy seat of a district with three thousand families. A hundred and twenty highly colored monastic buildings of the Red Cap Sect ranged in parallel lines upon a mountain spur create one of the most spectacular lamasery cities I have seen. At the base of the monastery are clustered several householders who till the valley flats. In the main temple three or four hundred monks pray daily before their chief deity, Padma Sambawa, who was the founder of their sect. In a smaller temple is Shampa, the God of Love, as the central figure, flanked by some copulating deities. The outside walls of the buildings are colored in white, red and blue stripes running from the ground to the eaves. Four hundred prayer wheels enclose the temple area. While the lay population of the town is perhaps twenty-five there are about two hundred people in homes scattered throughout the narrow valley whose stream flows into the Yangtze.

On the outskirts of Pehyee is a graveyard (Photo No. 56). Each grave is placarded at the head with a paddle-shaped board adorned with designs of the sun and moon at the top, and the heads of animals below them, followed by three blank rectangles and lastly, at the bottom, an inscription in Tibetan. The animal heads represent the year in which the deceased was born. One placard bore the head of a hog. Another had the head of a bull and also of a horse where a mother and her infant, both dying at the same time, lay buried. Each Tibetan year composing a cycle of twelve has a different animal name and each year has also the name of an element to the number of five. These two elements are paired into a cycle of sixty years. After the sixty years is finished another cycle is run. Ancient dates must be compared with known contemporary events in foreign countries to place Tibetan dates accurately. The inscription is translated "the clasped hands of disease or an unfavorable burden have been separated by the doubt barrier of the grave." It seems the corpse is first buried and then burnt but the interring place is marked by a rectangular mound of stones the length and width of the corpse. Poles with attached prayer flags are stuck inside this mound making altogether a striking situation especially upon a barren hillside.

During the second day of our delay here I hire two horses for Dingtzin and me to ride to the Yangtze River. We follow the small Ngee river northward to its mouth and then ride down the Yangtze to the end of the trail. I am not satisfied so I leave my horse with Dingtzin and alone walk through thorn bushes and over rocks and around mountain spurs for about a mile and a half until halted by an impassable cliff. White men have never trod around these bends and I can see where the Yangtze comes from the southwest and then south toward Pehyee (Photo No. 57). At the mouth of the Ngee stream this mighty river goes northeast and then northwest, thus in its curves describing three-fourths of a circle. There must be a marvelous canyon if the few unknown miles I am viewing, cliffed as it is in both directions, continue for some distance. I can throw a stone across the Yangtze here and about twenty-five feet up the opposite bank.

Leaving on February the seventh we make a long day's journey of twenty miles. We ride mostly through evergreen forest, surmount a double pass, the Nguzo La or Silver Pass with altitudes of 16,300 and 15,500 feet. At the end of this chilly, sunless day we lodge in the Red Cap Monastery of the Kahgyurpa sect called Kathoh on top of the mountain resembling the first letter (Ka) of the Tibetan alphabet where four hundred priests reside; although two thousand monks are said to be on the roll (Photo No. 58). Famous as a Nyingmapa training center Kathoh is now distinguished in the erection by a wealthy Chinese Lamaist a few years ago, of an indescribably beautiful chorten-pagoda with a base about sixty feet square and rising to four stories. Half Tibetan and half Chinese in architecture, each corner is decorated with dragons, lanterns, bells and elephants which enclose a central cone-shaped structure with curved Chinese roofs at each pagoda-story and the whole topped by a Tibetan chorten. In a nearby shed is a four-wheeled wagon for conveying the "idol god," Tsepagmed or Immeasurable Life.

I wander over to the main temple to watch a lamaistic Buddhist service conducted by some fifty priests sitting in rows before Tsepagmed. They are performing the usual ritual with the mumbling of prayers in long rolling throaty tones, the intricate genuflexions of fingers, the ringing of silver-toned bells and the menacing shaking of the dorjes or thunderbolts (dumbell-shaped exorcising instruments). They pause suddenly to take a sip of tea and the silence is so deep and profound that the air seems to be pregnant with the holiness of communion.

Leaving the main temple with its uncanny realm of devils being exorcised I stroll over to the unusual chorten-pagoda, presenting here and there the figures of deer, yak-heads, and unicorns (prong-headed antelope which have lost a horn or were born defective). The lowest floor is ringed with prayer wheels. The second story features the idols of the wizard Padma Sambawa with his wives and followers in front of him, some of them obscene figures. Upon the walls are eight of his manifestations. The third floor is dominated by the God of Mercy Chenrezig with one thousand painted figures of Guatama Buddha on the walls. The fourth and top floor shows Immeasurable Light or "Odpamed" accompanied by one thousand Buddhas painted upon the walls.

Horbu is our next stop after a short trip through wooded valleys spotted by inhabited clearings. Here roads lead up its river, the Dzin, to Gangdzi and down to Dege. Across the Dzin river on its left or south bank is a hut where I visit an old woman reputed to be a witch and 134 years old. However, she gives me her birth year and she is either 74 or 134 years old. As she looks to be 74 I conclude that is her age and I likewise doubt that she can float through the air as is reported although she is thin and light enought for the wind to blow her around. The fields here are visited by hundreds of pigeons who furnish us with squabs for supper.

In the morning we soon descend westward four miles down the Dzin to the Yangtze which seems smaller here than at Pehyee. We turn right, up the Yangtze, at times riding along the water's edge, and other times at variable heights up the bank. We ford or cross on bridges numerous mountain torrents but on the steep face of the opposite western bank only rivulets flow down into the Yangtze. The wooded western range has probably been severed by the Yangtze in its great arc through the Pehyee region. No trail leads southward for several days, which in Tibet indicates the Yangtze has impassable canyons. Flanked by scrub covered mountains on our right and steep evergreen slopes on our left we slowly rise higher with the Yangtze for two days, or about thirty miles, before we turn up a small stony tributary fifty feet wide which we trace upward to Dege arriving February 12th, 1935. Opposite the mouth of this branch, known as the Zee Chu, and across the Yangtze is a huge black rock crowned by altars and prayer flags. At the base of this rock are sands which serve as a landing place for skin boats that ferry over tea for caravans. This crossing of Gangthoh Drukha is very important as it serves a vast region westward to beyond Chambdo (Chahdo) giving a more direct route to that city than the ferries northward at Drima Lhakhang or southward below Batang. Once across the Yangtze, however, caravans must climb the opposite canyon wall through a narrow cleft and over a pass about 15,000 feet high.

Through a long barren red sandy valley and over a wooden bridge spanning a blue glacier torrent brings us into Dege (Derge) which is rated by Tibetans as one of the great religious, industrial and political centers of eastern Tibet (Photo No. 59). This city of one hundred twenty-five buildings inhabited by fifty lay families and six hundred monks cluster around three buildings, a huge temple to Tsepagmed, the palace of the Dege Prince and a large structure housing thousands of blocks for print: ıg the Buddhist Bible. More than half of the buildings shelter monks who assemble daily in their Sakya temple whose outer walls are blue with adjoining stripes of red and white. Prominent among the lesser figures in the temple sits Padma Sambawa the great exorcist.

As we approach from the south and cross the bridge a large chorten silently turns us to the left around it, for orthodox Buddhists keep sacred objects on their right and circle them clockwise. We ride past a long row of prayer barrels half-hidden in a low porch which encloses a dumpy structure. A ragged, winding street leads up the valley which runs eastward to precipitous mountain crags whose peaks are bare but whose ravines show patches of snow. Maps show snow ranges here, but my eyes and reports of the people indicate there are no perpetual snow peaks easterly for three days journey not until one strikes the great snow peaks of the ranges along the northern route through Gangdzi and Dzohchen.

We walk into the temple of Tsepagmed and watch the monks in their usual morning routine prayer-chant but they soon come out into the sunny courtyard for the final exorcism. Before the service ended all pause, and out of the kitchen in an adjoining leanto near the main entrance, paced by the throb of a huge drum six feet in diameter, rushes a long line of young monks. They bear on their shoulders thirty-eight gleaming brass and copper teapots (headed by a silver teapot for the abbot and two clay ones requested by aged lamas); and forty-six buckets all filled with a steaming yellow tea which is quickly emptied into the varnished wooden bowls carried by every monk inside the blouse portion of his cloak. During the progress of the prayers tea is served every half hour and this pause is used for the relieving of nature which takes place in public outside the courtyard walls.

The not imposing palace of the Dege Prince is now used by the Chinese magistrate and the Prince lodges in a large ordinary structure more befitting his reduced status. Once autocratic ruler over seventy thousand families, he now has fifty thousand and governs them under the sovereignty of a Chinese Mayor whose ideal is the collection of enough taxes to enrich himself and satisfy his superiors. The Prince is left to administer all matters among the Tibetans which do not involve Chinese and also must compel his subjects to furnish forced animal hire as required by officials, soldiers and others, including foreigners, when travelling with travel permits. The Chinese are not able to secure much money in taxes, yet this reduces a Tibetan court once brilliant to a shabbiness which is painful to Tibetan pride.

The bronze teapots, bells and dorjes which are manufactured by hand in small villages within a day's journey from Dege are famous all over Tibet. I buy some new ones which naturally are cheaper than elsewhere. Gegen Atring and I visit a home and watch the making of paper which is one of the chief products of Dege. The bark of a shrub (probably Daphne) is peeled off, soaked in water and the outer black layer removed and discarded. The residue, a whitish tough fibrous material, is stewed in wood lye water until soft and then macerated on a stone until the pulp resembles wet paper. Washed in a flowing stream and strained it is spread on cheesecloth in a rectangular frame and placed in the sun. With a bright sun about three hours dries the paper which is peeled from the cloth. The paper, although somewhat rough, is now ready for ordinary use in writing but the thicker grades are rubbed smooth and glossy. For the finest books the paper is later inked black and the characters written in silver and gold to produce the most expensive hand-written editions of the sacred scriptures. One sheet, about two feet square, costs two cents and a thick sheet six cents in American money. A day's wage being ten to twenty cents paper is consequently restricted to the wealthy for personal correspondence and for religious books whose purchasers are the rich and the pious.

We call on the Dege Prince, a sad-faced young man twenty-two years of age and dressed in a dirty lambskin-lined cloak. The scrolls and brassware furnishings of his home evidence a former glory and better settings. His courtiers reflect the defeatism of their lord in demeanor and dress. Although friendly and asking us to photograph them (I gave them prints before I left as is my invariable custom) we sense a definite reticence because of our Chinese connections. Unable to hire animals we have asked for oolah (requisition of pack animals) which the Prince must compel his subjects to furnish. We soften this tax by paying well above the regular rate and by personal presents to the Prince.

According to legend the narrow, steep-sided, dead-end valley in which the Dege Monastery nestles was once a lake. A Tibetan magician, Tangtong Jyepo, drained the lake by covering it with his cloak. The present terrain which rises very slowly from the draining stream, does indeed give evidence in form, limestone structure and moraines of once enclosing a glacial lake within traditional time. Furthermore, the limestone cliffs below Dege have a cave where once dwelt a hermit who was reputed able to fly, especially at night, so that Tibetans do not lack imagination to aid nature in the creation of marvelous changes.

Figure 53
Chungtsang Mehya snow peak from the west near Batang where the group of
seven peaks are called Tsirashee

Figure 54
Tibetan homes north of Samar built for defense

Figure 55
Roasting barley before grinding into tsamba; at Pehyee. Namjyeh, one of our
men (in far background), supervises them

Figure 56
Tibetan graveyard near Pehyee

Figure 57
Yangtze River below Pehyee emerging from impassable gorges

Figure 58
Kathoh Monastery of the Kahgyupa sect, taken from the east. Trail zigzagged
down on left

Chapter X

BY YAK TO THE YANGTZE AND THE YALUNG

The oolah (transport) from Dege are yak. Such ponderous beasts have not carried our goods since last October when the Washi tea caravan transported us to Batang from Litang. From now on yak are with us all the time; in the daytime either moving sedately and slowly with us over rocky trails, or pasturing upon the grassy hillsides under the eyes of our men until dusky evening when snorting and belching steam from lolling tongues the wild-eyed brutes charge in a mass down to our tents. Tail plumes erect they wheel just before running down our camp, and collecting in a group, wait to be driven individually to the long staked-down tie rope to which they are fettered about every four feet apart by a short fore-foot loop. At night the smell of their refuse and their grunting sometimes awakens us. In the daytime our previous long and fast marches of twelve to twenty miles made by our hired mules are reduced to eight to twelve miles so our yak may feed the rest of the day. Our camping places are determined by grass and water. The irregularity and slowness of our marches prove to us that a caravan like an army moves on its stomach.

Appeals to officials for wheat and barley which we cannot buy and which they supply for a good price out of their taxes in kind, enable us to leave within four days. On Feb. 17th, 1935, we ride northward up the Zee river treading much of the day in its bed through colorful walls of limestone six miles long. Sometimes we wade in the water and sometimes we sprawl along on the ice. At places the gorge walls close in and our loaded animals can scarcely pass. Looking upward the cliff faces towering a half mile high reveal stars through a narrow slit of light. Where the torrent spreads out and the cliffs angle to a climbable slope we see caves in which reside hermits with magic powers. I have visited such recluses a few times upon other trips but we must make a distant camping place this short day after the usual late start. In the dismal dark recesses the rocks display many hues, but more interest is centered upon a waterfall one hundred and fifty feet high now frozen solid. Gold nuggets ranging in size from a pea to a baseball are found frequently in this valley where gold dust is panned in the summer.

With the onset of dusk we lodge in the stagehouse of Khorlomdo where roads and valleys meet. Eastward can be seen two trails, a northern one leading to Dzohchen and a southern one leading directly to Gangdzi (Kanze). Along these trails, in an east to west trending valley, is a sixty monk Sakya monastery with Guatama Buddha as the chief idol and the God of Mercy, Chenrezig, on the left as the supporting figure. The Tibetan women here as elsewhere throughout the kingdom of Dege wear on their foreheads a coral or a turquoise jewel set either in an engraved silver disk or in an amber circlet.

From Khorlomdo it is a short trip of two hours on the morrow before we reach another Sakya monastery with Guatama Buddha as the principal deity. Sixty monks are enrolled in the temple around which are piled richly colored and deeply carved prayer stones. The day's course is mostly northwest past nomad tents and gold diggers' stone huts. The gold diggings exist in black gravel and slate. Throughout this region the valleys are mostly grass but when wooded have generally juniper on the south slopes and spruce on the northern sides. This particular day's journey is through wooded valleys. We follow the Zee river all day and find no snow mountains to the south or southwest.

On February 19th we still ascend the Zee river going northwest seven miles between undulating slopes and evergreen forests, and then over the Zee Pass of 14,500 feet altitude to descend a thousand feet, treading a light snow which fell last night. By noon, when we eat our cold water lunch of dried raw beef and gokway (hard biscuit) sitting in bright sunshine, the snow is gone. In the afternoon with two well-placed shots I kill three snow pheasants and wound a fourth who flops an escape through juniper shrub. We continue to descend and around twelve thousand, five hundred feet pass a few houses with cultivated fields. Not long afterwards when it is almost dark we stop at some oolah-changing huts. Our quarters are miserable and cold but we sleep well enough through the grey foggy night.

In the morning our course is gradually downward and north-west for five miles along the Mahrong River to its junction with the Nyoh River which descends westerly into the Yangtze. How-ever, we must turn east and later northeast ascending for about two miles over undulating ranges to Gohzer monastery of the Sakya sect. The main temple features Tsepagmed or Immeasur-able Life, a minor temple centers Tsongkhapa and in a third edifice the chief idol is a Chohden (saint).

Before reaching Gohzer as we pass the last village on this smooth partly barren upland, the Lingtsang Prince, escorted by a retinue carrying banners attached to spears, halloes to us as they gallop furiously to meet our caravan going diagonally to his route. His gay entourage impress us as compared to the stay-at-home reception of the Dege Prince. Both parties dismount and meet with upturned palms and bows. The Prince, a handsome Tibetan youth in his late twenties, leads us uphill to the home of his father, the King now retired, to prayer and meditation in a hill-side retreat. The King is pleased to converse with us in spite of his retirement and serves us sweetened tea. He is a benign, be-whiskered gentleman perhaps sixty years of age. While available for important consultation he has turned his principality over to his son. He is following the usual custom of important men who, as they reach old age, retire to make amends for the bad acts which the affairs of state or business have imposed upon their souls during their youth and maturity. We retire in a short time and seek the comfortable quarters assigned to us in the Gohzer mon-astery.

Nearby on a precipitous promontory stood the Lingtsang King's castle and adjoining it the Nyingmapa monastery of Dzonggoh containing as its chief figure the statue of Padma Sambawa. One hundred monks reside in this lamasary and serve the immediate interests of the Lingtsang rulers who adhere to this sect. Farther up the valley is a Kahgyupa monastery of sixty monks. We visit the castle to meet the beautiful wife of the Prince and his brother, the abbot of the Red Hat monastery (Photo No. 60). The prin-cess is a sister of the Dege Prince but this alliance had not re-stored to the Lingtsang Prince his former territory which had been reduced by seizures of the Dege Prince and the Chinese until his fifteen to twenty thousand families are now only five hundred in number.

The Lingtsang Prince feasts us on rice and meats and then escorts us on our way for some ten lee. As we ride along together he recites the wrongs inflicted upon him and invokes my aid. I express my sympathy but regretfully tell him that I am only a guest passing through the country. He leaves me rather disappointed but cordial.

We move with our yak caravan for over twelve miles westward crossing low passes from whose tops we can see the broken dip of the Yangtze river course. We have been parallelling the river since leaving Dege but hidden from it by a rocky range through which the Yangtze has cut an immense canyon impossible for a trail to traverse. The Yangtze continues only as a rift until we near Namjyeh Ling when the river emerges upon the undulating plateau which we have travelled since Khorlomdo. Namjyeh Ling (Monastery) which houses us for the night has sixty monks of the Kahgyupa faith. The town is all monastery with a few humble lay-servant huts. It lies a mile north of the Yangtze at an altitude of about twelve thousand feet above the sea.

On George Washington's birthday we reach Drehma Lhakhang (Tankhoh to the Chinese) after a fairly straight course westward for fifteen miles. We parallel the Yangtze upward but see it only at intervals amidst dry grassy hills until within two miles of Drehma Lhakhang. The great river is narrower than where we saw it below Dege and curves through a flat boggy plain which is a mile or more wide. This plain supports about six hundred people including four monasteries, three on the north side and one called Chungkhor across the river in Inner Tibet. Three lamaseries are of the Gelugpa sect and one of the Sakya. The most prominent is Drehma Lhakhang which features as its chief idol the Goddess Drehma (Drima) who saves one from transmigration. This particular idol is reputed to have flown from China a long time ago. We arrive in time to enjoy a royal feast with the Chinese military commander and the Mayor.

As we must continue to drive yak-oolah the securing of pack-yak and the replenishment of supplies keep us five days in Tankhoh, the Chinese seat for a magistracy of fifteen hundred families.

While waiting I spend the day crossing the Yangtze and visiting
the Chungkhor monastery. The river is about two hundred yards
wide and takes two minutes to cross in a skin boat as we are
carried downstream some little distance. At a point not far above
us the river is reputed fordable on horseback at the very lowest
water. Sining troops looted the monastery during the Sino-Tibetan
war two years ago and this may have been the reason they were
unusually gracious to me who speak to them in their Tibetan language with words of peace and kindness. I am given a rare invita-
tion that of visiting the room of fearful deities where I picture
the local Zhidah or guardian deity (Photo No. 61).

At the point of departure I watch the Tibetan headman and
the Chinese mayor wrangle as to who should have the oolah
money. The Mayor wins the thirty-three rupees. The owners of
the yak are indifferent to the squabble as they receive nothing in
either event, an extortion which we regret but cannot prevent for
the first stage. We turn northward and at right angles to the
Yangtze follow a rocky steep valley fed by a small river twenty-
five feet wide which steadily grows smaller until limestone walls
festooned by juniper and a few spruce give way to grass. Night
falls and while the yak are with us some of the steers (substituted
for lack of sufficient yaks) are so far behind we decide to stop at
a nomad tent of the Ngoja tribe. As chance would have it our
food and bedding are on the skinny steers who do not wobble in
until midnight. We eat a nomad meal of dried cheese, tsamba,
dried raw beef and buttered tea. Then we go to sleep upon the
ground slightly softened by felt pads and sheepskins until our
rubber mattresses arrive.

After a grimy broken night we rise and eat but forego washing in the icy atmosphere, understanding by experience why Tibetans rarely wash in winter. Icicles, formed by the freezing of
water clinging to the long belly-hairs of the yak picked up by
fording the icy stream which we continue to cross back and forth,
jinkle like tinkling glass rods. To such congealing music we at
last rumble onto rolling plains of withered grass which lead northward over Chutshuh La about 15,500 feet altitude. Ice on frozen
streams has worried us since Batang and my mule has fallen more
than once but I nimbly get my legs out from under and jump to

let him fall on his own ribs rather than on my bones. It's down and up again for some animal most of the time upon snow-covered ice amidst falling snow which develops into a fierce squall dropping six inches of snow in which we sprawl and zigzag. The blizzard is born out of a cold northern tempest which replaces the comparatively warm morning wind from the south which had given us clear skies since leaving Tankhoh. In this blast pitching our tent is a difficult task. A cold supper in a constantly dropping temperature, as the wind dies and a white sun appears, only to set, precedes what promises to be a dangerous night. The white and yellow race pile side by side in the one tent forming a human carpet and we are hapy to find ourselves unfrozen by morning with the thermometer five degrees below zero Fahrenheit.

Seven hours or about fifteen miles passing a hundred black tents scattered upon the gently descending plain brings us to Jyur Gonpa of fifty monks and 13,500 feet above sea level. Adjacent to Jyur monastery is the Chinese yamen of Sershee whose mayor rules about 2,000 tents of nomads. The mayor boasts he has the only strictly tent magistracy under Chinese control.

Now in the land of wild asses we harangue the officials for five days securing permission to make a trip over the Yalung to hunt the Tibetan wild ass. In this interval I take Tringleh with me on a five hour ride northward to the Yalung (Dza Chu in Tibetan) in whose basin we have been journeying since crossing the Chutshuh Pass. We ford the Yalung which is only fifty feet wide and three deep but so swift and icy that it is not easy to cross (Photo No. 62). During the trip I shoot a golden-eyed duck, chase a wolf on horseback and help take out a live steppe fox caught in one of our traps.

Our sortie northward beyond the Yalung begins on March the 8th and lasts eight days. In the beginning we have an eight mile march northward through smooth grassy hills lightly speckled with three inches of melting snow. We count 150 tents of Goloh whose dialect the men discover is the same as the Washi confirming what the Washi told us months before. We ford the Dza Chu or Yalung which is split here in two segments by a small island which shallows the water so that it is easier to wade. The river runs almost east and west in a two-mile wide plain which has such rich black earth that, as it lies at only twelve thousand feet altitude, will some day raise hardy vegetables and likely millions of potatoes. We ride on northward, ahead, up a tributary valley leaving our burden-bearing yak to follow more leisurely. In a short six miles we lodge in a black yak-hair tent set up for our special use by the nomads as a part of oolah service. We tip them two rupees for this extra effort which has never happened to me since the visit to a Red Cap shrine in 1925, and our first upon this journey.

In this narrow plain trending north and south about one fourth of a mile wide and bordered by slightly rugged hills with out-croppings of reddish shale, we stay over a day to hunt the wild ass. The herd of sixteen animals which I stalk the next morning for nearly five miles have been fired upon recently and are extremely wary. The clever asses can smell and see me first upon these grassy plains where no cover exists. I finally fire at three hundred yards dropping an adult who struggles to her feet to slowly follow the herd. I mount my horse and chase the wily ass for at least ten miles. Wounded in the foreleg she is joined gallantly by another. Knowing wolves would undoubtedly pull down the wounded animal I wish to finish her but they are able to keep ahead of my steed burdened as he is by my weight and travelling at an altitude of around 13,000 feet above sea level when one blows at the slightest exertion. Every time I stop to shoot, the two brown asses top a rise and disappear. We finally emerge upon a vast plain deeply roughened by hummocks and with icy stretches of swamp.

On a wide strip of ice the brave ass slips and falls. She struggles long enough trying to rise that I close in to 125 yards. I dismount and shoot her but she succeeds in rising and sets off, going perhaps fifty yards before I see I must fire again before she falls dead. It is then that I regretfully discover that I have shot a female (Photo No. 63). We skin her in the gathering twilight. One of my men and a Tibetan guide have stuck close to me else I would have had a difficult time finding my way back among the endless hills. In inky darkness we approach our camp beside the Tibetan encampment that has loosed their Tibetan mastiffs, who set upon us with such fierceness that it is only by constant lashing

with our whips that we keep them from pulling us off our horses.
It is nine P.M. when we ride elated into camp. The ass skin now
adorns our parlor floor while undoubtedly most of her former
companions long since have lost their skins to vultures and wolves.

Later many times I am much closer to the herds of wild ass,
sometimes not over a hundred yards. However, having killed one
beast I prefer to photo such noble animals and never shoot at
another. I never tire studying them, in grazing and in flight, as
wheeling they watch me curiously and then as I approach, canter-
ing away with heads high and tails arched. The Tibetans claim it
is a greater sin to shoot the wild ass than any other animal as
they are special mounts for the local protective deities who may
become angered at their slaughter and send calamitous storms
upon the offending area. The wild ass, known as kiang (jyang)
by the Tibetans, is light tan or yellow-brown in general color,
whitish underneath with almost white legs and a dark narrow
spinal stripe. Weighing from 500 to 700 pounds they are about the
size of the Tibetan horse.

We set out on March the tenth northward over the grassy
plains, covered in the moister places with straggly desert shrubs
up to one and a half feet high. Some slopes are entirely barren
denuded by millions of mouse hares (Ochotona) who honeycomb
the turf with countless tiny holes connecting endless tunnels. Yellowish brown steppe bears, light yellowish steppe foxes, golden
brown weasels, eagles and hawks keep them under control unless
man destroys too many of their enemies when they ignorantly repay their benefactors by eating the grass roots to extinction and
the rich barren earth is left to the erosive power of water and wind
so that both the simple nomad and the simpler mouse-hares de-
prive themselves of food.

We surmount a low pass and slide easily onto the western end
of an immense tussocked plain five to ten miles wide which trends
northwest and southeast for a length of twenty to thirty miles.
Upon it roam vast herds of wild ass in groups, as I count them, of
five hundred to a thousand. In the bright sunlight the atmosphere on the plain was like that of an African veldt perpetually
shimmering with light radiations to the point of forming lake
mirages against which the herds extended in mile long lines, now

invisible and now fantastically evident in double images. Now and then can be heard their harsh neigh repeated at short intervals and combined with a bray. We round peculiarly pointed peaks thrusting upward barren rocky points a few hundred feet above the plain. As usual the morning is clear but in the afternoon clouds envelope our patch of sky bringing cold winds which blow up and down the valleys no matter which way they run, although in this region they trend mostly north and south.

We still see tents of the Goloh subtribes here called the Getsegongma but north of us reside the Wanah who control the country up to the mountains of Machen Pomra [Oni (Amnyi) Machen] whose snow peak commands the plain. Machen Pomra is the nearest perpetual snow mountain and is an estimated eighty air-miles away. Around our present travelling area the snub-nosed peaks are about 16,000 feet and even now no snow exists on their southern slopes. The everlasting snow line must be 17,000 to 18,000 feet at this latitude with its twenty inches of rainfall which falls mostly in the summer months.

This Getsegongma tribal area is red sandstone but the numerous mani stone piles exhibit a few blue slate prayer slabs. The piles extend in long rows. The longest I measure is 1800 feet long, six to nine feet wide and averages five feet high. Alleys break its continuity for passage from one side to the other. Many of the reddish sandstone slabs are not carved, or only slightly etched, perhaps they have been weathered to smoothness again. In niches are the finest engraved slabs with god figures and the text "Om Mani Padme Hum." Peculiar-shaped white quartz stones are sometimes laying in front of the god figures. Occasionally a few pieces of granite have been inlaid in the center of a flat side to create a bizarre effect.

We move northward for two days over the same grassed and shrubbed type of hillside until we reach the divide between the Yalung and the Yellow rivers. Two inches of snow now forms a hard crust through which the longer grass stems and the dwarf shrubs of acacia and sage brush stand out ragged and prickly. Then our Goloh hosts refuse to penetrate farther northward into the cold bitter ranges. We have seen no people, and no people are living now in the winter season for the next two days to the

Yellow river. The nomads along the Yellow river are enemies of
our Goloh guides who own our hired yak so we are helpless and
much against our desire must return.

As the caravan men break camp on this farthest northward
point during the early frosty hours of March 14th I take Namjyeh
and climb the highest range to the north. A bitter south wind
freezes me on the summit as I try to pierce the drifting clouds for
a glimpse of Machen Pomra, "the gathering place of the world's
gods" say the Tibetan books, which also state that King Gesar,
the god of war, took all the jewels of the world and divided them
among the tutelary deities giving the finest to Machen Pomra. I
am not sure that the white mantled peaks shining through breaks
in the clouds include Machen Pomra whose height from comparative descriptions given to me by the Goloh is probably around
twenty-one thousand feet above sea level. To my surprise Dolan
joins me having the same thought of trying to see the goal of
this northerly thrust. Misty adventurous fancies race through our
minds as we gaze at the seemingly endless ranges rising and falling like ocean waves, perhaps sixty miles, before obscured by the
clouding horizon. We photo the undulating plateau of rolling
hills and U-shaped valleys whose vegetation thrust above the light
snow cover like a man's whiskers. Keenly disappointed both of
us take a long last look at the promised land and slowly descend
the slippery slope to rejoin the obstinate Goloh for the return to
the Yalung.

Our backward course is more directly southward through other
but adjoining valleys and this north-south trough brings us to the
center of the great wild ass plain which we cross diagonally
toward our former trail. Mirages of lakes and reeds appear upon
the lumpy surface. Battalions of wild ass gallop and wheel alter-
nately approaching and fleeing until we enter a side valley to
camp among the Goloh.

Another short jaunt retraces our old trail to the Yalung but
fords it at another point not far off. Ice on the river and snow on
the land are rapidly melting which has slightly deepened the
stream. I shoot two spur-tipped geese which are among the thousands of waterfowl nesting in this region. Baby antelope are seen
so a few at least are born at this time. Our camp is pitched beside

sheep pens whose one foot wide walls are solid yak dung cakes piled six feet high with doorways guarded by chained mastiffs.

On the sixteenth we come back to the Jyur lamasery, passing on the way the remnants of Tsang Wen Chin's horse which had become exhausted on the trip out and later abandoned by the nomadic owners within our view. We had watched the crows pick out the eyes of the dying beast and then wait nearby for the final breathing to begin work on the tough remains.

The magistrate secures yak for our loads and we leave Jyur Gonpa or Jyur Monastery on March 19th, tracing for a short time the trail back toward the Yalung but soon turn westward and in the vicinity of the Yalung cross over a low grassy pass, about 14,500 feet altitude, and deploy down an east slope to a flat hard turf plain covered with tundra grass. Directly opposite is Sershee Monastery nestling like a jewel at the foot of a half-bowl-shaped range flanked by two sliced shoulders (Photo No. 64). The extraordinary beauty of the lamasery enchants us and we hasten to reach it but the level plain deceives us with its width for it proves to be three miles wide. As we approach some of the enchantment is lost for gorged vultures stand stupidly upon one of the shoulders after a heavy meal of man steaks. We have just missed the carving and feeding of a corpse to the naked-headed birds.

Sershee is of the Gelugpa sect with one temple to the God of Love Jyampa (Shampa in Batang dialect) and another to the reformer Tsongkhapa or Lozongdrapa. We sleep in the house of the monastery's Living Buddha. Although the quarters are comfortable and comparatively clean we move on the next morning for five hours westward before pitching our tents beside the summer corrals of yak cakes. As windbrakes for tents and protection for timid stock they are ideal although needing yearly repair because of weather erosion. Such walls likewise provide dry fuel for emergency use when snow covers the scattered yak chips.

The Goloh, who live on these yellowish-brown hills which change to fiery red under a clouded sun, are from the Achog tribe on the Yellow River. They fled from the oppressive Mohammedan rule of Sining, capital of Tsinghai Province and were given refuge by the Dza river tribes and the Chinese magistrate of Sershee, Szechwan, our late hosts. Sharp rivalry and envious greed exist

between the Szechwan authorities and Tsinghai rulers over territory and tea taxes which sometimes leads to armed conflict. Naturally the Goloh are not averse to utilizing this jealousy. Incidentally the Goloh are more hairy even to heavily whiskered faces than
the valley Tibetans, which may indicate an Aryan strain in these
nomads who are probably the true Tibetans.

The Goloh usually have tent lamaseries of the unreformed sects,
mostly Red Hat but a few are Black Hat. The Wather tribe who
occupy this area have a thirty-monk tent-monastery. They furnish us oolah but their dialect is difficult even for my men so I
must use Gegen Atring as interpreter.

We continue westward for one of our longest days nine and
three quarter hours or about twenty miles. The wide grassy trail
leads up a red sandstone valley, with black soil along the streams,
upon which the nomads to the number of fifty tents are pasturing
their flocks. It is March 21st and the cold wind which brings both
clouds and sunshine during the day has the feel of incipient
spring. On the long upward slope is a prayer stone pile called
Ridri Mani. Letters carved one and a half inches deep have little
moons within each letter, the engravings tinted artistically in red,
yellow and blue. Over Ngangpa La of 14,500 feet we drop quickly
westward, working out way slowly through a blinding snowstorm
in the late afternoon which accompanies us to Zhewa. Above some
wretched huts upon a steep cliff clings a spectacular Sakya monastery enrolling fifty monks who worship Shampa, the God of
Love, as the chief idol.

Shortly before crossing Ngangpa Pass in the early afternoon
we met a long Goloh caravan split into fourteen nomad groups of
about fifteen persons each. Last year in the fifth month (our
June) they had left upon a pilgrimage to Lhasa and India. They
had departed from Lhasa after the New Year which occurs from
the last of January to the fifteenth of February and now almost a
year later are homeward bound to the great lower curve of the
Yellow river still a month's journey away. As usual the nomad
women are gaudy, the black apron portion of their sleeveless skirt
resplendent with four to six silver plaques hanging down below the
waist and jangling with every movement of their hips. The Goloh
men are wild and fierce in appearance with long straggling locks

of hair reaching to the antelope-pronged flintlocks on their backs. In their hands they grasp for immediate use tasselled spears twelve to sixteen feet long.

From Zhewa, altitude 12,250 feet, we clatter down a stony valley with a hundred scattered homes kept by tiny fields. The houses clustered in twos and threes present an air of settled agricultural peace and prosperity strangely contrasting with the moving nomad-settled plains we have just left. Ten miles from Zhewa and our ravine drops into the Yangtze river valley at Dripomdah 11,500 feet above sea level.

We sleep the night at Dripomdah and in the morning before the sun rises cross on the jammed icebridge over the Yangtze (Photo No. 65). Open water at the rapids below and at another race above the ice, with the coming of warm air in the spring, indicate the breaking up of the icebridge so we go over in small groups for safety. Yet, at the opposite bank some of the yak stray from the central path and break through but are saved by desperate plunges to the shore. A week later, from Jyekundo, Dendru took a message toward Gangdzi, and in crossing here while leading a single horse, broke through. He reported on his return that the bridge separated entirely on the last day of March. Ice now is mostly along the shore but lower down we pass another icebridge which is still used by men.

We step warily along the narrow cliff road on the south or right bank of the Yangtze (Photo No. 66). Sometimes rotten piling and loose stones support the road so we are glad to see the finish of these few miles which go in a southwesterly direction until the Yangtze swings at right angles to continue southeast through an unknown canyon. At this point we turn west up a tributary, the Ba river, whose winding course has a twisting trail through scrub bushes and trees, varied at expanded plains by fields, which support twenty villages totalling 400 homes, in the length of fifteen miles to Jyekundo. The Bah Chu is generally about twenty-five feet wide and swift to turbulent. When swift we ford it at these wider expanses, but when turbulent we cross on narrow wooden log bridges.

It seems a long trail but we finally reach, three miles east of Jyekundo (Jyekumdo), possibly the largest Mani or prayer stone pile in the world (Photo No. 67). The first mani stone which began this monster pile is reputed to have been selfevolved. I measure the rather irregular four sided strip of ground occupied by the pile beginning at the southeast corner and going clockwise. In feet its four sides are 1071 x 228 x 774 x 273, and the greatest height is 15 feet. This space is filled with prayer stones of white limestone, of all sizes and shapes, carved, plain and in brilliant colors, with and without moons, Buddhas, animals or sacred symbols, but all bearing the sacred six letter prayer "Om Mani Padme Hum." Mostly on the east but extending around on the south side are eighty-four small and three large prayer-barrels sheltered beneath a long porch. A godhouse adorned with wall scrolls is attached on the south. After a cursory trip around to the north side of the pile, which I examined later in detail, I ride swiftly to Jyekundo ahead of the others. Immediately upon my appearance in the street I am surrounded by a crowd of the passersby which constantly grows in volume. No white man has been in Jyekundo for ten years and he but for a few days and all affirm that they have never seen a white man before. It is the twenty-third of March as I inquire the way to the Mayor's official residence to seek for an assignment of quarters.

Jyekundo (Yushu to Chinese) is about 198 miles from Dege by the most direct route. The town, a straggly collection of a hundred houses with a population of 2500-3000, lies on a flat onion-shaped bulge of land concentrated around the junction of two streams, one from the west and one from the south, which form the Ba Chu. Each house is a huge array of connected dwellings occupying the three sides of a courtyard whose fourth side is a wall with an imposing doorway in its center. Most of the buildings are squat but spacious, adobe structures of one story but a few have two stories and we are lodging in one of these upon the east side of the town. The streets are wide and irregular and of the natural yellow clay which erodes into dust that is then blown into the houses. Usually six to eight families reside in a courtyard with its horseshoe shaped house.

To the east of the city beyond a stony ravine rises a Sakya monastery crowning the end of a tipped up mountain spur. Five hundred monks are registered in the monastery. North of Jye-

kundo slopes the precipitous side of a mountain range over which
lies the shortest road to the Yangtze valley and to the Yellow
river sources which are halfway to Sining (Ziling), the capital
of this province of Tsinghai. Westward above the town there
ascends in gradual incline a broad U-shaped valley where fields
are cultivated for perhaps a half mile until the valley narrows
into a grassy ravine which leads over a pass to the Yangtze river
by a trail that joins eventually with the Sining road. South is the
Ba Chu whose green meadows trace the southern fork upward as
a constantly dwindling torrent that finally splits upon a broad
plain into three streams whose sources are like the branches of a
tree.

Jyekundo lives by trade. As a tea-port it is second to Tachienlu in importance. Tea, dispatched from Tachienlu by small
yak caravans of two hundred animals or less, halts in Jyekundo
to accumulate for a great migration. Yak, hired in herds of two
thousand, converge from all directions (particularly the southwest), on Jyekundo after the fall rains cease in late September or
early October. Tea which leaves Tachienlu in March and April
arrives in May and June just prior to the onset of the monsoon
rains. Much of the tea is sold locally within two hundred miles
but the remainder leaves by battalions of two to three hundred
yak travelling near enough for protection yet far enough apart for
plentiful grass around separate camps. The caravans arrive in
Nyachukha in November and December, and in Lhasa before the
New Years' festivals. The tea traders barter with the 15,000 to
20,000 pilgrims in Lhasa for other goods and depart from that holy
city in March, April or May. They arrive back in Jyekundo in
two or three months just in time to prepare for the next journey.
In this schedule the trip to Lhasa consumes a year.

Two hundred loads with twenty-four bricks of tea to the load
(about 100 pounds) leave Tachienlu each day for the interior,
most of it going to Jyekundo. Perhaps an eighth of this amount,
or twenty-five loads a day, on the average is conveyed into the
Lhasa area. Caravans returning to Jyekundo transport wool worth
six to eight rupees a bale (half a load); or hides (five yak-skins
sewn in a sixth) valued at nine rupees a bundle; or grey wool
homespun cloth costing twenty rupees a roll and packing ten

bundles to the half load. The tea in Tachienlu costs 48 to 60
rupees a load, freight 18 rupees to Jyekundo and 10 to 12 rupees
more to Lhasa. Thus the tea costing about 78 to 90 rupees in
Lhasa brings a high profit when sold there at 110 to 160 rupees if
one does not consider the losses on the road from climate, thieves,
storage charges in Jyekundo and the personal travel expenses of
the merchants who must accompany their goods or pay for a
representative to safeguard them. Risks are so heavy that the tea
trade is either in the hands of petty pilgrims, families who own
yaks, or well capitalized merchants with thousands of yak-loads
and long-established connections. It is the eight to nine thousand
loads of tea sent to Lhasa which is exchanged for miscellaneous
cloth, hardware, gems, and religious equipment imported into
Jyekundo that keeps the city prosperous.

Figure 59
Dege Monastery from southwest

Figure 60
The Lingtsang Prince and his Princess at Gohzer

Figure 61
Local Guardian Deity or Zhidah at Chungkhor Monastery in Inner Tibet
across Yangtze at Tankhoh

Figure 62
The Yalung River (Dza Chu) near Jyur Gonpa

Figure 63
Three wild asses—the author, Tibetan wild ass (Jyang), and Tibetan guide
beyond the Yalung

Figure 64
Beautiful Sershee Monastery of the Gelugpa sect hugs the flat spur tip in
center where they transmigrate their dead through vultures

Figure 65
Crossing Yangtze river on an ice bridge at Dripomdah, March 23rd

Figure 66
The Yangtze Gorges near Dripomdah where white men never tread

Chapter XI

IN AND OUT OF TIBET

The stars decide our departure. We plan for the eleventh of April but our men consult the astrologer lama who discovers in his book on stars and planets that this is an unlucky day. For the sake of the men's morale we leave on a lucky day, the 12th, after nineteen days in Jyekundo (Photo No. 68). Our objective is Sining and to safeguard our journey for the forty days of scantily inhabited and barren country we have purchased fifty yak and thirteen horses and mules. Our permanent staff of eleven Orientals ride and our temporary guides and caravan men walk, driving our fifty-five loads of food and equipment.

Our departure is not under auspicious skies. It is cloudy and threatens snow. The gloomy day matches our general depression. We have signed affidavits releasing the Chinese authorities from responsibility for our safety and departure. The men are accompanying us into an area hostile with Goloh nomads and barren of food except by the shooting of game. The insecurity of our position, however, unifies our group and we feel ourselves to be as one man against the world. This attitude is heightened as the sullen priests and indifferent populace coldly watch our departure past the Sakya monastery levelled forty-five years ago by an earthquake leaving ruins and slides still visible.

Our course lies northward up a steep stony ravine which in three hours leads us over a pass 14,200 feet in height. On a dipping plateau we proceed for an hour and a quarter before camping. The next morning we emerge in an hour and a quarter upon a widened saddle pass called Thangbumdah at an altitude of 14,500 feet. We have scarely entered upon this comparatively placid elevation when the hitherto scattered snowflakes thicken into a blizzard so dense that I cannot see my hand when extended before my face. I ride sidewise because of the bitterly cold wind and the driving snowflakes, leaving the horse to find his way along the hidden trail. I soon get off and lead my horse to keep from freezing and follow the trail as the horse was wandering. Our caravan is not able to keep contact and when the blizzard suddenly lifts after a half hour we are widely scattered in four directions. If the blizzard had lasted longer, or even an hour or two unquestionably some of the party would have become lost in side ravines and perished. Already some have suffered severely and are on the point of exhaustion and freezing but the sun comes out immediately. We thaw out as we are consoled by tales of men and animals frozen in past years upon this pass. We can verify the death of animals by the skeletons of yak and horses which we pass.

In two and one-fourth hours we camp at Sajyasumdo, 13,000 feet above the sea, where three valleys meet and where three winds hit us at once. In sight of this place the explorer, Du Rhins, was killed near the end of the nineteenth century. According to our guides the people are still noted for their anti-foreignism but they seem friendly to us.

On the 14th of April, 1935, we continue down the barren valley of stones and leafless shrubs, most of them thorny, acacia and mimosa, until we strike the banks of the Yangtze after six miles of winding trail. The Yangtze one hundred and fifty feet wide flows between canyon walls downstream but we ascend into gentler slopes rising behind tiny grain fields carved out of the narrow stony plain. We skirt the fields to the Gaden monastery of Ranyah with four hundred enrolled monks and proceed up the Yangtze valley to where a second lamasery is perched high up on a low spur. Of the Kahgyupa sect and called Bumden, the outside walls and the monks' cells are pure white, the god temples a solid red, and the incarnated abbot's home all yellow. Four hundred lamas are said to reside here. From Bumten we trace the Yangtze two and a half miles to Dzindah, a large village of thirty houses on the edge of the Yangtze at an altitude of 11,750 feet. Here is a monastery of the Sakya sect with fifty lamas. The women wear on their heads immense pieces of yellow amber and irregular red coral while crosses of silver and shell hang from the waist extending down the front of the leg to the hem of the dress at the ankle. We spend the night in an illy ventilated room.

A short jaunt of six miles up the narrowing Yangtze valley brings us to the ferry of Landah, about 11,775 feet altitude. On this side in the cliff face are caves containing a row of chortens and across the river opposite is a large stone prayer-pile with a clay figure (dorma) shrine-hut and nearby a large chorten, all connected by ropes of cloth prayer-flags. Our goods and horses are ferried over the 150 yards of water in a boat forty feet long, nine feet wide and four feet deep with five compartments and three oars, each about fifteen feet long. Three trips are required in this barge which drew about two feet when loaded. Each crossing takes but three and a half minutes but the current drags the boat so far downstream that a day is consumed for the three crossings. The yak are stoned into swimming the river.

We no sooner are settled for the night when a lieutenant from General Ma at Jyekundo tries to get us to return on alleged telegraphic orders from Sining. We refuse to parley short of Trindo, the seat of the next magistrate, and therefore continue up the Yangtze valley on the north or left bank four and one-half miles before turning right beyond Rawo. We now leave the Yangtze and ascend a U-shaped valley, battling against four different blizzards in three aand one-half miles before camping at the foot of Par La, about 13,500 feet high. To secure fuel in the falling snow at dusk we all gather yak chips and then I shoot a Kulung, or snow pheasant, for supper.

We cross the Par La the next morning in the midst of a snowstorm and descending past two Sakya monasteries, three hundred monks in one and a hundred in the second, ride through the Trindo valley to four miles beyond the Mayor's residence before we camp in a smooth grassy valley. The Mayor comes to visit us after we send our card to him as we go past. He is not pleased but we did not give him a present, which he probably expected, since we had given so many expensive presents to the Jyekundo officials in order to secure permission to proceed northward.

Our difficulties in combating the officials have so increased that Dolan leaves secretly after nightfall for Sining to contact the Governor of Tsinghai Ma Pu Fang, taking two men and the three best mules. This is a very courageous adventure of more than four hundred miles through barren country, the first half of it

subject to Goloh raids. By traveling at night they missed the
Goloh and eventually reach Sining. The rest of us stay behind
and wrangle terms out of the Chinese officials for continued hunting.

The caravan leaves northward the next morning, April 18th,
while I take Tringleh to call on the Trindo Mayor with the purpose of concealing both the secret departure of Dolan and the
continuance of our caravan to the Yalung. The Mayor receives me
coldly and in a long parley refuses my application to be given a
guide in order to seek General Ma (who has gone to fight, or at
least collect taxes of the Goloh) and secure permission to hunt
the wild yak. He announces that I am his prisoner which I
accede to calmly but ask for something to eat as it has been a
long time since I had breakfast and it is near lunch time. Food
is brought and I eat to impress him that he will have to feed us.
After another two hours he releases me and permits the lieutenant of General Ma, who had tried to stop us at Lamdah, to accompany us to Drijyuh (Source of the Wild Yak) lamasery, a
forlorn and dirty place near the banks of the Yalung river. We
leave to the firing of a shot which went through the roof, whether
accidently, or to scare me, I have never been able to fathom and
hasten after the caravan. After a ride of ten miles past some fifty
nomad tents perched among the undulating grassy hills we pull
into Drijyuh lamasery (Photo No. 69).

Drijyuh has the most desolate setting. The valley of the Yalung bulges out here into a wide flat plain about two miles across
and four miles long. The surface of the plain which is boggy in
the rains is covered with low bushes scattered among the grass
but the enclosing hills have only bunched grass broken by jutting
rocks to vary the dreary monotony of a comparatively smooth
landscape. No steep walls and forbidding canyons such as we had
left on the Yangtze. The Yalung winds in gentle curves through
a placid valley. In this windswept plain squats the monastery with
its poorly painted temple and decadent monk-cells hugging the
base of the western hills. Water is carried from the Yalung, now
at its lowest size and only twenty-five feet wide. Drijyuh has two
hundred of the ugliest monks I have encountered but they worship Gautama Buddha as the central idol. However, his flanking

deities are in keeping with the outside shabbiness for the God of Mercy, Chenrezig, in two aspects assists the main idol. In one aspect Chenrezig has six arms but in the other figure he is copulating with a fairy on his lap. The monastery is of the Kahgyupa sect. Roosters are set in the outside walls beneath the roof and deer horns of both the white and the red species adorn a prayer tower.

After a day's rest in the monastery we hire a one-eyed backsliding monk (he has taken a wife) as hunter guide and move northwest tracing the Yalung for five miles before entering a left-hand tributary valley where we camp. Weather has eroded some of the hillsides after the grass was killed by the mousehares who have been unchecked by their natural enemies, steppe bears, wolves and weasels, which have been driven out by the modern rifles of the nomads who formerly carried only lances twelve feet long.

Snow falls the first night and continues every day, forming a hard crust which horses cannot paw through to secure sufficient grass. They had fled back one night to the monastery when turned loose and it takes an entire day to bring them back. This extra exertion and lack of food is causing them to eat the hair ropes by which they are tied and also the hair of each other's tails. We wait for the storm to cease but on the fourth day admit our defeat and return to the lower altitude, about 13,400 feet at the monastery, where the melting snow has uncovered the grass.

On the 26th of April the snow having melted on the higher parts of the mountains we leave again and camp on the banks of the Yalung near the old grounds. From this camp on the 27th of April I have one of the most disappointing and strenuous days of my life in the hunt for the "bear I didn't get."

I make the mistake of taking along the one-eyed renegade lama hunter who I soon discover knows where the bears are but cannot see them with his one so-called good eye. The bears upon these plains are a steppe grizzly colored in yellow grey and black. Riding our horses we ford the 25 foot width of the Yalung as it is only two feet deep and not frozen at this point. Mounting up a gradually ascending valley northward we soon come upon fresh diggings where a grizzly has been uprooting Droma, a sweet root about one-half inch long and about the diameter of a lead pencil. Bears are very fond of this root after their long winter hibernation and it grows extensively upon the grassy plains.

I know we are in the possible vicinity of a bear and so does the hunter. We dismount and I caution him to stay with the horses and not expose our riding beasts while I creep ahead. As soon as I am out of sight the hunter disobeys and follows me slowly at some distance. Creeping around rocks and keeping under cover of rough protuberances of the terrain I spy a bear. He is busy digging up a root and I begin to crawl closer in order to get a better shot. The wind was coming my way and he is still a little far to shoot with no clear view. Suddenly he lifts his head and starts at a gallop up a ravine as if he had seen something. I look behind and soon here comes my bleary-eyed friend leading the horses as if he sees nothing. The bear evidently saw him rather than me.

When my hunter arrives I tell him I have seen a bear but he declares he has not. I suppress my rage and tell him to follow slowly up the ravine into which I ascend with speed, climbing rapidly as the bear has left footprints in both patches of snow and on soft ground although on the bare rocks I must guess his direction as the ravine winds in and out. Perhaps he fled on from general principles for after a thousand foot climb at an altitude of about 13,500 to 14,500 feet I gaze up a very steep slope abounding in huge limestone rocks. There is my bear sitting on his haunches near the top of a ridge on a flat stone amidst the large boulders. He is calmly watching my ascent like a spectator in a stadium at a ball game.

The bear does not seem to be over a hundred and fifty yards distant. I halt a moment to catch my breath and rest my gun on a rock as the bear started to walk broadside which further excited me but I drop him at the second shot. He struggles to his front legs but does not seem able to move away so I conclude he is too badly wounded to escape. He is my first bear and this is a mistake. I am about to go closer to finish him but I think what a splendid opportunity to obtain a picture of a live steppe grizzly. I resolve to take a chance and gaze downward at my guide 500 feet below me and slowly struggling upward. I motion to him but he continues his snail pace and I wait, gazing at the bear to see if he will be able to move onward. The guide is leading our two horses but he takes at least a half hour to cover what I had walked up in ten minutes. Just as the guide nears me I see the bear starting to drag himself over the large rocks big enough to hide him as he passes behind them. Not being able to see the bear by kneeling and resting my rifle on a rock I stand up and excitedly fire three or four shots, thinking I must surely hit him before he mounts over the ridge. All of my shots are wild and the bear disappears quickly over the rocky top. I tell the guide to follow and then run uphill after my bear.

We are close to fifteen thousand feet above sea level and I stop only a moment to view the pool of blood where the bear had been hit and then dashed over the ridge. My bear is not visible but after a slight drop the ridge rises higher and I guess the bear has fled along the slope and is now hidden by a ravine. I am right and in a few hundred feet see drops of blood upon the snow which exists here and there in depressions with barren stones protruding over most of the surface. I follow as fast as my winded condition allows but at this altitude one does not run far without stopping frequently to recover breath and strength. I think surely he is too badly hurt to go far and I try to keep enough vitality to battle him if I should suddenly round a rock and discover him. At first the rocks are small with only sudden depressions but I circle around a basin and appear amidst huge granite boulders some five feet in diameter which are ideal for hiding. I approach them cautiously and reach the edge.

It is very dangerous to track a wounded grizzly. I have no pistol but feel my hunting knife to insure its use and with cocked rifle approach the edge of the rocks. The guide is about five hundred yards distant appearing over the ridge with the horses. I stop to survey the tumbled rocks which reach to the top of the range, about five hundred feet above me, and scan all directions carefully. I pause to rest so as to overcome my pounding heart and trembling legs. Suddenly, not over fifty feet distant, my bear leaps up and starts around the rocks. I am too exhausted to hold my rifle steady while standing and wait a few seconds before taking snapshots as the bear is clambering between rocks hoping he

will hesitate or present a better and longer view but he disappears
behind the boulders and around the slope. I rest a couple of
minutes, believing it is wise to hold my fire since that will acceler-
ate his going. I move forwards and view the bloody stains of his
resting place before following the direction of his flight.

I emerge from the stretch of boulders and top the range, probably about 15,500 feet altitude, and find myself viewing another
basin covered with a few inches of hard snow which glares under
a bright sun. I see tracks but no bear. The snow tracks indicate
that the bear is dragging one hind leg uselessly leaving faint smears
of blood. I trail downward and around the circular basin with
the ridge to my right. After dropping about five hundred feet
and going perhaps a quarter of a mile, the track suddenly turns
left, crosses a tiny frozen rivulet and climbs up over another
range equally high. I have not seen my hunter-guide since he
travels about as far behind me as the bear does in front of me.

I have now come to the conclusion that this is going to be a
long chase and I may as well take my time in order to retain my
strength. I climb the next range more slowly and move along a
slope of a still higher range getting close to 16,000 feet where the
snow almost disappears upon a slope of shale and fades out the
bear tracks which are now more difficult to follow. I sense he will
not climb higher but will keep a fairly level keel to conserve his
strength. The shale finally changes into another group of huge
rocks cluttering the side of the mountain. I see here a footprint
and there a drop of blood but the trail grows fainter and fainter.
I come upon another resting place but the blood stains are less
in quantity and in such a steep rock pit that I know he is recovering. I begin to lose hope of catching him as it is now the middle
of the afternoon. I have had nothing to eat since early morning
and only snow to quench my thirst. To climb up one thousand
feet one must walk at least a mile and the air is only two-thirds as
heavy as at sea level and I have kept myself winded since first
seeing the bear.

I rest a bit and then move on more rapidly leaping from one
boulder to another and find a third reclining spot but practically
no blood and only slight traces of my bear's presence. No sight
of the bear as I come to the end of the rocks and soon around the

end of the slope appears a wide valley dipping down a thousand feet. The bear tracks lead downward and I follow but the snow soon vanishes and with it my ability to see tracks. I have almost given up hope of killing my bear and I am tired but resolutely go to the bottom and sensing that the bear would as usual seek the opposite outcrop of large naked limestone blocks lining a slope leading to a pass, I still accept the challenge and mount upward, clambering boulders and seeking tracks. I am not sure that I see any but leap from top to top and rarely slip although I hit a knee until it aches a time or two. I reach the top of the pass but there is no bear in sight. My heart is full of disappointment. The top of the pass reveals nothing but endless grass with patches of snow or more of the huge boulders lining the mountain slopes.

It is now late and I am not less than sixteen thousand feet above the sea. The sun is reaching the tips of the mountains. I see no trace of my guide. I must not be benighted without food. I have not lost my sense of direction and wearily retrace my steps to the bottom. I sadly reflect upon my lack of knowledge in hunting and tracking big game. I now remember what I have been told about wild animals recovering quickly from wounds and that their blood coagulates much more quickly than that of domesticated animals or of man. I know that the bear's hind leg is broken. He must have been hit high in the thigh and now I hope he recovers for my bear has led me a magnificent chase and deserves to live.

There is no sign of my guide so I wearily mount the thousand feet weaving back and forth to reduce the grade and turn left to go diagonally back to my starting point if I have to walk. I find myself upon a basinlike plateau and sit down. Before going farther I must gaze carefully around. My halfblind hunter has followed my tracks and is now nearing the valley having short-cut my trail. I shoot off my rifle when shouting fails of response. He sees me so I rest while awaiting his arrival.

The sun has set when he reaches me and it will soon be dark. I tell him to find the best way back to camp. I shall never forget that ride. Our horses are fairly fresh and strong as they have taken it easier than I have and by short cuts have saved miles of the devious wandering for I often went up and down the slope hunting for clews among the rocks to make sure my bear had not turned aside suddenly.

While I sit in weary silence our horses descend slowly in the twilight into a long valley which I sadly and tiresomely ride for what seems hours. The guide and I eat some cold antelope beef and bread; he had eaten a noon meal of tsamba in cold water and gnawed on some raw but dried yak beef, yet did not object now to sharing my supplies. The moon rises after a short period of gathering darkness and our horses walk with less stumbling. Because of the darkness my guide had chosen a more roundabout but gently sloping valley which requires two hours of steady riding before we drop steeply into the narrow valley plain of the Yalung. We find ourselves about two miles above where we were in the morning turnoff. Now we sometimes ford the river, sometimes in the shade of high cliffs we cross it on ice, but always, through swamps and slippery banks we weave from shore to shore, until finally we arrive in camp where I tumble into bed about ten o'clock. I had climbed four passes, chased a bear for seven hours and ridden five hours on horseback.

The next morning with the hunter and Drashi I go back to where I had left off the night before but no trace of the bear could be found and we were unable to pick up the tracks after the bear had reached the barren valley floor. They are probably lost amidst the huge limestone boulders or perhaps the bear has holed up among them. We return to camp. I feel so low in strength that I rest the next day in camp and reflect that for the first time in my life I must have approached complete exhaustion.

Our caravan moves again up the valley of our previous sortie but this time we continue another three or four miles, under leaden skies threatening a storm, into a dead-end ravine, to camp. During the night a blinding blizzard whose imminent advance made us camp as we were prospecting for the purpose of surmounting a pass, descended upon us, and raged so fiercely that we break camp on May the first and race back to the protection of Drijyuh monastery.

On May 4th we retrace some of our steps to Jyekundo going by a slightly different but shorter route from Drijyuh past Loh monastery which houses 500 monks of the Gelugpa sect. On the drier ground the small yellow flower of fourteen petals called Donkey flower by the Tibetans and some yellow poppies are thrust above the dead grasses but in the bogs are seen only pink primroses. When we recross the Yangtze at Lamdah the waters are one and a half feet higher, due mostly to melting snows. The ferry requires five minutes to cross. The terrain all through this region seems to be mostly of a slaty formation with some quartz.

Wheat is up and the villagers are sowing barley. Priests from the Sakya monastery of Tharlung, several miles north of the Yangtze left bank, are blessing the sowing by thrusting into the ground red, blue, and white flags upon which are inscribed prayer characters. Monks also sow the first handfuls of blessed seed as a starter. Men lead the yak and women handle the plow which is the reverse of the Batang custom. The yoke is also different, being of padded felt borne by the neck of hornless yak, while in Batang the heavy wooden yoke is supported by the horns making horned plow-yak a necessity. Again iron points, as the plowshare here, contrast to the Batang wooden ones and the uncovered manure piles of the Batang plains are opposed by dirt-covered dung piles of this region.

From the Yangtze river basin we mount over snow-covered passes down to the city of Jyekundo where the barley is tiny green blades. While awaiting official action regarding our future course I attend local functions of the Jyekundo community. On the eighth of June I go with Dendru, Namjyeh and Drashi to the power-giving ceremony at the Sakya monastery on the eastern hilltop (Photo No. 70). On the 14th and 15th of May Tringleh, Dingtzin and I watch the devil dances at the Tranggoh lamasery three miles up the valley on the road toward Tankhoh (Photo No. 71).

Also on the 14th commences the annual fair when nomads come from long distances to exchange their produce for the merchandise of the shopkeepers or for the products of the farmers. The first and most important half of the fair is held across the Dza river from the Tranggoh monastery which is upon a slope on the east and right bank. The fair is opened by the monastic lamas in a grand procession from the monastery gate to the river's edge where the devils are propitiated and the good spirits pleased

with bands, banners and chanting. Chief monks in the colorful
parade sprinkle grain and wine upon the rushing waters of the
river as other priests chant to the blare of trumpets and the
whine of conch shells. The market stayed here three days before
moving to Jyekundo where a lesser crowd haggled three or four
days outside and inside the city.

At the monastic grounds the market resembles a county fair in
America, only here the display is more to sell and less to show for
future trade and not at all for prizes. Tents of cotton and yak
hair cloth are pitched along a highway forming a market street
upon which crowds amble slowly, aimlessly stopping at the tent
booths to price or purchase from displays of goods. There are
one main midway and two short side streets. Chinese merchants
show cotton and silk cloth, tea, tobacco, candles, aluminum ware,
candy and toys. Tibetan merchants display a wider range with
hemispheres of brown sugar, felt pads, wooden plowshares, pack
saddles, water casks, bolts of coarse yak and goat hair cloth, home-
made swords, copper and clay teapots, copper and wooden dippers,
wild yak horns for whiskey, yak tails as fly chasers and decoration,
besides a wide variety of religious musical instruments. The
articles attest to a higher skill on the part of the nomads and
farmers than their simple life implies. I am also a buyer and
purchase some silver plated trumpets, a gaily painted clay-flute, a
bronze idol and a dagger. If one can be trusted, Chinese guns,
bullets, and gunpowder are available in quiet places. There is a
wide choice in horses, mules and yak but prices are high and we
decline.

Some deals are by barter but small articles are bought with
Chinese copper coins. Expensive goods are purchased with silver
rupees having the last Manchu Emperor's head engraved on the
face and coined by the Chinese for the Tibetan trade as the wily
nomads refuse to accept anything else, not trusting the increasingly debased Chinese dollars, and under no circumstances taking Chinese paper money which comes and goes with the warlord
who issues it. Large deals are by the exchange of goods in bulk.
Bargaining openly with jest and laughter is the rule unless large
amounts are at stake when clasped hands in the long loose sleeves,
with the sums indicated by seizing of one or more fingers, reveals
the offer solely to buyer and seller.

I wander with the crowd accompanied by Drashi and Dendru. Their escort is a wise procedure facilitating interpretation of difficult Tibetan dialects which often puzzle them and also enhances my prestige in the eyes of the crowd especially when drunken young men swagger down the midway with sword in hand expecting all to give the right of way except the escorted rich and powerful. Many have never seen a white man before and some have never heard of him, so I go easy with the timid and am not annoyed when crowds press me to touch my flesh or finger my garments.

As the days pass negotiations with the Chinese merchants grow increasingly difficult in order to secure the transfer of cash which we promise to repay in Tachienlu. Our debts are heavy. The officials and merchants expect me to stay in Jyekundo as collateral for these debts and against any escape of the rest of our party to Sining. However, finally our financial position becomes so desperate that the merchants and officials agree that it is best for me to go to Tachienlu and finance our credit. There is one possible drawback in the reported approach of the Communists to Tachienlu. For the last three weeks a hundred Jyekundo soldiers in addition to militia have been mobilized around Tankhoh to prevent or at least discourage a possible Communist advance into Tsinghai province. I do not relish the prospect of advancing into Communist hands but long experience of Chinese news and rumour enable me to rightly judge conditions are not as desperate as reported.

The Jyekundo officialdom grant me power of oolah to Tachienlu, 424 miles away. My official paper authorizes all enroute to furnish me with transport and quarters. Leaving Gegen Atring to represent us and manage our affairs I take with me Dendru and Drashi. We ride our own horses but use the forced yak transport for bedding, food, and the loads of our skin collections. We leave on June 17th and ride southward up the Ba river fork in whose waters I had one day discovered red and black hair snakes. We pass the site of the former fair and the Tranggoh Monastery where now only hawks disturb the monotony of cold walls. After leaving the bulging Jyekundo plain the valley narrows for a time but after passing a huge rock upon which is imprinted a faint self-evolved figure of Drehma, the ravine widens into a valley of yellow limestone ridges dotted with scrub cedar. After ten miles the heavily pronged mountains fall away and we turn southeast into an immense plain.

We enter this plain about three miles from its western end which is the source of one of the three streams which unite near our entrance point to form the branch up which we have travelled. The plain thickly covered with grass is one and a half to two miles wide, and easily seventeen miles long generally trending east and west. The altitude is about 12,000 feet and comparatively level but slightly sloping toward the center from each end. Southward are ranges known as Dzajangpo trending east and west and reaching up to 16,500 feet with the highest having eternal snow in ravines and possibly in some years on the tip. We spend the night at the Kahgyupa monastery of Pehchen with its one hundred and fifty monks. Awaiting oolah is the wife of the Tankhoh Mayor who is sending her to Jyekundo as a precaution against the near approach of the Communists.

Early the next morning we traverse the remaining seven miles of the plain before rising over the 13,500 foot pass of Thra-o so easily, we hardly notice it. However, we are now in independent Tibet as the pass is the boundary point. We drop somewhat steeply through an increasingly large cedar forest followed by a hundred Chinese soldiers going down to repel a possible Communist invasion. Together we ride into Kharsa where the Tibetan border tax collector obtains revenue.

The population increases the next day as we continue to trace an expanding Yangtze tributary. Past a huge chorten forty-five feet square at the base and located at our stream's junction with a small tributary, we reach the Yangtze in another two miles at Jyonggon, elevation 11,750 feet above sea level. Here is another Kahgyupa monastery but only fifty lamas enrolled. High above it amongst many poplars and evergreens is a small beautiful Gelugpa temple of about the same size. At this point the Chinese soldiers cross the Yangtze to regain their own country but I stay in Tibet. I continue to secure oolah but with a little difficulty as I have no Tibetan permit and I must drive it in my general position as a foreign official. Northwest from here the Yangtze is running in a deep canyon with steep slopes but now expands into an upper terrace about three hundred feet wide through which it flows in a narrow cut about two hundred feet deep.

Nine miles lower down on the Tibetan side of the Yangtze river is the Dangthoh lamasery of the Sakya sect, housing about seventy-five lamas and used by us as a night lodging place. Farther up but not far above us on the Chinese side and the left or north bank of the river is another Sakya monastery of the same size which lodges our travel friends, the Chinese soldiers. Fir trees begin to appear again and with spruce are said to forest the south side of the range which has followed us on our right but which show only scattered patches of snow as the highest points are only about 16,000 feet high.

Through this stretch the Yangtze is a yellow flood cutting a narrow limestone gorge which soon drops from two hundred feet in depth to less than fifty and later into a plain which is never more than a quarter of a mile wide. The bluish limestone gorge is tinted in red and grey at places and rarely over a hundred feet wide through which the river rushes with terrific speed. At one point a huge rock has cut the channel into two streams, one seventy-five and the other twenty-five feet in width. This would be a splendid place for a bridge. The fairly steep mountain slopes are masses of color with yellow poppies, golden buttercups, pale lemon colored violets, and yellow loosestrife relieved by pink mallows, pink primroses, blue sweet williams and white bridal wreath. Gooseberries are half size and green.

The day's ride on June 20th is a rather long one of 18 miles, crossing the Yangtze at about mile seventeen. It is a brilliant and warm day but like all days in Tibet one becomes cool as soon as one is in the shade of a tree or a cloud. Clouds also soon create winds which blow with bitter fierceness and are dangerous at narrow trails in deep gorges. We change our pack yak several times; pass two small monasteries and go over a shoulder pass 13,500 feet high where the Yangtze cuts through a spur and forces us upward. The valley continues to widen slightly and near the ferry we are on a boggy flood plain. From the plain gullies push upward through the fir forests with trees seven-five feet high and one foot in diameter.

The location of the ferry is marked by eleven white stones each inked with a Sanskrit charm character. Each stone is placed one and a half feet apart in a straight line down to the bank with the last three stones beneath the water. On the opposite shore is one lone white stone. The ferry is a skin boat which takes three minutes to cross but is swept so far downstream that twenty min-utes is required to complete the round trip back to the white stone marker starting points. The coracle holds but two of us, the boat-man and our baggage necessitating several trips. In crossing the Yangtze we are out of independent Tibet where we have spent three days. Gehsar is our night lodging village and at an altitude of 11,350 feet is the lowest we have been for almost four months. Almost at the edge of the Yangtze, we feel as if we have reached a lower altitude again.

Riding the next morning through the high tufted grass of the swampy plain I spy a baby sheldrake about one-third grown. Cov-ered with grey fuzz and distinguished by a black stripe on its head, its inch-long yellow feathers on its wings indicate that it is prob-ably a month old. I pick it up, pet it and then let it loose. How it runs while the anxious mother who has tried to lead me away from it flies in low circles. Shy partridges slip through the grass as we ride near their stands and we sometimes hear their call which resembles the croaking of frogs. All day we go slightly southeast and after sixteen miles on the fairly flat surface of the expanding flood plain reach Tankhoh. The fir forest ceased with the limestone cliffs at the eight mile mark where a Sakya mon-astery of twenty-five monks is located.

We spend a day in Tankhoh awaiting oolah and as a guest of the Mayor at a review of troops participate in a target shoot with Tibetan home-made rifles. It is my first shooting with such a gun. The target is a board three feet high and seven inches wide with a black circle four inches in diameter. Placed fifty-five paces dis-tant the board is pierced only ten times by the seventy odd men, mostly militia (Tibetan) aided by a few of the officials and my-self. The black circle was touched only three times but seven others including the author managed to hit the board with the erratic high shooting muzzle loaders. The shoot is held in honor of the dismissal of the Tibetan militia who are being replaced by the one hundred Chinese soldiers who have come with me from Jyekundo and who are considered sufficient to serve in the fading menance of Communist advance. Of the two Red columns which threaten Tachienlu, the one coming northward from Yunnan province has passed by; but the second moving southward from Sungpan is still causing anxiety which is not altogether relieved by the rumoured arrival of 2,000 troops in Tachienlu.

On the 23rd of June we leave Tankhoh going over the same trail described in Chapter X for the first two days, although we spend the night in a new village called Bahzhah, eight miles west of Namjyeh Ling, where we stayed Feb. 21st. The grass is green now instead of grey patched with snow and blue poppies peek amidst granite rocks. Hot white sulphur springs two miles west of Gohzer are too hot for me to thrust my hand in a second time for a sip without cooling. We pass Amdo priests measuring their length to Lhasa (Photo No. 72). Hands placed palm to palm and the thumbs touched to forehead, lips and heart are then extended full length in front of the head as the worshiper prostrates upon his face. His finger tips trace a line in the dust. Rising, he repeats the performance until tried of moving forward his outstretched length each time. Alms and lodging are given by local inhabitants who thus share the merit he is earning for his future life.

Patches of spruce seem to grow only out of the crags but the fir spread out into the grass. We move out of Gohzer past the sacred evergreen trees of the Lingtsang Prince's grove which are guarded against being cut as they symbolize his dynasty and represents its continuance. The Prince's palace on a promontory is surrounded by twenty-five homes. We pass by without stopping as we have our longest stage before us. Our course lies over grassy hills rising gently from long, easy sloping plains. We scarcely notice ascending the Latsekhering or "long-waisted-tip pass" about 14,000 feet above sea level, and the descent is just as gradual.

The region of the pass marks one of my rare interferences with Tibetan domesticity. Not knowing the basis for quarrels and beatings and as it is difficult to ascertain the real causes I usually pass up such incidents but today an old man driving my oolah horses beat up an old lady so senselessly and persistently that I order my men to rescue her and command the old boy to cease his brutality. I hope he does not take our interference as cause for further beatings when they are at home later.

We arrive at Dzohchen Monastery at nine in the evening after riding easterly for 14 and three-quarters hours or about thirty miles. We have difficulty arousing anyone at the stage house and so churlish is the attendant that my men lay their whip upon his back to secure obedience. I remonstrate with him in Tibetan and order my men to cease such forceful methods. He thinks I am a Tibetan until he brings a light and finds I am a white man whereupon he sticks out his tongue in humble compliance. I am flattered that he does not believe the assertion of my men because my Tibetan is so good, and readily overlook his lack of civility as he prepares our drafty quarters. We eat tsamba and hot buttered tea as our loads have not arrived and, when they do, are ready to slide quickly beneath the covers of our bedding.

Figure 67
Possibly the largest prayer stone pile in the world is eastward of Jyekundo

Figure 68
Jyekundo from the East. Flat roofed Tibetan homes of pounded clay

Figure 69
Drijyuh or "wild yak source" monastery on the Yalung River

Figure 70
Power-giving ceremony at Sakya Monastery of Jyekundo. Priest with teapot
pours out holy water and scarf-carrying lama receives gifts

Figure 71
Annual fair across Dza River from Tranggoh Monastery

Figure 72
Amdo priests prostrating their length to Lhasa

Chapter XII

RIDING INTO THE RED REALM

Dzohchen Monastery in Eastern Tibet is the center of the Red Hat or Nyingmapa sect whose lamas congregate here to receive their final scholastic training. Five hundred monks are enrolled which is a larger number than the few buildings, located south up a ravine behind a spur, indicate. The setting is magnificent. At the head of the deeply incised valley broods the Dzohchen granite peak tipped with everlasting snows below which slide glaciers that fill the scarred ravines. The altitude is around eighteen thousand feet above the sea. Below the ice begins a thick ever-green forest tangled with rhododendron and other underbrush which fades out just above the grassy and slightly wider monastic alluvial plain. The ground surrounding the monastery is boggy with a height of thirteen thousand feet but the monks appear healthy. The main temples are irregularly spaced amidst the scat-tered dwellers of the monks, conveying the freedom of an un-walled village and contrasting refreshingly as compared to the usual congested and walled monastery. Still lower down, the val-ley widens to hold some tiny log huts which contain millstones for the grinding of grain and are perched over water wheels turned by the onrushing mountain torrent (Photo No. 73). Below the huts the ravine pours into an expansive bulbous plain studded with granite boulders. High ranges divided by four stream val-leys surround the plain which measures three miles in diameter and is spread with grass which in flood is immersed slightly in water, so low and level is the ground. Trails lead out through the four valleys which lead east, northeast, northwest and west but to the south is the solid wall of the Dzohchen range.

Dzohchen seems to be the dividing line between grasslands to the west growing on a red sandstone soil broken by slate outcrops, and low shrubs one to three feet high which cover the sandstone and gravelly soil pierced by a few limestone crags amidst granite boulders to the east. Westward are rolling downs and eastward are steep mountain slopes. The change of landscape added to the species of deer for here are first encountered the small, three feet high tailess roedeer with sharp, many tinned horns whose reddish brown color and dainty form are an odd contrast to the big red white-lipped deer and the equally large greyish white elk which roam over most of eastern Tibet.

Rumours of the Communists are so varied that we grade down the tales but safeguard ourselves by careful questioning of all travellers headed toward us as we continue to ride eastward and then southeastward to Tachienlu. My two Tibetan fellow-travellers are Drashi, once a monk who studied in Lhasa, and Dendru, a one-time soldier, the first from a neighbor family in Batang and the second from an official's personal bodyguard at Batang and knowing me longer than I have known him. Jolly and licentious they frequently break out into the high-pitched falsetto notes of Tibetan songs. I ask them to sing slowly so I can write down the words since their jesting smiles indicate conflict and coarse wit.

Drashi tells me of Dingtzin, one of our party left behind in the Jyekundo area who parodied a chant about Dendru shortly before we started on this trip—

> "Dendru at the time of coming,
> Thought a coral would be enough.
> Dendru at the point of going,
> Looking and thinking, up and down,
> Dendru thinks a child will be coming,
> Dendru gives the girl sixty rupees."

Thereupon Dendru, who is also clever in composing, with a laughing and embarrassed defense, sings me his answer as of that time—

> "For Segah (Dingtzin's girl) was said to be sick,
> It was said that she is with child,
> Dingtzin, 'To the borders of Sining
> I will quickly return,' said he."

So my two men sing back and forth snatches of verse and parodies which they have learned or composed all to the same tune, correct in rhythm but careless of rhyme.

On the 26th of June we hurry on our journey over the grassy plain of Dzohchen into the scrub of steeper slopes, over a low pass, and then over a more important divide, the Muri Pass of 15,250 feet, before descending along a southerly grassy slope. The northern mountain slope was a contrasting mass of purple furze. Black mouse hares with orange tipped ears scamper in all directions and I marvel that my horse does not stumble more often for tiny holes dot the ground. A huge grey owl blinks at me from a mani stone pile which we encircle to make sure he is not asleep. We pass him fifteen feet away but he holds his perch and I hold mine without disturbing our mutual dignity. We ride by fifty nomad tents during the day for we are never below 13,000 feet and crops are still impossible. This lowest altitude we find at our Yee river camp which we reach after twenty-two miles.

The next day we go southwest six miles following the Yee Chu through a grassed valley, and over a two hundred foot high divide. Steppe foxes abound but they see me first and are off through the tall grass and brush. The river is fordable until a tributary at the end of our first four miles joins from the west but undoubtedly it it always fordable everywhere during the long dry winter season when not frozen. The bottom of these valleys have rich black soil which ought to yield quick-growing vegetables even at this elevation of about 13,000 feet. Four miles southeast beyond the divide through a parallel valley we meet the Yee river again and cross it to our left where we lodge at the village of Yeelung in the house of the headman. The snow range on our left or south side of the valleys which we have followed from Dzohchen first shifted to dolomite snow peaks and then became rounded summits of lower altitude and covered with forests, mostly spruce. According to Dendru, who is a Tibetan authority on trees, there is little or no fir among the forests north of a line drawn roughly from Gangdzi to Dege and westward and that most of the larger evergreens northward are spruce, which grows on favorable especially northern slopes, but also in some deep eastern and western ravines. Southern slopes tend to grass or scrub juniper. Such a division

of south and north slopes holds true southward until regions of
heavier rainfall are reached.

The Yee river plain is immense for Tibetan terrain, extending
lengthwise for eight yak hours or about 15 miles and generally
one to two miles wide. Steppe antelope are numerous and being
in need of meat I shoot one but the pleading eyes of the dying
beast make me resolve to let others kill such a graceful, gentle
creature.

We leave Yeelung exactly at five in the morning and in an all-
day drizzling rain proceed as usual slightly south by east. We follow the river but after eleven miles the deep stream, fifty to seventy feet wide, begins a mile long horseshoe bend through a gorge
and turns northwest to enter the Yalung. However, we continue
eastward through scattered spruce forests between which are
pitched nomad tents. Prostrating Lhasa bound pilgrims mostly
from Amdo to the north and Menya from the south, are passed
more frequently than at anytime since leaving Tankhoh where
they cross the Yangtze and go into independent Tibet for the remainder of their journey. At a slight rise we ride by shrubs
wrapped in prayer flags where three men had been killed and
robbed. Over rolling grassy hills we wind in and out to reach
Rongbahtsa after twelve and one quarter hours in the saddle and
twenty-five miles in distance.

One mile west of Rongbahtsa is a hermit retreat of white
painted houses decorated in blue stripes. Here a fair sized mountain stream rushes through a tunnel in a huge cedar-covered limestone rock which evidently fell off the mountainside ages ago. The
area of Rongbahtsa has 350 to 400 houses in twenty different hamlets. In addition three monasteries totaling four hundred monks
represent three different religious sects. We are in the beginning
of a well-settled valley about twenty miles long and from one-
fourth to three miles wide which extends in the Yalung valley for
ten miles south of Gangdzi. In this stretch of plain not less than
12,000 lay population and five thousand, seven hundred lamas and
nuns reside. However, this priestly number is partly drawn from
the adjoining areas.

The next morning, June 29th, is a ride through the valley plain
largely settled with homes who raise their barley in the adjacent

fields. In the four miles to Lingtsang where the Yalung emerges from a deep cleft in the northern mountains, we pass the mud walls of the recently burnt Gelugpa monastery of Dajyeh which before 1932 housed 700 to 1,000 monks. The gist of the war which was finally fought to a conclusion in the battles of Batang seemed to be a dispute at least partly religious between the Dajyeh (Yellow Cap sect) supported by the Drewu chief, and the Red Cap monasteries of Nyara (Sakya) and Guluh (Nyingmapa), both located in Bero, aided by the Rongbahtsa headman who was later slain. The Chinese, true to their ancient diplomatic policy of "divide, ruin and rule," supported the Red Caps, probably because the Dajyeh Yellow Cap monastery was supported by the Dalai Lama who belongs to the Yellow Cap sect. The Bero palace of the Yellow Caps and the Dajyeh monastery of the Red Caps were burnt thus evening affairs locally. The Chinese lost the Yenchin salt district and the Tibetans lost the principality of Dege which equalized matters nationally. The sorrowing relatives of the hundreds killed on each side were the ones who paid the principal price in the eternal result of no gain in war.

At Lingtsang near Darjyeh monastery where we again met the Yalung, the river has become a mighty torrent as compared to its size at Drijyuh monastery north of Jyekundo. Between those two points the Yalung has received numerous tributaries which have, with the parent river, been swelled by heavy rains, and their combined influence has enlarged the Yalung into 200 to 400 feet wide at Bero which we reach after riding eastward for eleven miles from Rongbahtsa.

A five-span bridge of the cantilever type crosses the Yalung at Bero and just beyond it on the north or left bank is the Gelugpa lamasery of Bero with five hundred to seven hundred monks. The Sakyapa with 400 to 600 priests and the Nyingmapa with 75 lamas are on the south or right bank, the former near the burnt out palace of the chief. This residence is now being rebuilt inside the old clay walls which enclose an area of fourteen by fifteen fong or squares (each square is 112 x 112 inches). The first story is complete and the second story, where we lodge, is partially finished out of an eventual four stories to be constructed.

Gangdzi (Kanze) is reached on the 29th of June after a seven mile jaunt. We cross the Yalung by a wooden cantilever bridge constructed in two lengths, one 600 feet long of five spans, and the other 100 feet long, over a smaller channel divided by an island from the main stream (Photo No. 74). The bridge seems well constructed to twelve feet wide. After crossing we jolt past the Chinese style temple erected over one hundred years ago in honor of a Chinese princess, Wun Chen, who married a Tibetan prince about 900 A.D. during the Tang dynasty.

We do not see Gangdzi, which is hidden by a spur one hundred feet high, until we are at its edge (Photo No. 75). The houses lie in a dip or small valley trending N.E. and S.W. between two mountain spurs with the palace of the chief on the northwestern slope of the southern spur and the monastery confronting on the southeastern side of the northern spur—a symbolic set-up with the lay Tibetans squeezed between government and religion so that he has little for himself. This Gelugpa monastery enrolls three thousand monks ruled by a Living Buddha bearing the big ears and sloping forehead which are essential characteristics of incarnations. This Living Buddha is very pleased to have me photo him in his ecclesiastical robes before an elaborately-carved altar of golden color (Photo No. 76). I also picture, in her gown of silk brocade, his beautiful sister who is the Tibetan ruler of the local tribe of Hor Kangsar whose domain is Gangdzi and the adjoining territory (Photo No. 77). She leads a hectic life beset on the one hand by the exactions of Chinese magistrates and on the other hand by Tibetan lovers who seek her hand and dowry since she divorced her headman husband who finally disliked sharing her charms with other sweethearts.

The chief temple of the Gangdzi monastery is dedicated to Tsongkhapa while in the nearby red building sits Paldan Lhamo upon her mule to give power to the exorcising priests. The temples surrounded by monk's houses are substantially built and line crowded aisles upon a fairly steep hillside. From the roofs of buildings one can see the triple sacred snow peaks of Khawalaring (Long Pass snow peaks) to the southward, the highest seems to be the center one, estimated at 19,500 feet as the snow line here appears to be about 17,000 to 17,500 feet above the sea (Photo No. 78). The peaks are probably limestone structure and either

near or between them the Yalung pierces their range with a tremendous gorge, which is over a mile deep.

We delay four days in Gangdzi (altitude 11,750 ft.) and succeed in hiring fifteen mules at fifteen rupees each from a renegade
lama of high rank who, against his vows, took a wife whom he
must support by going into business. Using his former connections
to secure a propitious forecast he lands our juicy contract in opposition to a competitor whom we had hired but who later myster-
iously backed out. Continued questioning of my men reveals there
is some hidden pressure which they think may have been applied
by an unfavorable astrological forecast against our first contractor.
I resent this underhand method by the lamas but am unable to
remedy matters.

On the fourth of July we set out for Tachienlu distant two
hundred and ten miles. With our mules, who are faster than yak,
we move rapidly, first easterly four miles along the Yalung, which
then turns south to cut its canyon through Khawalaring to Nyahrong. However, we keep an eastern direction over a low shoulder
and then trace in four miles a tributary of the Yalung northeast
to the village of Lozhung who welcome us for the night. During
the day's journey we have passed two Gelugpa nunneries, one on
each side of the Yalung, and each registering about forty nuns.
Although one has a male abbot, neither he nor any other male
are permitted to stay overnight at the nunnery. We also see other
small monasteries, one of the Sakya sect.

Mustard plants wave their yellow heads amidst the barley now
in head, a little farther advanced than Gangdzi which also raises
some wheat, potatoes and quick-growing vegetables but, as here,
only a one-crop region. Morning breaks with a drizzling rain and
we move east twelve miles through the remainder of the Gangdzi-
Yalung valley to surmount a low pass of 13,000 feet called Latse
and wind slowly down in the Bu river valley. After some northeast turns we reach a beautiful lake some one hundred and fifty
acres in extent, and put up at the muddy village of Kharsar,
smelly with twenty-five dung-plastered stone-houses.

We are leaving early during these days and on this third day
out of Gangdzi we ride from five A.M. arriving after two miles at
the Bu river, seventy-five feet wide and now unfordable. On the

left bank is Drewu whose headman was decapitated by the Chinese
for aiding the Dajyeh Monastery during the late rebellion. In
their huge castle one of the family lies badly gored by a yak. They
had sent a messenger to me at Gangdzi requesting me to come and
render medical aid but I found it was not a recent wound so I informed them I would stop on my way down. I ride across the
bridge and inspect the groin wound, and, suspecting syphilis, I
give treatment for both possibilities. They present me with five
rupees or five days' wages for a laborer, one of the largest fees
ever given to me as a doctor. I seize the opportunity to look
around the almost barren fortress which is eleven by ten fang (88
x 60 feet) with walls seven feet thick at the bottom and four
stories (60 ft.) high. In the ransacked godroom lie remnants of
the Buddhist scriptures scattered by the Chinese soldiers.

Our trail continues through the prevailing red sandstone country up and down grassy hills along the right bank of the Bu river
until the stream bends to cut a gorge through a spur and we rise
over it by a gentle climb. In nine or ten miles we reach Bahmdah
where gold diggers are still tunnelling holes in the black earth. I
count forty excavations. We also pass the first Sakya monastery
since Gangdzi, one of forty monks called Zhaleh.

Old fields and decaying houses confirm the local statements
that once there was a greater population in these valleys now reduced by the comparatively frequent earthquakes which has left
cracks and faults in many places, especially in the Zhe river valley
between Dawu (Taofu) and Drahngo. The earthquake in 1923,
about the time of the Yokohama tremor, shook the life out of
half the people and flattened most of the houses. The last shock
occurred this year in May leaving fresh scars but tumbling only a
few poorly built huts. Its center seemed to be at Gahradrong.
Population increase is so slow in Tibet that this area does not
seem to be able to repopulate except where the Chinese swarm in
to despoil the fields by mining gold.

The general trend of the Bu valley is northwest and southeast
and we continue following the Bu river on July seventh for eleven
miles when it flows into the Zhe Chu which is only a bit larger
than its tributary. The united stream is about one hundred and
fifty feet wide as I could not quite throw to the other side. The

population increases, as we plod for fifteen miles slowly down the
Zhe valley, passing four hundred and twenty houses and the
thousand priest Gelugpa monastery of Drahngo, before stopping at
Yesu. During the day we see poplar trees six feet in diameter
and seventy-five feet high as well as numerous wild pear trees,
some of them three feet in diameter. During the night a terrific
attack of fleas drives me to the roof but a few robust jumpers, in
spite of a light rain, follow me to that ordinarily insect-free resort.
Our landlord is one of the minority polygamous households as he
has married two sisters who seem happy, lugging babies on their
backs and keeping the house tidy. Generally in these cases, the
husband has been adopted into the family in lieu of a son, and
thereby keeps the inheritance intact.

Another early start and a fifteen mile trip southeast during
which we cross the Zhe river over a Tibetan cantilever bridge of
spruce logs in two spans, one ninety feet and the other one hundred and thirty feet in length. Built at a narrow twist of the river,
logs of one hundred feet long were required to span the center
above four layers of huge beams supporting the ends. A tributary
from each side, each about thirty feet wide, have entered the Zhe
Chu and helped to enlarge the swollen torrent. About noon we
pass at least a thousand pits left by twenty-five households of
Chinese golddiggers who have ruined many fields, probably without proper compensation to the owners. We stay the night at
Chahjya.

Still trending southeast with the Zhe river we reach, after ten
miles, another bridge over the river but do not cross the one
hundred and eighty foot span since this would lead us into Nyahrong. We stay on the east and left bank for two and a half miles,
when, turning a projecting spur with a very narrow path, we find
ourselves almost at the edge of Nyeetsho (Two Lakes) monastery
of the Yellow Hat sect. Its fifteen hundred monks daily worship
before the two chief idols of Tsongkhapa, the great reformer, and
Champa, the God of Love. Beyond the lamasery are two hundred
dwellings housing about four hundred families comprising Dawu.
A French Catholic priest, Alphonse Doublet, with church and
school, is pleased when I call upon him according to custom, and
for the same reason I pay my respects to the Chinese magistrate.

At Dawu we hear the Communists are about sixty miles to the east where they have seized Rongmi Drango (Tanpa) as temporary headquarters. No one seems to know what these Communists forces will do next but constant watch is kept in recently constructed outposts on hills commanding the ravines leading into the valley. The air of uneasiness which prevails over the town is shared by me and my two men, Dendru and Drashi, as our road trends toward the territory now under Communistic control and eventually joins the Rongmi Drango road before entering Tachienlu.

At Dawu we have reached a lower warmer altitude where we find wild apricot trees with ripening fruit. Prickly (holm) oaks become plentiful again and from their depths the greenish-blue thrush (Jole) calls out, "Yes, I'm here," and the cuckoo repeats its name in constant cadence from a far-off rock. I notice the light green spines of tamarack for the first time.

Out of Dawu we ride up the fertile valley past the cleft where the Zhe river breaks through the western ranges to disappear amidst high mountains among which the stream will join the Yalung river between thirty to fifty miles southwestward. In five miles we pass the junction of another road leading eastward to the Rongmi Drango strongholds of the Communistic forces. After two and a half miles more we stop for the night in Chapoh containing ten houses and a Gelugpa monastery of seventy-five lamas. During the day we pass in seven and a half miles 585 houses, probably 3,000 individuals and a Gelugpa monastery of twenty-five monks, making this valley one of the most populous in eastern Tibet. All day our route has been fragrant with the scent of mock orange and red elderberry bushes. Trees are numerous in the ravines showing species of hemlock, fir and spruce. On the grassy level areas brown marmots, standing upright above their holes, whistle cries of warning before diving into their refuges which reach twenty-four feet in length and three feet below the surface to end in a rounded nest.

Thursday, July the eleventh, is spent following six miles up a raging torrent over the grassy pass of Mijhi, 13,000 feet high. Large tamarack seven feet in circumference and seventy-five feet in height are numerous in this stretch. Tracing another tumbling torrent down the pass we stop after four miles at Mijhi Castle noted as the junction for a road leading up a wide valley to Rongmi Drango. After a cold lunch of gokway and boiled mutton during which I discover that the shoulder blades of sheep are always broken and cracked to avoid ill-luck before being cast away, we continue southeastward ten miles. In a valley between the three shoulder passes, all about 13,000 feet in altitude, our caravan dog Goseh (Yellow Head) claimed by Drashi as his own, tackles a big marmot who puts up a gallant fight and successfully defends himself as he works toward his hole. Another dog of the muleman arriving and also attacking the marmot I see it is an unfair battle, with the marmot the eventual loser, so I ride over and snap one dog off with my whip which enables the marmot to escape. In the final grassy valley are many cultivated fields surrounding the village of Garthar or Tailing where we lodge in a suburb.

We rest a day and visit the Gelugpa Garthar (Gar's escape) Monastery enrolling some four hundred monks. Built in 1723, in the form of a huge square, the high sundried brick walls surround a large temple and the quarters of the priests to present an imposing spectacle. Tradition affirms that the famous Gar was detained here while on his way to China for the purpose of asking the hand of the Chinese Princess for his King Songtsangampo. Gar finally escaped to continue his journey to Peking but the monastery and town were named after him. Nearby is a square tower of unknown age similar to those in the Menya valley two days westward.

On the 13th of July we set out southwest, taking the western route to miss the Zhara Pass where our road would connect with the road to Rongmi Drango where the Communists are in power. We ride down with the Garthar stream until it joins the Mijhi La stream and there we meander past a Red Cap monastery perched on a conical hill to our left. As usual this minority sect have the smaller lamaseries, here but fifty monks, as contrasted to the dominant Yellow Cap whose monasteries contain hundreds or thousands. Following the united stream where fifty gold diggers are busy shovelling the black soil, which is underlain with slate, whose outcrops lend additional color to the landscape in varied hues of green, brick-red and purple. There is no cultivation here as the height is over 13,000 feet. We forsake the gold stream and ascend over a grassy plateau with a scant sprinkling of evergreens and scrubby thorn bushes until we arrive at Bahodrong near the Sakya monastery of Jelung with fifty monks in residence. We camp in the open where our desire for clean grassy camps instead of muddy stinky courtyards is featured by wolves snagging one of our horses during the night so severely that he had to be left behind at a farmhouse.

In a half-mile the next morning we top Mule Pass (Dreba) 13,750 feet. To the south we see the ice-cream cone of Boh Gongkar, 24,900 feet, and nearby to the east the hat-shaped Zhara, 19,400 feet. We ramble a little downward, mostly south but a little east, following the contour of a wide pleateau-like slope cutting over shoulder passes and dipping into transverse ravines to camp at Nahjhapuh, comprising ten houses. We travel about fourteen and a half miles today.

The next morning with Boh Gongkar in sight at 165 degrees we go quickly past fifteen nomad tents over two shoulder passes and after eight and one-half miles southeast, surmount the eastern Jethoh (Jedo) Pass which is about twenty-five feet higher than the nearby western Jethoh leading to Litang. Then forking into the regular Tachienlu to Batang road we leave the caravan encamped over two miles below the pass and reach Tachienlu after a rapid ride of five hours. In this last stretch we pass five dead horses and two yak corpses, relics left during the late hasty exodus of the Tachienlu population upon the approach of the Communists in May. As we ride into the China Inland Mission compound we are warmly greeted by Mr. J. Huston Edgar, who is the only Protestant missionary left in the city (Photo No. 79).

Last spring the Reds had been advancing in a great northwest circle from Kweichow Province and as they approached the cities, people fled before them. As they neared Tachienlu by two routes, one along the Tung river road from Lutingchiao and the second from the south to the east of Boh Gongkar Peak, almost the entire population fled including all the foreign missionaries. Although damage to the common people's lives and goods were small, the treatment of foreigners was severe. They were fortunate to escape

with only severe beatings and stripping but some were sawn as-
under or disappeared in other ways without a trace. Mr. Edgar
had gone on a trip into the Menya country to await the Red retreat or defeat. The Tachienlu soldiers had fled but for some un-
accountable reason the Reds had stopped at the pass on the south
trail and above the Luntingchiao bridge. Maybe they feared being
trapped in such wild and inhospitable country. Anyhow, they
marched back across the Tung river and then moved northward
on the east side of the Tung river to Rongmi Drango where they
are still threatening Tachienlu. Mr. Edgar had just returned a
few days before I arrived but many of the people are still absent
and business is at a low ebb.

In ten days I am able to sell ten thousand rupees through merchants in Tachienlu and deliver this sum to the branch of the
Jyekundo firms with whom we are dealing. I promptly dispatch
Dendru back to Jyekundo with the receipts and orders for drawing upon the Jyekundo merchants to pay our debts and await my
return there. Before I leave Tachienlu I deem it wise to see that
the part of the animal and bird skin collections, now forty loads,
including ten loads which I had just brought from Jyekundo and
thirty stored in Tachienlu, are transported to Yaan where they
can be immediately transferred to rafts and floated down the river
toward Chungking in the event of a Communist advance southward again (this actually happened when we left Yachow). I hire
a Chinese named Wu to escort them and accompany him with the
goods two days downstream as far as Lutingchao to see the valuable cargo across the swollen Tung.

I find the Tung river is in full flood and the only safe transport
across an unstable old ferry boat. The iron chain bridge over
three hundred feet long, cut during the late Red advance and now
lying on the river bottom, has been replaced by a bamboo swing-
bridge consisting of five six inch cables supporting thin boards
(Photo No. 80). Two smaller side cables with some frail open
interlacing bamboo withes attached to the floor are useful for
grasping if one sways too far. A six-inch cable overhead has rings
which can be grasped and slid along as one progresses with drunk-
en steps. I cross it back and forth and then order a man with a
small load to go over. His wobbling almost gives me and the other

carriers heart failure and I can see that the wide cases borne by
two men will never be able to move between the narrow railings.
The looks of relief upon the faces of the other carriers as I tell
them to go back to the ferry I shall never forget. I hire the ferry
boat which crosses safely a thousand yards above the bridge, although a few days before one of the boats had overturned, drown-
ing two men, and can be seen now resting on rocks at the rapids
below the bridge. The loads safely across, I bid farewell to Mr.
Wu who arrived with all goods in excellent condition at Yaan
where we picked them up on our way out.

Returning to Tachienlu I depart northward toward Jyekundo
with Drashi and a new horseman, Lozong. We travel light and
fast with two pack horses conveying our food and bedding. We
are accompanied by an independent missionary, R. R. Holder,
with one load of gospels and tracts for distribution. Mr. J. H.
Edgar bids us farewell at the north gate on August 19th as we
take the road toward Rongmi Drango where the Communists are
still in control. We are a little uneasy but all are armed and on
fresh horses, so we can retreat rapidly in any direction if necessary.

The north road leads up the long narrow Yaranong valley
whose flats are cultivated by Tibetans and whose slopes are washed
for gold by two hundred Chinese miners. Scrub covers the hills
and scattered evergreen trees fill the ravines. We ride eleven and
a half miles and camp at eleven thousand feet. In the morning,
ascending four miles higher, we near hot springs whose temperature is about a hundred degrees Fahrenheit. The pool, fifteen feet
across and two feet deep, is in the open and the air not being
warm, none of us feel like a bath although Drashi and Lozong, as
is true of most Tibetans, are sadly in need of soap and hot water.
We furnish both freely but they do not always use them.

Another stretch of seven and a half miles and we stop for a
lunch of tsamba, yak beef and buttered tea in a grassy clearing
hedged by wild cherry, buckthorn bushes and stunted growths of
spruce, fir, mountain ash, mountain willow and juniper. In the
afternoon we climb six miles to an altitude of 14,000 feet where
we pitch our tent overshadowed by cathedrals of granite-gneiss
rocks rising up to the bare cone-hat of Zhara peak. Five hundred

feet above us the fir trees peter out and here begins the road to
Rongmi Drango about three days journey or forty miles distant.
A black stump seen faintly in the bushes so closely resembles a
bear that all of us are deceived until we come closer.

The morning breaks in rain and mist so thick that one cannot
see over a hundred feet and, as frequently happens, our horses
have strayed during the night. We spend an hour finding them
but eventually get off northward and in three miles surmount the
Zhara Pass, 14,750 feet above the sea. The pass is broad and
beautified by four lakes nestling in grassy hollows. We yell,
"Ohlasahlolo," throw stones upon the prayer cairn and dismount
to walk down hill. Long slopes of grey scree on our right guard
the pass to Rongmi Drango. Cliffs of granite-gneiss line the steep,
narrow defile through which we descend into evergreen forests.
Looking back we watch the play of sunlight upon the silver surfaces of three glaciers. We eat lunch in a dense woods, mostly
tamarack, some trees eight feet around and one hundred and
twenty-five feet high, and then descend, still in a northern direction, through a ravine ever widening and decreasing in slope.
After eleven and a half miles from last night's camp we turn left
at right angles over a thirteen thousand foot pass, and slowly wind
our way, during the last six miles blinded by rain and deafened
by thunder. At the edge of Garthar, where we stay the night, we
pass the birthplace, in 1838, of the eleventh Dalai Lama. The
adobe structure, of commonplace Tibetan size, about thirty-five
feet square, is signalized by a yak-hair cylinder, resembling a
closed umbrella, perched upon the roof.

We are now on an old trail and from this point we retrace our
previous journey daily toward Gangdzi. The constant riding and
familiar scenes are broken by new lodgings for we rarely stay in
the same villages where we stopped on the downward trip. Being
later in the season we enjoy the golden color of the ripening
wheat and watch the cutting of the silver-white barley in the
Dawu valley. As we ride up the Zhe river we are often forced to
detour above the trail as the river is six to eight feet higher, due
to unusually heavy rains (Photo No. 81). At one time a landslide compells us to climb along the mountain contour over a trail
so steep we must lead the horses.

Enroute to Gangdzi at Dajyeh we spent such a fearful night battling fleas that Drashi curses and paddles one of the landlord's children who cried because of bites. Fleas have to be pretty thick to disturb a Tibetan. From this point we hasten as the Zhe river bridge is threatened with collapse by rising water, but in spite of losing an hour by a detour and fording a swollen stream three feet deep, we cross the weakened bridge. At the end of this day my faithful grey gelding which I had bought from the Washi last October near Litang and has lasted longer than any of the other horses or mules finally becomes lame and gives out so completely that I trade him during the noon lunch hour at Gahradrong. We are now changing yak oolah once to four times a day, but our demands are for just a few yak who are fresh, so we push them rapidly and do not lose much time.

At Kharsar while our landlady is scouring her brass pots and pans with dried cow chips I count the number of braids in her hair. Including some mere lizard tails she has one hundred and sixty-one separate strands, many more than the required sacred number of one hundred and eight. From Kharsar by a long hard day, but with faster horse-oolah, we make Gangdzi on August 28 after eight days of hurry. Nearby fields are in the beginnings of the harvest but the triple peaks of Khawalaring are still silver with snow.

The Yalung river bridge at Gangdzi is cut by floods, the longest eastern span swept away, so we stay on the right or north bank the next day until we reach Bero whose bridge is used for crossing the raging torrent. I am riding a wild bay, sold to me cheap for one hundred and fifty rupees plus the quickly acquired nag given in exchange for my Washi grey. Two men seize the bridle, another stretches his tail and a fourth holds the lengthened stirrup steady while I approach stealthily, lift up my foot and with a leap I am in the saddle. The bay leaps the next instant and we are off at a furious pace. I must let him run on the wet slippery streets out to the grassy hillsides where I gradually direct him uphill where the altitude wears him down. When the steep slope slides him to his belly I jump off but mount him as he rises for another run.

Approaching Rongbahtsa we encounter Tringleh and Ding-

tzin of our party coming to meet me from Jyekundo. Our enlarged group move rapidly through the Rongbahtsa valley where
a road branches south to Nyahrong. Without pausing we move
over the grassy hills and camp in the Yeelung valley. To the
south the barren dolomite ridges, which stop just below the perpetual snowline, are now white. In the ravines are spruce and
juniper but fir and tamarack are absent.

Another long day is varied by passing up a valley, west of our
former route, and skirting a lake of about two hundred acres in
size. The only inlet barely touches into the lake's northern edge
and then flows out again showing it is merely a wet weather
feeder. Our new course eventually leads over the familiar Muri
Pass where we camp on the other side. No sooner is our tent
pitched than a terrific windstorm attacks us lashing us with hail
and two inches of rainfall amidst heavy blasts of thunder and
vivid lightning. The storm lasts much of the night, our tent leaks
copiously, and the men sleeping under their fly are soaked. We
rise bleary-eyed and bedraggled to continue our ride over an old
trail to Dzohchen. Enroute Holder shoots 2 fire or steppe foxes,
and here later on our return I shoot one at 125 yards distance.

At Dzohchen we extract news that the caravan under Gegen
Atring is coming from Jyekundo via Sershee. Hence we will not
have to make the entire trip back to Jyekundo but will go to meet
them. Consequently on the third of September we set out northward four miles having left our old trail to cross the wide Dzohchen valley to a stream junction and then to proceed up the
northwest fork which is swollen and unfordable after nightly heavy
rains. Running into a raging tributary after two and a half miles
I make the first attempt to cross but the water rises to the saddle
top and it is only the strength of my fiery bay which saves me
from being swept downstream to possible death. We are near the
mouth of the torrent so I order the men to go upstream where they
find a shallower place. They strip, hold their clothing in one
hand, and with their other hand clinging to the horse's tail, are
pulled safely across. I had grabbed my camera and had held it
dry but I am wet to the waist for the rest of the day.

Another four miles on the right bank and we cross the main
river in a long diagonal ford of multiple channels but the depth

of three feet make us uneasy as the stream is a hundred yards wide. Past fifteen nomad tents whose husky-throated mastiffs bark until we are out of sight, we ride northwest through flooded valleys amidst grassy, rolling hills for ten and a half miles. Darkness finds us opposite the Gelugpa monastery of Jhoru (Jhowo) where a hundred dirty monks reside. It is too dark to undertake the dangerous fording of the river between us so we are offered shelter in a small poverty-stricken nomad tent, since Holder with the tent loads does not arrive. We bed down beside the nomad men and women with only our clothes and a few stiff felt pads for cover and wish we had sheepskin cloaks, as they have, for clothing. We pay our hosts well for sharing their crowded quarters as otherwise we would have had the rainy sky and boggy soil for a bed. While their odor is bad, their tsamba and buttered tea are refreshing and their hospitality is appreciated.

We hear that Gegan Atring is but a day's march in front so we remain with our nomadic hosts until the afternoon when Dingtzin and I ride up northwest for two miles to meet the caravan. What a happy reunion after an absence of over two months! We camp overnight with the caravan and in the morning, after a rainless night, the river has dropped to two feet in depth, we ford it safely. Three hours below Jhoru Monastery is a huge mani pile 90x75x10 feet which I estimate has three hundred thousand prayer-stones. I observe yak being driven around the pile a number of times to gain merit for their herder, and act as a charm to protect the beasts from harm.

We travel fourteen miles and camp after crossing the river which has begun to rise again as it is raining. Since the source is not far off it would soon become unfordable. I lead the way through the three foot depth of the ford and splash merrily across the flooded plain. Mostly there is a foot of water when suddenly my horse is swallowed in a five foot hole, but he gives a mighty leap with such quickness that the water does not have time to close in and wet my camera. We camp upon a sodden plain, beside the swollen stream which two days before had almost swept me away.

Veering to the right the next morning we take a short cut to the main Denko road and travel it to Dzohchen. Here we stay overnight and leave the next day with our reunited caravan, making the third time I ride the Dzohchen-Tachienlu trail. With fifty yak loads we proceed slowly and generally stay in old camps. In the Yeelung valley Holder borrows my open-sight rifle for a two-hour hunt on the mountainside where he sights four M'Neill's Deer and eight musk deer. By killing a four point buck (horns are in the velvet) and wounding a second elk, Holder has the honor of being the second white man to shoot a buck of M'Neill's Deer.

Our return trip is marked by cooling weather with more snow on the mountains and hoar frost in the valleys. As we pass through Rongbahtsa on Sept. 10th peas and barley are being harvested, the barley being piled on the house roofs to dry and later to be flailed out in leisure time. I break my watch crystal and the minute hand comes off, so I cease keeping time of travel. The Bero bridge is swept away and we go on to Gangdzi for the crossing which must be by skin boat.

Six skin boats, each with a capacity of 750 pounds besides the boatman, serve passengers and baggage but the animals must swim. The horses are led behind a skin boat and the yak stoned across in groups. Our crossing is hazardous as the Yalung is swollen eight hundred feet wide and running like a mill race. Our horses snort and struggle, sometimes behind tthe coracle and sometimes towing us dependent upon their fear and strength. We work half a day driving the yak with stones and even club them from coracles in which I exhaust myself. They are worried by the shifting current and width of the river and keep swinging back even when half way over. While resting I ask for a drink of water but strange no one has his bowl, and borrowing one from a curious lama discover he has only a human skull-cup, but I am so thirsty that I do not hesitate to use it. Intrigued I buy it for a high price and have it as a memento of our battle with the yak. Since only twelve yak succeed in crossing I instruct Gegen Atring to sell the others on that side while we wait for him in Gangdzi which we leave on the 16th of September.

Earth cracks are seen around Gangdzi showing that this whole region along the trough of the Zhe river and its enclosing ranges is subject to frequent sliding. The rivers on our trip down to Tachienlu again have fallen as much as two feet since our trip up two weeks ago but are still high enough to force us into the same detours. Oolah is such a problem that we split the caravan into two sections which are a day or two apart. One of our landlords steals a yellow slicker from one of our men, we recover it accidentally, and he is glad to grant us free lodging as a punishment. At Garthar I leave Gegen Atring to follow with the loads and ride rapidly over Zhara Pass into Tachienlu. I am astonished in meeting an old friend, one of the Boh Gongkhar climbers—Jack Young, with whom I share a room in Edgar's home.

Then follows hectic days of getting money, boxing the collections of bird and mammal skins, hiring carriers, buying a few trinkets and paying off the men. Each of the men are given a year's salary in cash or goods, a horse and their expenses home. Gegen Atring as the caravan leader has first choice of horses and an extra reward for taking money and goods into Batang for Mrs. Minnie Ogden and the mission workers. These and a multitude of lesser tasks finally are finished.

On October 15th Batang people now in Tachienlu and my own Batang men, Gegen Atring, Tringleh, Dendru, Dingtzin, Norje and Drashi, follow me ten li down the road toward Yaan where in a scene never equalled for heart-rending grief and controlled tears, I bid goodbye, perhaps forever, to the brave men who have followed me for more than a year in all kinds of weather, amidst bandits and undescribable dangers through the wilds of eastern Tibet.

The trip out to Yaan is not marked by mud avalanches and constant rain but by a new route described in Chapter IV, from Hualingping to Yungching. With new scenes and different inns we enjoy the pleasant days and cool nights until we arrive in Yaan on October 22nd.

Meanwhile the Communists have left their Rongmi Drango stronghold and are advancing slowly toward Yaan. I immediately hire three rafts with the aid of Mr. Fred Smith, a Baptist missionary at whose home we are staying, and load the collection sent two months ago and also the last part brought with us. We embark on our bamboo rafts the 28th of October and the next day the Communist forces surround the city of Yaan cutting off all down-river traffic. They besiege the city for about three weeks but fail to capture it and slowly retreat northward. We evade them by one day and save the expedition from delay, and possible damage to the skins from humidity and rats. We rescue ourselves from the racking, uncertain strain of a prolonged siege.

Reaching Loshan on the 29th we float down the next day in junks to reach and leave Ipin on the first of November. By steamer to Chungking on the evening of Nov. 2nd, and Shanghai on the second of December and then I have a ten day vacation in Peking. I arrive home by the President Lincoln and Union Pacific Railway on January the tenth, 1936, after an absence of twenty months. I am glad to be free once more from China's internal wars and doubly happy to escape the triple threats of the Communists in my three long rides through the Red Realm of western Szechwan and eastern Tibet.

Figure 73
Water mills grinding grain at Dzochen

Figure 74
Cantilever type bridge over Yalung River at Gangdzi

Figure 75
Gangdzi from southeast. Abbot's home and main temples in the right center
and lay ruler's palace in right foreground

Figure 76
Living Buddha and Abbot of Gangdzi Monastery

Figure 77
Sister of Living Buddha and Queen of Hor Gangsar principality which includes
Gangdzi

Figure 78
Triple Peaks of Khawalaring from Gangdzi

Figure 79
Dendru on my right and Drashi on my left arrive with me at Tachienlu to
stay with J. H. Edgar

Figure 80
Temporary bamboo-cable swing-bridge over Tung River at Lutingchiao

Figure 81
Road after land-slide along Zhe River

Figure 82
A summer palace of former King of Jala where we lodged

Chapter XIII

RUSTICATING AMONG THE RONG

J. H. Edgar as the premier traveller of Eastern Tibet, conducted
many a novice over the Jethoh (Jedo) Pass to sip rancid buttered
tea from the darkened hands of handsome Tibetan nomadic maid-
ens in the peaceful valleys of Rong. While not exactly a novice I
seize the opportunity in the fall of 1932, after we had come out of
Batang following the battles of Batang and while awaiting the
abatement of the cholera epidemic in the lowlands, to go with
Mr. Edgar on a short trip which would give me a closer view of the
famed snow peaks of Boh Gongkar or Menya Gongkar. At this
very time four Americans—Moore, Burdsall, Emmons and Young
—were attempting to climb the highest peak, in which attempt
they succeeded, arriving in Tachienlu shortly after our trip was
finished.

Mr. Edgar likes to rough it and I am not averse to a little hard-
ship or a great deal if necessary. However, when one can have
one comfort why not enjoy it? so we take along a tent, as the
rainy season is not yet finished and sleeping under the stars is
pleasant only in the dry season. I decide to try Mr. Edgar's custom of using a door upon which to place my bedding as he does
or the floor when no doors are available. We also take some supplies since entire dependence upon the native food is not wise as
to quality or quantity. In past times, by necessity, both of us had
lived off the country for extended periods. Likewise believing
that man's soul should be ministered to as well as his body, our
loads like ancient Gaul are divided into three parts—one load of
bedding, one of foods, and one of religious tracts and gospels—
which Mr. Edgar distributes by the thousands among the Tibetans
in itinerating trips along the Border.

Leaving on the 27th of September we pass through the village
of Jethoh where we spend the first night. True to tradition Mr.
Edgar takes the door of his room off its hinges and places it across
boxes as the foundation for his bed. The second day we continue

southwestward up a pass over a road whose makers never rode
horses else they would have been more careful about scattering
so many stepping stones all over the highway. Snow begins to fall.
This white mantle smooths many of the inequalities to the eye but
not to the horse's hoofs which constantly slip into the hollows between the stones of granite-gneiss. After Mr. Edgar has knocked
the wind out of his horse when the beast falls under him, both he
and the horse decide to trust only their own feet. I stuck to the
saddle contemplating that four feet even with my weight are better
than two and then, Scotch-like, I hate to see a horse carry nothing
when he has been hired to carry something. However, the pack
animals cannot dump their burdens.

The blizzard increases, keeping us busy shaking off the snow
until we strike a decent road when the sky clears and we stop for
lunch, boiling tea and eating tsamba. As we climb higher the forest peters out and we enter juniper shrub which in turn gives way
to grassland. At last we top the western Jethoh Pass which leads
into the Teruh valley where we pitch our tent for the night. There
are at least five passes over the Jethoh range which circles the valleys centering at Tachienlu from the north to the southwest.

I soon find that my chief culinary duties are that of critical
guest. Fortunately Mr. Edgar is fond of cooking, being justly
proud of his famous stews to which I contribute the spice of conversation. I can fry eggs but we have forgotten the frying pan.
Later I killed pheasants and bought goats which kept Mr. Edgar
supplied with meat, although it was sometimes high for the stews
which formed our chief food for ten days.

The third day we ride over the southern Jethoh Pass with a
height of 14,600 feet and turn southwest through a shrubby valley
to top La Neebar, or the Second Pass, which my ameroid makes
a thousand feet higher. Just beyond La Neebar I dismounted to
take a picture of the Boh Gongkar ranges lying almost east of us
with the highest peak to the southeast. My horse promptly ran
off and being alone I immediately chased him and by the time I
caught him and returned to the same spot clouds obscured the
snow peaks and I never had another opportunity as good for pho-
tographs. The highest peak to the right is a pyramid of silver,
pushing its nose through swirling clouds while the snow below

scintillates like diamonds. Three peaks are visible at La Neebar, the central one being the lowest. The peak to the left seems to be the apex of a long ice ridge leading down to a white barrier in front. This barrier whose rocky teeth are softened by eternal snows rises like a whitewashed fence behind the lower grass covered peaks in front of it.

Silent and majestic in its solitude and wearing a mask of death, Boh Gongkar stands a true sentinel of Tibet, typifying its airless plains, its cold, merciless rivers, and its dismal, trackless forests. The silver peak seems to speak, "You who would enter, behold the Gateway! I guard the Land of Ice. Here is everlasting snow whose glare will blind you, unmeasured heights which will squeeze the last breath of air out of you, ceaseless winds which no furs will check, piercing cold which no fire can dispel and galloping rivers which roll huge boulders like pebbles. If you fear not these you may enter but my marbled tips you cannot reach for I have glazed my pyramidal sides with glistening ice."

We go through this portal of Boh Gongkar to meander peacefully down the grassy Yeelungshee valley to camp after a short southward jaunt.

"What are we going to use for wood, I suppose we will have to gather yak chips for fuel," I ask of Mr. Edgar.

"See those piles of brush," he replies.

"Yes," I answered, "those were gathered by the nomads for their use when they return next spring to pasture their flocks in this valley. However, we can ease our conscience by giving a rupee to the first nomad tent we encounter as payment since there is no landlord here. We are extremely grateful that the nomads are so thoughtful of future travellers in a woodless country." I keep a straight face so that Mr. Edgar merely eyes me closely.

Mr. Edgar is a great collector of artifacts and I can truthfully say that he knows a Paleolithic stone when he sees it. He finds me a poor student. I might have been a better one if he had not ruthlessly discarded a nice water-worn spearhead which I offered for his collection. Then he refuses to take me seriously when I suggest that a certain peat bed might be the barnyard where Paleolithic Man kept his cows. He watches me carefully when I fondle a nice quartz crystal artifact (the only one he has ever found). I threaten to steal it, as I could not find one in a thousand years, even if I had that much time. Mr. Edgar knows this fact, yet he decides against my possession of it. I, however, realize the value of his artifacts and later took them out for him when our family journeyed down into the lowlands. They arrived safely at West China Union University in Chengtu where they are now on display.

Still descending the Yeelungshee valley we accost the first nomads about noon soon after I had told Mr. Edgar that I wanted to see the numberless smokes of nomad tents which some of the novices had proclaimed as existing. These people are half nomadic, pitching tents from June to September for their summer quarters at heights of fourteen to sixteen thousand feet. Their herds of yak and flocks of sheep and goats may roam still higher. In September they descend to plains at thirteen thousand, five hundred feet or lower to spend the winter. During the coldest months of December to March they reside in well-built stone houses while their animals are enclosed at night within immense square or circular enclosures fenced with thorn brush. During the summer one member of the family remains behind to guard the house while the others live the care-free life of nomads.

As we approached the first black tents a few Tibetans came out and coolly informed us that we could go no farther as a cattle disease had existed for some time in these localities. Such a statement when we had already arrived and without prior information from Jethoh village that an epidemic was raging, aroused my suspicions (later confirmed) that a conspiracy for unreasonable animal hire had been hatched by our animal men. Further questioning extracted the notification that horses could go on but not cattle or yak. We agreed to send our yak back if they would furnish us three horses to carry our goods. It is an old trick for Tibetan tribes, especially nomadic ones, to hinder strangers from passing through their country unless they can profit by it. You hire their animals or pay them escort money and they will let you pass. In this case there is truly an epidemic of rinderpest which is unwise for us to disregard but which the men who had hired their yak to us had known about. Tibetans are very careful about losing their own funds but are always willing to take risks of financial loss when a rich foreigner is involved. We send our yak back after giving our animal men a bonus for not being able to use their yaks any further as we had first agreed.

While Mr. Edgar went ahead to pick up ancient stone weapons which even moderns do not hesitate to use when nothing else is available, I stay behind to superintend the loads. We are now driving oolah, or forced pack animal hire. As we start off the rattling of the cans in our carelessly packed food box frightens the nomad's horse who hasn't reached the tin can civilization as yet. With a leap he starts galloping but his master, holding on to the bridle, forces the animal to run in a circle but not to stop. Round and round he goes while I meditate on the damage. The horse in trying to break loose resorts to plunging and the boxes begin to break open as his owner with whitened face tries to save the goods. The thongs break and the boxes come down with a crash upon the ground which does not satisfy the horse. I laugh as the animal circles again and backing up to one of the offending boxes deliberately kicks the helpless container. With a resounding whack out comes eggs, tin cans, hunks of meat and loaves of bread seeking rest. Such a disaster scares our man worse than the plunging of the snorting beast—for what will Mr. Edgar say. I help gather up the fragments which are remarkably small, about three dozen eggs, some of which show signs of strength. My hilarity as I describe the disaster turns most of Mr. Edgar's anger away from his man to myself for which the Tibetan is grateful. Mr. Edgar is soon appeased and I secretly believe he enjoys such a mixture of our staff of life which is still good for stew. He has hired the man who has charge of the animals, while I contribute the cook and both of us share in the general expense.

We pass numerous flocks of black and white sheep and herds of long-haired black yak until we reach the former palace of the late King of Jala (Photo No. 82). Past sixteen prayer wheels up the steep stairs of the mansion we dart into one room but do not stay long for two decaying yak carcasses prove too strong for us. We retreat to the main temple rooms where the gods of gaudy clay regard us with serene eyes although we do not like their musty odor. Both yak and gods are dead but one has never been alive which makes it less smelly. We borrow the idol's butter lamps to which they offer no objection.

The palace is a typical Rong house built of stone set in clay.

The walls are extremely thick, four and five feet at the bottom. The back half rises to three stories and with the front two stories supports a double roof, the first of clay and flat, topped by a second slanting covering of rough clapboards held down by stones. The clapboard roof is not perfectly tight but catches the bulk of the water leaving the scanty drippings to be absorbed by the clay. The windows, whose frames are whitewashed upon the sides and bottom, present striking "U" figures of white. The first floor of the palace houses the animals, the second serves the general living needs of the family while the third and attic contains the storage, where turnip tops and grain can be seen scattered upon the floor.

The King of Jala drowned, possibly voluntarily in despair, some years ago when he was trying to escape from prison and found his retreat cut off. Since then his palaces, except those appropriated by the Chinese, have been occupied by relatives and retainers. In this palace are merely an old servant of the former King and her child.

The next morning we wander downward to the cultivated sections where barley is encountered at an altitude of about 13,250 feet. Lunch is eaten near a temple at Sobu whose monks are sculpturing gods and painting frescoes of deities after both had been extinct for many years following their cremation by Shangchen raiders. Forty Chinese soldiers who crowded into the temple at that time accompanied the gods on their journey. The lama artists are very clever and I wish our itinerary would permit us to stay several days to watch the modelling in clay and the working in color. Some state that painting and sculpturing are hazardous professions since any imperfections may cause the death of the artist (Photo No. 83). An artist in Batang died in 1932, a few months after completion of a statue of Champa, the coming Buddha. I think this artist had tuberculosis, although I did not see the youth, but knew he was sickly like several members of his family who had succumbed to that disease.

That evening we camp upon a plateau covered with evergreens, above Meje and a short distance south of fields which culminate at our spur that forces the river into a canyon. A short but lucky hunt adds a 'Kulong' and a 'Shagah,' both labeled snow pheasants, to our larder. Just before dark the daily clouds which had been robbing us of fine views of the Boh Gongkar ranges as we had paralleled them close at hand, drift away, and we have a clear view of the snow peaks. Then as the mists float around the peaks the clouds outline the exact shape of the snow cone against the clear sky—a cloud illusion which is so unusual to both of us that we leave our supper to enjoy it. The weather has been so uncertain most of the time, with hail, snow or rain during the night and clouds in the day. The cloud illusion of Boh Gongkar charms us and we go to bed at peace with the world but during the night we are awakened by nearby bursts of Dorje Lutru, Tibetan God of Thunder, whose close lightening floods the tent for two hours with constant flashes.

The following morning we leave the cultivated fields of the Yeelungshee valley to plunge into heavy spruce forest whose somber lines are relieved by the lighter green of larches. Going northwest to the junction of the Yeelungshee and Chentse rivers we cross and follow the Chentse westward down to cultivated fields. Above on the ridge are two monastic establishments housing about fifty monks each. One of these is the winter quarters of the priests from a monastery on the slopes of Boh Gongkar where during the remainder of the year they minister to the spirits of the snow peaks.

We soon arrive at Serurong, previously visited only by Sorenson to whom the forty families surrendered for protection against Shangchen raiders and accepted missionary teaching. While this seeking of foreign missionary protection saved them from being looted by the Shangehen there is now little evidence that their submission had led to a permanent desire for Christian teaching.

From Serurong we desire to trace an unknown road down the Chentse river to the Yalung but find the trail is impossible for horses after two miles, so we retrace our steps for an hour back to Lelekhuthe which we passed yesterday. Here we turn left in a northerly direction, ascending through an oak and pine forest. The honking of the Shagah snow pheasants stir my hunting blood until I grab my shotgun and charge up the mountain. I knock over two of the big black and white birds who flop four hundred feet down the hillside which is so steep and dense with underbrush that I lose sight of them and only by careful trailing, here a feather and there an overturned leaf, am I able to pick up their corpses near the base of the mountain.

After a goat stew dinner enjoyed while sitting upon a grassy knoll we go over a steep pass and then drop down a declivity on to a gentle plain where I again chase snow pheasants but they outrun me. Pheasants can always outstrip a man up a slope and hares can leave the fastest hound behind when chased uphill. At least that has been my experience and observation at these high altitudes.

Emerging from a fir forest we spend the night at Zhohlu, sleeping in the kitchen with all the household; that, however, did not keep Mr. Edgar from using his favorite door as cot method. These homes have immense rooms for kitchens with ceilings so high that the smoke does not choke one as it does in Tibetan homes farther west where ceilings are low, sometimes one can touch them with the extended hand.

The kitchen in Tibet is the "best room" in the house (Photo No. 84). It is generally located in the central part of the home and many of the other rooms open out of it. Upon one side of the kitchen are rows of brass, dragon-mouthed teapots, shiny yellow plates and round gleaming dippers. Near these stands a huge brass kettle which holds the family supply of water. Beside the stove is the brass-hooped wooden churn topped by a strainer full of wet leaves, the remains of the last buttered tea. The leaves will be used over again by the poor or if tea is scarce, but eventually they will be mixed with barley flour and fed to the horse or donkey. This custom has created the proverb, "If the master has no barley, How can the donkey expect barley gruel?" On the other side of the kitchen leading to the doorway will be at least two immense prayer barrels chuck full of "Om Mani Padme Hum" printed on paper and the pious will always pray by turning the barrels as they go in and out.

No nation has made a closer study of prayer and efficient methods of performing it. The agencies of nature are called into cooperation. The sighing wind whispers, "Om Mani Padme Hum," as it flaps the prayer flags on bridges, over streams, on poles in the courtyards, on the house, sticking out of altars, or suspended

from cairns on high passes. Water-powered prayer wheels, hand
turned ones, huge casks in temple doorways, medium sized barrels around the walls of a temple, and small ones turned by roadside brooks grind out the appeal for mercy and produce merit to
end the terrible round of existence. Even seeing this prayer carved
on a stone worked into the grass of a mountainside will be efficacious.

The fireplace is not a built-up stove of stone and clay as found
farther west but an iron tripod within a square tract of clay
fenced by six inch high square timbers which make a very con-
venient rest for the knees of the cook as she stirs the tea or broth
in an iron pot upon the tripod. Above the stove is often a triangular stretched rope decorated with feathers which is a substitute
for a prayer flag, one man informs me. The smoke is supposed to
go up through a wide opened space in the roof but the blackened
timbers and personal experience proves that some of it goes elsewhere.

Unlucky is the household which does not have a cat whose
figure is featured also as lying on the left arm of the King of the
North and concurrently the God of Wealth. I unwittingly wrap the
skins of my pheasants in paper which unthinkingly I leave outside
my bedroll. During the night at Zhohlu the cat dines on my
pheasant skins doing this within two feet of my nose while I
sleep.

The coldness of the weather leaves us comparatively free from
attack by the tiny predatory inhabitants of the house, those 'beas-
ties' who stick to the sheep skins which by day are piled up in a
corner but at night are spread upon the floor as bedding. We
have visual evidence that Tibetans sleep naked piling their day
clothes upon the other bedding at night. We try to make our bed
in a corner far from the stove and sleep well in spite of closed
windows and occasional wisps of smoke from dying embers.

On the right of the stove is the seat of honor where sits the
family priest grumbling and moaning out sacred texts from a
large book on the low table before him. He is a member of the
family, a younger brother, condemned to prayer and celibacy.
He receives good portions of food and well-buttered tea but "the
home priest rises with the crowing of the cock, while his land-

lord sleeps until the cow rises." Sitting upon a comfortable mat he must mumble all day but frequently he turns his eyes toward the evergreen forests where "while the mouth is repeating the name of Buddha, the eyes pursue the white pheasant afar off." Reciting from daylight to dusk, when he closes his book, the housewife bustles over to the prayer-wheels and gives them a turn. This completes the day's religious rites which is supposed to insure the household from the visit of evil spirits and brings to the family, prosperity in all of its undertakings.

Called Menya by themselves but known as Rong to the Tibetans, our nightly hosts upon this trip resemble the Mosu of northwestern Yunnan more than the Tibetans of Lhasa or Eastern Tibet. Their skin is lighter and their features finer while aquiline noses and long heads are common. Some of them would pass for Italians or Greeks in America. They may have some Aryan blood carried down from some remote ancestors of Central Asia before being driven southward (probably by Mongols) centuries ago. Tall and slender they seem more intelligent and peaceful than the ordinary Tibetan. They have a distinct language whose words they sometimes mix with the Tibetan language which makes them hard to understand.

The Rong men wear the usual loose Tibetan grey woolen cloak and earrings in their left ear. The women have a distinct tribal custom in binding around the forehead a chain of rupees or white flat, round, bonelike stones set in a band. Sometimes their skirts are made of white and black bands of wool cloth. Different clothing or jewelry distinguish almost every Tibetan tribe or administrative area.

The towers are another mystery—who erected them and when? Some say Gesar, a king, ruling in Shensi about 750 A.D. when he conquered this country (Photo No. 85). Others affirm that the Chinese built these towers as forts about a thousand years B.C. My guess is that the Rong themselves built these towers for home defense. One is used for this purpose at the present time. The workmanship is similar to that of small towers erected as part of the homes and often used as the family godroom. Layers of wood still remain in parts of the tower walls and this wood possibly of walnut would have long since rotted if the towers were very ancient, although these might possibly have been inserted in the repair of later years. If the towers were of religious significance they would probably have not been left to decay. Likewise there are very few temples among the Rong since every home has its own temple room where the gods sit before the flickering butter lamps and on festival days are wreathed in clouds of incense. Most of the towers are square but many are octagon while a few are twelve sided or four rectangles joined together. One, nine feet in diameter, is nine cornered. The average height is fifty feet but may reach ninety feet. The walls are three feet thick at the bottom, tapering to one foot at the top. The construction material is blue limestone slabs or bluish slate which are laid to break the edges and sometimes leveled off with long slabs of stone or even wood. I climbed one which had five separate floors, the first two I reached by notched Tibetan log ladders but the last three I scaled up the rough stone wall. Each story has tiny rectangular slits for windows, enlarging inwards and large enough for accurate firing with arrows at an enemy.

Rong homes have flat stones for their walls. Their windows may be constructed of white stones or painted with whitewash. The two sides and bottom of the window frames are given wide white borders and the top of the frame fringed with white disks eight or nine in number. These white frames resemble great white eyes from a long distance or in the obscuring darkness; and it is not too farfetched to think of them as painted eyes to scare demon spirits.

From Zhohlu we move northwest down a forested valley, noticing that black and white birch, and maple share the hillside with fir and spruce. On past Dronohbong we enter a region of long needled pine extending in open forests. Near here we eat our dinner followed by an hour's ride which brings us to the junction of the Zhohlu and Li rivers. The Li is large enough to be fordable with safety only in the dry season. It flows into the Yalung four days southwest of here but although passable for horses the road, according to people, has never been travelled by a foreigner and the course of the stream is still a dotted line on the maps. It is remarkable that considerable exploration of untrammelled trails can still be done within a few days of Tachienlu.

From this junction where there is a village called Trundo we trace the Li river northeast and soon cross to the north or right bank over a bridge one hundred and fifty feet wide and possessing a central span of ninety feet. We travel among pines whose furrowed bark of silver and black are camouflaged masts in a green park. The river below us is a roaring yellow flood which indicates much rain around its sources. Heavy rains have fallen at night during the last few days with the days marked by a few short showers, although the sky is cloudy most of the time. The end of the monsoon is at hand.

Tonight, the eighth out of Tachienlu, we stay at Chorurong in a home once wealthy before impoverishment by raiding of the Shangchen about 1916. The kitchen displays carved wooden paneling lining the walls of stone. This immense stone house with flanking round towers of grain piled on the roof reminds us of medieval castles in Europe. This home is blessed with the highly honored cat which sits by the kitchen fire contentedly purring "Om Mani Padme Hum," at least that is what my buxon landlady affirms.

In the Li valley are many trees like some found as far westward as Batang. The back and leaves of one species resembles the pear but the yellow-red fruit is the size of cherries and has the taste of crabapples. Their tartness soon chokes our throat, a quality about which the people have warned us. The local name is Omasu but farther west near Hokou they are called Ramasu. The first name may mean red throat fruit and the second red goat fruit, its sharpness fits both names.

After being forced to send back our yak on the third day, the hiring of oolah horses, without a road pass, becomes an increasing vexation. The Tibetans dislike taking their animals far from home lest they meet with robbers or be striken with disease. They have sufficient lands and flocks to make their lives comfortable. Money would have to be hoarded if earned by oolah which brings in half a rupee a day if the traveller has a road pass and one rupee a day without the pass. Then of course they show reluctance in order to squeeze more out of the rich foreigner. It is not the greater cost which irritates but the daily, sometimes twice daily, wrangle for an hour which is necessary to secure animals for the

next stage. My cook, Gezang Tsering, develops unexpected elo-
quence and resourcefulness in coaxing and forcing oolah. Neither
Mr. Edgar nor I favor the use of oolah but here we are compelled
to employ every threat and remonstrance to secure beasts of burden at a high price because we have no road pass.

October the fifth and our ninth day of travel finds us moving
north and northeast along the north bank of the Li river, crossing
however to the south side at Midizamba, near which is a white and
yellow striped temple surrounded by four towers well preserved
and two others in ruins (Photo No. 86). Juniper smoke from
altars sailing heavenward and encircling the towers recall factory
scenes in the homeland but with this difference—juniper smoke
is pleasant to smell. We pass the remains of forty towers during
the day. Mani stone piles become numerous, at one place I count
eighty-one separate squarish mounds adjoining each other and
forming a long prayer stone row and nearby is another with forty-
five mounds. I have prayed more Mani prayers going around these
stone piles keeping them to the right during my thirteen years in
Tibet than I have any other prayer. Before the end of the day
we see our first building whose outer color of dark gray is varied
by wide stripes of whitewash poured down the walls. Such a custom is permitted only to the upper class in Batang.

At noon we reach Athedrong and eat our tenth installment of
goat stew killed three and one-third days previously.

"Mr. Edgar," I remonstrate, "I smell like a goat, I feel like a
goat, with ten days growth of beard I know I look like a goat and
if you keep on feeding me on that decayed goat stew I might
soon act like a goat."

"I hope you don't reach that last stage," he replied, somewhat
irritated since he hated criticism of his cooking (Photo No. 87).
He was a good cook and his stews were very tasty but his thirty
years of roving among the Tibetans had dulled his smell of high
meat. Fortunately I am pretty well acclimated and not particular
as long as the meat will hold together.

At Athedrong Mr. Edgar and I part, he to continue northeast
following the Li river upward to Dzonggo from where he will
follow the Batang-Tachienlu road homeward over the northern-
most pair of the Jethoh passes. His route will bring him to

Tachienlu in three or four days but mine, over a shorter more direct trail will take me back in two days. I wish to have another close view which his route will not give and possibly a better photograph of the Boh Gongkar as the weather is now clearing.

Before starting I ascend one of the ancient towers whose inhabitants at the bottom are two wretched beggars who obtain alms from me, and on the upper floors numerous pigeons whose sudden flights as they jump out of unsuspected crevices almost make me lose my hold on the stone slabs. After descending Gezang Tsering and I mount immediately and ride swiftly east, first up the Athedrong and then the Ajedrong valley. Enroute snow pheasants gobbling and walking leisurely uphill to roost in evergreen trees cause me vain regrets but night is falling and our inn house is still out of sight. We pass two triangular plots of prayer flags stuck in the ground above an altar halfway up the mountain side in memory of the dead who have long since fed vultures (Photo No. 88). Just at dark we reach the last house up the valley and lodge for the night.

Before being allowed to sleep we must pass three hours of expostulatory pressure for oolah. Threats finally of walking off in the morning and leaving my luggage in their hands to be retrieved by soldiers sent from Tachienlu procured promise of three animals at the reasonable price of a rupee each to Tachienlu. After they gave in my hosts are amiable and as always perform good-naturedly their agreement regarding the carrying and delivering of baggage but they certainly have time to wear out the foreigner whose impatience and possession of cash make him the loser.

Leaving Ajedrong in the morning we pass north up the valley where three flocks of snow pheasants raise their raucous cries as they retreat into the pine forests. I am anxious to attain the pass while it is still clear as it generally clouds up in the afternoon or I would have made them respect me. I again sadly left the males honking and fighting while the females feebly cheeped to their lords not to be so lusty.

The different varieties of pheasants like the various species of trees have their well-defined belts of altitude in which they will be found. The lowest is the purple-blue Johshah or valley pheasant found from six thousand up to above eleven thousand feet prefering cultivated fields except during the nesting period. Where the holm or prickly oak and the other evergreens begin around eleven thousand feet the timid mottled Bogoh, the greenish blood pheasant Tsereh and the red-eared snow pheasant Shagoh will be seen feeding on acorns and seeds from the evergreens' cones. The snow pheasants gather into the largest flocks sometimes as many as twenty-five birds. These three rarely go above the forest line which may take one up to fifteen thousand feet. In the upper forest reaches is the Kulung while above the forest line ranging among the bare rocks which closely resemble its iron-grey feathers is the Gomuh which I have hunted up to seventeen thousand feet.

In regard to evergreen forests, lowest down are the prickly oak about eleven thousand feet and extending at least two thousand feet higher. Other evergreens begin with the oak but climb up higher, such as spruce, fir, and larch which are seen in a few cases about fifteen thousand feet but usually not much above fourteen thousand feet. Beyond the limit of the larger evergreen species range the juniper which keeps creeping up with twisted gnarled forms spreading out in an umbrella shape, for another five hundred feet where they give place to scrubby rhododendron whose beautiful flowers of blue and yellow may follow one over sixteen thousand foot passes. Of trees not evergreen the birches and poplars range with the prickly oak but maple will be found below them. Walnuts and fruit trees grow still lower although wild cherries may be found as high as twelve thousand feet.

Ascending the Ajedrong valley is slow and deceiving work but we finally reach the Aje La. East and slightly below it one can get a glorious view of the Boh Gongkar group if the weather is clear. My luck is bad for even an hour's wait did not dispel the clouds which persisted in hovering over at least one peak, especially the highest cone. Sorrowing, I top the Aje Pass which is covered with two inches of snow. Beyond it we move another hour east and cross the southern Jethoh Pass which we had come over ten days ago. To Jethoh village that night and early next morning in a heavy fog to Tachienlu are just more pleasant repetitions of previous days.

The Rong or Menya valleys which surround Tachienlu on

three sides are some of the most pleasant vales in Tibet. Wide undulating hills covered with grass and occasional forests, and the lower valleys producing wheat, barley, peas, turnips and potatoes enable these Rong Tibetans to have both a semi-nomadic life in summer and a varied menu in winter which is denied to the higher altitude Tibetans farther to the north and the west. Although set in the midst of nomadic country the valleys such as the Li river are heavily populated for Tibet. I counted a hundred and forty-four houses in the Li valley between Chorurong and Ajedrong, a day's journey. As a final remark I may say that the Rong men are often handsome and the women, ah, the women, invariably beautiful.

Figure 83
Lama sculptor cutting "Om Mani Padme Hum" stones

Figure 84
Tibetan kitchen of the "just comfortable" class

Figure 85
Menya homes and towers in upper Li River tributary valleys

Figure 86
Li River near Midizamba with towers and early morning incense smoke

Figure 87
Our noon lunch of goat stew with J. H. Edgar as cook

Figure 88
Altar flanked by prayer stone carved with "Om Mani Padme Hum" where
bone remnants of dead are burned. Out of sight up hill are prayer flags

Chapter XIV

RAFTING THE RAPIDS OF THE YA

The bamboo raft will be forty dollars for the eighty-six mile trip from Yaan (Yachow) to Loshan (Kiating)," blandly remarks the Chinese owner in answer to my question of cost.

"That much! I will give you fifteen dollars which is the price if I am not mistaken, the last time I went down the Ya river," I reply with the carelessness of a confident, experienced traveller.

"Where is such a price? What son of Han would give such a cheap rate to a great man and a foreigner?" explodes the crestfallen raft master as his visions of extra profit vanishes.

We wrangle back and forth and I finally settle for $22.50 with the promise (which I know will be broken) that no other goods are to be carried besides my own. But such a promise I can utilize to create an argument if necessary, to keep off enough goods so that the raft will not be overloaded.

We have just arrived from the Tibetan plateau making the trip from Tachienlu in ten days. It is late November and the cholera epidemic has dried out due to the winter cold. Enroute from Tachienlu I noticed that the cholera stopped as if blocked by a wall at about six thousand feet and below that altitude only one unburied corpse was lying by the roadside and another man was a possible victim as he was barely alive. We had taken the utmost precautions on the road and delayed six weeks in Tachienlu while the cholera was killing its hundreds, including one white woman missionary in the hot, humid Red Basin of Szechuan. Our party consisted of my wife, oldest son John Kenneth, daughter Marian Louise, and youngest son Robert Malcolm in addition to our cook Tsang Wen Chin and his wife Dendru Lhamo (formerly one of our Tibetan orphan girls) with an infant son whom she carried on her back when not feeding him, which is frequently for Oriental women nurse their babies every time they cry.

With our bargaining price settled our next task is loading the raft. Tsang Wen Chin calls a gang of coolies through a coolie hong or association and a long procession in the evening of November 20th carries our stuff to our new bamboo-raft home. Boxes are stowed in the center and bedding under the curved bamboo-mat roofs. Tsang sleeps on the raft to guard our goods and we walk down the next morning about eight o'clock on November 21st. We bid goodbye to our hosts, the F. N. Smiths and R. L. Crooks, at the raft. As we board the raft it weaves up and down under our weight.

The bamboo raft, called patse, looks like a frail structure upon which to float down the Ya river to Kiating (Loshan) for in this distance of about eighty miles the river drops eight hundred feet over thirty-three major rapids and forty-seven minor ones. However, the fragility of the raft is its strength for it gives transversely and laterally, yielding at one place to save another spot from being crushed by a blow, and adjusts itself to the contour of the force as a willow branch sways in a storm. A bamboo raft is practically unsinkable.

Our raft is made entirely of bamboo poles from the giant bamboo known as Nan Chu (Photo No. 89). Each pole is about five inches in diameter and ten to fifteen feet long. The poles are laid side by side with the joints broken to make a structure seventy-five to one hundred feet in length. Our raft is ninety to one hundred feet long (as I stepped it off) and 24 poles or about ten feet wide. The outer edges have a second bamboo pole on top as a six inch guard or reenforcement. The tapered bow is curved upward with twenty foot long poles which are braced by ten foot long cross pieces. Each bamboo pole is bound to the next by bamboo withes one-half inch wide which constantly break and give way under the strains of tumbling waters so that one man is continually putting in new ones. However, each pole is bound by wire to another two poles away so that when the withes break the wires still hold.

The five foot center width of the patse is raised by uprights to one foot above the floor level and here freight is stacked to a height of four feet. In this center, sections are cut off and laid with sleeping mats protected by round bamboo-mat roofs. Each one of us has such a hut for our sleeping quarters. On each side of the raised center are the passageways over two feet in width.

Tholes for oars to guide and propel are placed, one in front on the right side, one near the middle on the right side, and a third on the left side at the rear of the raft. Our patse will carry two to three tons of goods in addition to another ton (fifteen to twenty persons) of people. The largest rafts made are said to be one hundred and ten feet long, and twelve and a half feet wide, of poles up to ten and twelve inches in diameter and will carry five to seven tons of goods and people. Patse are constructed in two weeks and cost $600 in Mexican (Chinese currency) or about $250 American money. Yaan and Loshan are the manufacturing centers.

We have a crew of five men, two at the front with punting poles and oar, one replacing withes, one cooking and the fifth manipulating the rear or rudder oar. The cook has his clay stove in the rear end and mans the middle oar when necessary. The punting pole is used to push the raft, preventing it from striking a rock, or to propel it in shallow water. The patse draws three inches when empty and six inches when loaded to capacity which is reached when the bamboo floor poles are covered by an inch of water. Then we feel like a submarine as the raft snakes beneath the surface. Going up river the five man crew is augmented by extra men as trackers. The trip up from Loshan to Yaan consumes two to three weeks with the raft making five to ten miles a day, depending upon the height of the water. The trip down takes one and a half days to three days with the patse floating, under the impact of the current, up to five miles an hour.

Patse have broken up but only if overloaded or poorly managed by being allowed to hang on a rock since their draft permit them to be pushed through a three inch depth of water with a fair load. We have about a ton of our own goods besides several surreptious bundles of the crew's friends. I watch this extra cargo carefully, letting a few of the friends ride with their luggage so I can demand that others be denied. As soon as I arrive on board I order the laoban or master to cast off quickly so that other free riders cannot come aboard.

As we float down the quietly flowing stream the raft-pontoon bridge is opened for us to pass through. Lashed bamboo rafts are cabled to basket anchors full of rocks to hold the course for the pathway of planks, upon which people but not animals can walk. This pontoon bridge is utilized only in winter. In summer during the high water a wooden ferry boat is used for crossing.

It is pleasant and peaceful to sit on the patze and watch the shore-life slip by; women gathering leaves for fuel, farmers tending garden, coolies burdened with loads of coal or rice and children making mud pies by the water's edge. The high brushed ridges enclosing Yaan diminish to terraced hills and then slide into rice plains as one goes down river. Mists play over the distant mountains and sunshine follows shadow as we move around curving hills and past valleys of rice paddies. All is quiet.

But our musings are soon broken by the road of rushing water. We approach our first rapid with trepidation. The crew springs to the sweeps and rows frantically. We gather speed, as the raft, is forced by rowing, to point its head toward the center of the curving race. We toss and tip, the timbers heave and groan and before we can glance around we are past the crest and floating quietly and almost imperceptibly in the placid deep waters below the rapids.

I count the patse coming and going. Those bound upriver are generally more heavily loaded than those going down river. Cloth, salt, wine and rice ride up while coal, iron pots and lumber float down (Photo No. 90). The wine is from Ipin (Suifu) and is held in large earthenware jars each of fifty gallons capacity. Each jar is encased in a bamboo framework to protect against breakage. Thirty jars strapped in a single row down the center of the raft constitute a load. The largest of these rafts upstream have two steering oars at the rear and thirty-one men were groaning and chanting as they pull the craft upward over a powerful rapid. Once beyond the rapid six men will suffice until the next torrential race is encountered.

As we pass Hungya, ten lee beyond the third way mark, we see a five storied pagoda peering above a temple whose four corners are also pagoda-like towers. This pagoda protects Hungya from unseen evils. Three-fourths of the distance down to Loshan is a seven storied pagoda almost hidden by trees. All pagodas have an odd number of stories as odd numbers signify the Yang or male element which is the emblem of activity and luck.

Each rapid is a new adventure and we soon become careless in our regard of them until we are shocked into a proper respect of their power when the boatmen fail to keep the raft headed straight. They shout a warning. Louise and I grab the children who are sitting next to us in the center of the patze where we stay during the passage of the rapids. We brace our feet and hold on which proves to be a wise precaution else we might have been washed overboard as the raft heaves, buckles, and rolls to a thirty degree angle. One basket and the lightly laden box used for daily cooking supplies slide overboard. The contents spill out of these cases and sink if tin-canned goods but float if light wood. Other baggage pieces are securely lashed in the center but these which we use from constantly have been left carelessly sitting on top. For the next fifteen minutes we are poling the raft over to our floating goods which we rescue. Meanwhile, the repairman is busy replacing an unusually large number of broken withes. The raftmen are fearful lest we charge them for the can of meat and vegetables lost but I assure them we are grateful that this is the only loss and that no person has received any more water than what their shoes hold. We have learned the power of a rapid and after this mishap sit securely braced in the center to enjoy the lashing waters as our patze rides them safely.

We glide downwards sometimes hugging three hundred foot high bluffs of sandstone where the water is over twenty feet deep and the canyons narrow to three hundred feet wide at the top and only one hundred and fifty feet wide at the surface of the water. Again at other places the river spreads like a lazy lagoon so shallow that the raftmen get out and push the patse over stones which rip out withes so rapidly that the witheman swears softly at his task.

Chienfungi, fifty lee southeast of Hungya, lives up to the meaning of its name—One Thousand Buddha Cliff, for row on row of colored Buddha figures sit in niches on the standstone cliff of the left or north bank (Photo No. 91). A narrow road has been carved out of the cliff face and many travellers are passing without glancing at the brilliantly tinted Buddhas, some lining the roadside and other peering calmly a hundred feet above the river.

It is a short distance below the Buddha Cliff early on the morning of the third day when our raft pulls over to the right bank where two of our crew go ashore. They will stay in their homes a few lee away and join the boat again on its way upstream. From now on the Ya river is wide and deep with no dangerous rapids. The raft master states there is no need for their service although I dislike to see our crew so reduced. At the same time three men, a merchant and two assistants, each with a fat bundle, hustle on board. I make a faint protest but they refuse to heed my objections. The boatmen because of the small tip which they will secure do not aid me although they had promised to take on no other cargo. I subside into resigned silence. At various times when we have stopped to buy vegetables or at our overnight anchorages, we have been boarded by as many as twenty soldiers who take free rides down the stream to another point. As they are a protection against gangs of bandits and a protest will not only likely be futile but earn their ill-will I have not complained. My three new merchant friends save me the loss of crew members as will be seen later.

An hour before dark our patse has tied up to a wharf the last two nights near a village where the water is quiet and deep. These are scheduled overnight ports, some rafts are already there and others will swing in with a silence that startles. Before dark the edge of the river is a continuous bridge of rafts on which I step from one to the other for two hundred yards. As our own patse docks the raftmen immediately jump ashore to purchase vegetables and maybe a bit of pork to be fried as side dishes for the rice now being steamed at the rear end brazier. Some build a fire on shore, which our cook does, to supplement our crowded stove in the preparation of the evening meal.

Supper over we put the children to bed who are soon drowsy after a long exciting day in the open air. Louise and I sit near them and enjoy the slowly gathering darkness as the fog and eerie quietness settle down over the river. Outside, upon the darkened banks, are seen fitful flickering lights and inside the nebulous blackness over the river, is only heard the gently slapping of water against the bamboo poles and the happy gurgling of baby whirlpools twisting around and between submerged rocks. Soon we slip into our bedding and sleep undisturbed until the first flashes of dawn when we are awakened by the bumping of raft against raft and the moving of our own patse as it is used for a backstop by the pushing poles of other craft getting underway. Within a short time we too release our moorings and move silently and majestically downstream. The fog still hovers over the village now more silent than a deep pool of water, save for the barking of a dog who likes not the sudden activity at the water's edge. We seem to be alone but the morning sun is lifting the veil of mist which has concealed, as if behind partitions, the early risers at their morning toilets.

On our third and final day we have not far to go. Our merchant friends give us disquieting news, troops of one warlord are retreating out of Kiating (Loshan) and other forces are moving in. We have come out of one war in Batang and do not like the prospect of being caught in another battle. We do not have long to meditate on this subject for the rapid current is carrying us relentlessly to a broad expanse of water where the Ya merges with the Tung. The Ya has widened rapidly but it is not as broad as the Tung or Tatu river which we had crossed about two weeks ago east of Tachienlu. We are ten lee or about three miles west of Kiating and are hoping nothing will delay us these last few but crucial miles.

As we approach the junction point of the Ya and the Tung where the flooded waters seem a half mile wide suddenly the sound of a rifle is heard. We glance around anxiously as we are one hundred and fifty yards from either shore. The raft seems to ignore the shot and then another but nearer sing of a bullet warns us that we must pull inshore. The raftmen propel vigorously and slowly the current swings us toward the bank at the junction point. Now Chinese soldiers can be seen waving their guns. The raftmen yell out between breaths that they are coming. I do not like the situation. We curve into the bank and a rope fastens us to a stake.

On the shore seem to be only a lieutenant and ten men. They

demand our raft and I counter with a request to see their captain. They recognize that I am a foreigner and finally after some consultation a soldier is dispatched to a nearby building. When the captain arrives he repeats the demand. We parley and in the discussion we find that they are leaving Kiating and need the raft to carry their goods upriver. I point out we have hired the raft, have our goods on it, have three small children with us, and what will we do under the circumstances. We are almost at the city and we can be stranded here for days and anyhow it will be slow work pulling the raft up the river.

It develops that they are really impressing carriers to carry their supplies and realize the raft would not only restrict them to the river bank but retard them to a few miles a day. They demand our three raftmen as carriers. I resist this suggestion stoutly asserting they might as well take the raft for who can steer down the flooded river into the city. While they engage in vociferous conversation with the raftmen and my cook, Tsang Wen Chin, the solution comes tumbling into my mind like the racing of a rapid.

"How many carriers do you want?" I ask Captain Lee who had politely given me his card.

"Teacher, we will need three men," he answers politely.

"Very good, you can have three," and I point to the merchant and his two assistants. "There they are and please take them. They did not ask my permission to board my raft." I blandly suggest to the Captain.

The merchant pales and turns disconcertedly to me. "But I am a merchant, I do not know how to carry a load upon my back. I know only selling and not bearing of burdens," he protested and his two assistants joined in his vigorous assertions which grow louder but to no avail. The boatmen are immensely relieved but say nothing and let me take the responsibility of making the sacrifice. The Captain seems glad to get out of the difficulty, to save his face and avoid the charges which would eventually be pressed against him if he left a foreigner stranded with possible injury to one or more of his family. The soldiers grin to see such a clever solution.

I politely invite the merchant to debark with his two assist-

ants and my request is enforced by the waving of guns of the
soldiers toward them. Loudly protesting the three move off the
raft as at my command the raftmen seize their bundles and deposit them ashore. Foaming at the mouth and throwing at us
looks of intense hate the three hitchhikers are escorted by the
soldiers toward the pile of baggage. I express my thanks pro-
fusely to Captain Lee, bow low and tell him we go at his plea-
sure. The Captain nods courteously with an amused smile at
such a happy termination and commands the raftmen to go. With
alacrity the raftmen spring to their positions and cast off as we
smilingly shout, "Please go slowly," to our captors.

We only glance at the merchants who stand by their new tasks
scowling resignedly. They will be forced either to carry a load, or
buy off the soldiers, or hire someone else to take their places
after carrying their loads a few miles. I am not vindictive and
truly feel sorry for my late guests whom I have had to place in
such a predicament. They are paying high for avoiding the paying of a regular fare and forcing themselves upon a chartered
raft. I have given scores of free rides upon my many trips
when I have chartered rafts, buses and boats. However, I always
appreciate polite requests for rides which unfortunately is not
the rule.

The united Tung and Ya seem immense as we glide along
easily and soon sight the Great Buddha 150 feet high and standing piously in a rocky niche where the Min river from the north
receives our combined rivers from the west. Kiating is hidden,
except for its walls and long lines of boats and rafts tied to
wharves around the gates, until we are almost abreast of the city.
When the terraced rows of tiled houses mount up before us, the
current is so swift that we see little of the city because we are
tensely watching the skilled raftmen swing us out of the main
flow and attach our patse to boats anchored in the backwash of
the united Tung and Min rivers (Photo No. 92). The swollen
streams have formed a mighty river three-fourths of a mile wide
and we can see its relentless waters riding swiftly southward in
an ever widening stream.

Everyone seems restless at the piers but we enter the city gate
before noticing what is wrong at this peninsular tip where we

have landed. Abandoning our raft and struggling over swaying boats to the shore has taken all of our attention. Now we look up and see grey straggling columns of dirty, scared soldiers pouring into the congested city of Kiating. The first ranks have not stumbled off the pontoon bridge over the Min, before people are scurrying in every direction.

Ricksha men unceremoniously dump their sedate whiskered fares into the street, seize their shafts and run down by-roads to their master's shops. Water coolies dressed only in shorts, tip over their buckets to form an increasing flood of water rushing down the cobblestone steps, and start upon a trot for their homes callous of the fact that some round-faced Tai-tai or magistrate's wife will have no water for tea. Country lads and lassies quickly gather up their vegetables into two trays, swing their pole over their shoulders and trot for the open fields, oblivious of the stray radishes filtering to the road. Shopkeepers grab bolts of cloth and trays of jade, shoving them anywhere out of sight, while clerks begin fitting the boards into the shop front as they do when closing for the night. Some leave a narrow doorway and exhibit empty shelves proclaiming they are only a small shop and not worth looting. Sedan chair carriers shout "to the right or left" and turn into large inns which were not their original destination.

All cannot get away. Shrieks and cursings announce that men are being seized at the jab of a bayonet to carry ammunition, umbrellas, guns, and bedding for wornout soldiers who are impeded in their flight by such impediments. Well-dressed merchants are kidnapped and loaded down with goods that revolt their refined fingernails until they can find coolies at the first resthouse and pay them outrageous prices to take their places. "La-fu" forced transport with its ill-treatment, uncertain food and unknown days of heavy carrying with their family uninformed of their journey is the cause of all closing of shops and the fleeing of all classes of people.

Frightened soldiers from the east continue to pour over the pontoon bridge spanning the Min river, pass through the city taking what carriers they can grab, and fleeing out through the opposite gate to the west. We have just come from that direction, almost losing our raft. Terror of looting and carnage is quickening the hiding of goods and people behind walls and rubbish, and the return of silver by burial in mother earth again.

We hasten our pace and quickly arrive at L. A. Lovegrens, dispatch Tsang Wen Chin back to guard the raft and then we hunt up coolies to bring our goods ashore accompanying the carriers to our new home where we settle down for our second siege.

Figure 89
Our bamboo raft is contacted by another one on the Ya river

Figure 90
Bamboo rafts loaded with wine jars from Ipin are tracked up Ya river

Figure 91
Buddhas in cliff-face along road beside the Ya River near Chienfungi

Figure 92
The river front at Kiating (Loshan) as we enter. Our raft in the foreground

Chapter XV
CAPTIVE GUESTS OF CHINESE WAR LORDS

Retreating troops usually pillage but orders have come from Liu Wen Hui to hold the city. The scared soldiers are gradually halted and some troops file back into Kiating. Local police cooperate with the commanders who also have forbidden the ransacking of shops and homes. As a result merchants suffer little loss, mainly in the form of below cost prices they are compelled to take from the soldiers for articles of small value when the troops do not have enough money.

However, the citizens must still endure other losses. Liu Wen Hui's forces prepare to defend the city against the oncoming victorious soldiers of Liu Hsiang who is a nephew of Liu Wen Hui. Now begins other enforced appropriations. Every available board, post, pole, door, and any loose timber of home and lumberyard are purloined to construct dugouts until the outskirts of the city resemble a new pioneer settlement. Men are impressed for the digging of trenches and guards with machine guns are mounted along the river bank.

No boats are left upon the opposite banks of the Min and Tung rivers. The pontoon bridge is severed and the boats scuttled near the shore where desolate masts marks the savings of many families who only desire a peaceful land in which to work out a meager living. The war-god of ambitious, careless men has seized their tiny business relentlessly.

Soon the city assumes the aspect of a beseiged fortification; yet no enemy is in sight. Empty shops cast forth the smell of stables as horses whinny where prim, long-sleeved Chinese merchants had sat before their shelves of silk. Wealthy families have fled to squalid quarters leaving only servants on futile guard thereby saving their most precious possessions and also close associations with hordes of weary soldiers who crowd into their huge courtyards where every available table is utilized as a bed to spread the silken comforts permanently borrowed from the storage chests of their reluctant hosts. Tea shops by day serve little round bowls of amber beverage upon the tables which by night support pallid heroes snoring out the opium fumes which ease them from the uncertainities of a warring life.

Still no enemy comes. The nervous people pace up and down to view the defenses against the foes of the soldiers in their midst. Neither side is friends to them. Days wear on. No sound is heard across the rushing rivers. No life appears among the rice fields. Nobody goes to and fro outside the city walls. No mail comes in. The only news slips secretly out of the military commander's councils and this is mostly rumors of impending troop movements or of attack. Kiating is as a separate island cut off from the world without by impassable barriers.

The only excitement is the parade of the martial law battalion. Twice daily with a stern visage a captain marches through the main streets with a column of men. Marching grimly behind a soldier bearing aloft a charactered placard authorizing summary punishment, are two men with shimmering executioner swords pointing skyward. The sight of those naked blades empowered to sever heads with a single immediate stroke of any culprit caught red-handed, restrain the most hardened criminals.

As tense days are succeeded by uneventful days, farmers begin to come in with produce. Shops make tentative sample displays of goods. The noise and bustle of dense crowds pervade certain inner streets but all move as if they are minute men ready for instant retreat. The guiding spirits in the merchants' guild and two of the leading foreign missionaries meet daily to hear reports and make representations to the commanders of the two warring forces, pleading with them to arbitrate their disputes. The merchants sip their amber tea, discuss the latest rumours without criticism intent on losing as little as possible of their worldly goods by pillage. It matters little to them who runs the government as long as taxes are bearable and they can make a little profit.

When everybody has just about hoped themselves into the certainty that an attack will fade into the usual conference adjustment, two aeroplanes roar over the city. Before the planes are seen the citizens dive like marmots into their dark homes, close the doors and windows, and fearfully yet fatalistically await the expected blows. They hope that their thin paper partitions and tile roofs will protect them. No bombs are dropped and the city soldiers take pot shots at the soaring enemy. The retreat of the soldiers into the city has been largely due to terror inspired by bombs dropped upon them by these planes as Liu Wen Hui has not fighters to defend his men or to retaliate against Liu Hsiang. Fear is the only damage of this first visit but it is enough to empty the streets again since the people are ignorant of the destructive power produced by the bombs and all expect the planes to return unexpectedly.

When everyone is wishing that the war was over, soldiers of the other side suddenly open fire upon the city from across the Min river, using cannons, trench mortars and rifles. The shots are aimed at the soldiers but hit the citizens. The soldiers in the city are behind heavy earthworks which absorb the shells with little damage but the citizen behind his thin wooden walls and under his heavy tiles suddenly finds himelf sprawling in his own iron pot while his family are mixed up with tile pottery, bamboo chairs and vegetables into a bloody conglomerate mess.

Whole families die amidst the debris of their falling homes. Shopkeepers with their clerks pour out streams of blood on costly silks before breathing their last. Coffin makers on Coffin street are hurled dead into their own product by bursting shells. Fragments of tile and splinters of wood sprinkle the streets.

The wounded pour into the United Church of Canada hospital. In stalks a stalwart son carrying his unconscious mother on his back, the stump of her right leg bound tightly with the leg of her padded pants. Behind tramps the second son bearing the bleeding leg. When the doctor appears he is asked to sew on the bleeding leg and make it as before. Had not the doctor taken out the protruding intestines of a neighbor yesterday, washed them and placing them back in, sewed up the patient who is still alive and expecting to recover.

Their soon follows a father bearing a young girl in his arms. The girl has only one good eye, the other being a pop eye that had become sightless when she was a baby and had sore eyes. Now a splinter from the home has pierced the good eye. The girl is betrothed to a neighbor's son and with a blind daughter he will have to return some of the dowery all of which has been used to feed the family long since. Doubtless the doctor can fix her up is the anguished father's cry.

As the only western-trained doctor is trying to keep up with the constantly incoming stream of mostly non-combatant wounded, shells begin to drop behind the hospital. The city defenders have planted a cannon beyond a wide ravine upon a summit above the hospital! The city cannon misses the hospital but the opposing forces in reply are not so accurate in locating the town battery. Midst bursting shells which fortunately never struck the building, the helpless are cared for.

While the soldiers are busy firing and hiding, the citizens tense with dread are shivering until the next shell drops when they discover whether or not they have another short lease on life. Then the hum of a distant motor is heard. It comes nearer and nearer until over the immense sitting Buddha at the fork of the two rivers, an aeroplane begins to circle the city. Most of the people, who know nothing of the power of aerial bombs, flee screaming to their homes and sit dumbly. The rest of us run outside, curious to see where the bombs are going to drop. Only two eggs are laid this time by the skybird. One falls into an open court hurting no one, but, tearing up the pavement, shatters a few walls. The second lands in a tin shop, lays out a visiting soldier and buries the tinsmith with his family beneath lamps, buckets, water sprinklers and knickknacks which he will make no more. Fortunately we are too far away to hear more than a dull report but near enough to receive the casualty news soon afterwards.

"Ayah if that is all, that doesn't matter, I thought a street of houses would be blown up," speaks an old wrinkled citizen as he lights his pipe but his thoughts are the thoughts of many among the less scared. Most of the terror for the airplane flees with the pilot as he disappears down the river.

Firing from the city begins against the soldiers whom we can see seeking shelter across the Tung river opposite the L. A. Lovegren home where we are guests. We order our children to play behind the high stone wall which fences in the yard and we adults do not linger too long in exposed places as we watch some of the shooting from our porches. Soldiers are stationed along the city wall below us. A bullet tears into the sideboard of the dining room and spoils a drawer. Others from the far east side of the Min river are too spent to do anything but just drop harmlessly from the plaster.

The days wear on and all become inured to the occasional sing of a bullet or the clatter as a fragment of a shell tears through a tile roof to bury itself in the earth below the cannon mounted upon the heights just outside the northwestern city walls. All plunge inside in spite of the fact that it would be too late to escape after hearing the noise. Then all rush outside again to view and discuss the damage.

"Ayah that almost hit my house. I was sitting here in the doorway making the sole of carpenter Chang's shoes he asked me to make yesterday. Pieces of the tile hit me on the head. My destiny is not yet come," shouts shoemaker Lee, glorying in meeting death so closely and yet to being passed by.

On Sunday morning we go to the Baptist Mission church and listen to an eloquent sermon by Rev. J. C. Jensen. He reaches his closing prayer but the "Amen" which is on the point of being uttered, is never spoken. At that moment an aerial bomb crashes into the adjoining house. The worshippers in a panic-stricken mob rush for the opposite doorway. We merely stand up and wait. A second bomb bursts at the window which falls into pieces. Iron hunks are shot in various directions. One piece strikes the first man who goes through the doorway and he runs about ten yard to drop dying. Another piece shears off another man's ear. A big fragment goes through the wall a few inches behind us we afterwards discover, but now we are too busy getting out and following the rest to the outside. Leading my son John and daughter Marian I walk past the stricken man and hesitate until I see that he is past help. He dies without a sound. We sorrowfully leave while Mr. Jensen and Mr. Lovegren with aid from a member of the church carry the man to his home. That was one of our closest misses by the carriers of death.

Tea shops are very busy whether they are paid or not and the proprietors know that it is useless to protest. All other businesses are silent, the merchants standing with hands clasped in wide soiled silk sleeves within the doorway of their shops whose empty shelves indicate that their owner may be on the verge of bankruptcy. Merchants are afraid to display their goods and the buyers are distrustful of letting others know that they have money to purchase. Those who have, are indifferent about making more money for who can say that they will be able to keep it or spend it. Those who have not must work as usual but they are glad they have nothing to lose and no worries about possessions.

Children play in the streets oblivious of the tragedy hovering over them unless it strikes in their midst. The women knit sadeyed, whispering low of loved ones, relatives and neighbors living a few days ago. Shoemakers pound mightily upon shoes for the soldiers. Coolies idle in hidden backgrounds to escape forced carrier service listening carefully for the tramp of soldiers at the front gates of the compound, and when the sound of marching feet is heard, slinking out the back ways. On the streets orderlies rush to and fro bearing messages of a sudden attack at some hidden point. Everyone watches for the daily visit of the aeroplanes whose few eggs wipe out a few households or plow a garden. Above the treble of bullets or bass of shells is heard the thud of hammers and the rasp of saws. The coffinmakers are striving to keep their depleted supply from vanishing.

There is no news except military which is unreliable and unsafe to discuss unless favorable to the side on which one happens to be. Bad news make men ugly and evil men dislike others hearing it. Most of the news is bad since the city troops seem to be losing ground. They are now largely confined to the city, all of the outposts having been driven in across the rivers but the road westward is open for the retreat to Yaan which took place after we left.

About Dec. 10th on the route westward there comes in from Yaan the three men who had climbed the Boh Gongkar, Richard Burdsall, Terris Moore, and Jack Young. We had left them in Tachienlu. They had transferred a fourth member, Arthur Emmons, who had frozen his feet in the climb, to the care of Dr. R. L. Crook at Yachow hospital and come on by raft. As the siege may last indefinitely they decide to continue their journey down river. Although news is very meager and uncertain we resolve to join forces with them since the river below seems fairly quiet. We notify the military authorities of our intention and each party engages a small junk.

About daybreak on Dec. 15th we are escorted by our hosts aboard our junk and we cast off after the crew have splashed chicken blood on the bow. We had feared our most dangerous stretch of the river would be at the moment of departure by soldiers from Liu Hsiang's besiegers firing upon us, but not a shot is heard as the six mile an hour current reinforced by oars bears us rapidly downstream. Perhaps the early hour, the slight night fog and almost empty boats idling at the wharves and no soldiers seen near them are favorable to non-molestation by the outposts. We gratefully enjoy the silent drifting with the current while the people on shore are yawning to life.

Our two boats rise high in the water. There are no smuggled cargoes aboard and our baggages are light. On our junk the passengers are merely my family, the same five of us with the cook's family that left Tachienlu and came down on the bamboo raft. Other Chinese have decided that this time of war is not propitious for travel and with only the crew we enjoy the lack of confusion and crowding. Each of our boats are the small shenpotse about 30 to 40 feet long and seven to eight feet wide. After safely clearing besieged Kiating we breathe freely and hope for no more trouble although reports of soldiers and possible trouble have been heard about Chien Wei Hsien one hundred lee down river from Kiating. However, we intend to anchor if there is any fighting and pass down the river after it is over.

Everything is quiet. The mist lifts from the river, the shore lines emerge and life seems free from fear and bloodshed. Our freedom does not last long. Soon after lunch we round a curve and hear the sound of distant firing. What are we running into now? Another curve and the reports ring louder as we come upon a large number of junks anchored at the shore. Downstream can be seen the dim outlines of a walled city which we find is Chien Wei Hsien. Our boats pull to the shore near the lower end of the parked junks and we step out on the bank.

Jack Young of the Gongkar party, being an American of Chinese descent and speaking Chinese as a native, takes the leadership. Terris Moore and I follow in his steps. Questions and

answers soon inform us that Liu Hsiang's troops are besieging
Chien Wei Hsien and an attack is in progress. The anchored
boats are waiting for cessation of the battle. The sensible thing
seems to be for us to wait with them but such active firing may
last for days. Being cooped up in a boat with constant fear of
looting or molestation by uncontrollable soldiery is not relished
by us so we resolve if possible to contact the commanders of the
besieging troops.

Jack, Terris and I, leaving Richard Burdsall to guard the
Gongkar party boat and my wife Louise with the cook Tsang
Wen Chin to watch our vessel, make a long detour through fields
until we are well behind the firing lines which we approach
cautiously. An outpost guard passes us through and an officer
escorts us through an embanked field where a few wounded men
are reclining. We are struck by the air of casualness which per-
vades the hospital camp and also among all the soldiers. No one
seems excited and none show fear. All go about their duties as if
performing an ordinary day's work. I reflect on this attitude and
conclude that battles between Chinese warlords are much noise
and little bloodshed. Fighting is necessary, incidentally, but ma-
neuvering and outnumbering the opponent are the main elements
of a campaign. This strategy is borne out in this battle and by
what followed.

We hump over and go through a dry ditch bed to a large
farm house where the General is sheltered. An aide comes outside and then returns to bring the General back and we are introduced to him. Jack does the talking and while he is thus engaged I saunter over to the corner of the house and peek around.
I am a little startled by our closeness to the front lines. The
high walls of the city are about 300 yards distant and a few men
can be seen here and there on the top. Between me and the city
wall and about a hundred feet in front of us are a row of troops
lying behind the hedged bank of a caravan road and firing into
the city. Such a ridge holds the water of a rice field and being
an embankment about two feet high makes an excellent breast-
work and with the bushes on top of it provide additional con-
cealment. A bullet occasionally whistles overhead and I reflect
that the thin mud-plastered walls and wooden partitions of this
straw-thatched country home will not stop a high-powered bullet.

A small grove of trees and bamboo shrubbery conceal the house and unless the opposing force can see their foes they are not likely to concentrate their fire upon it but a random bullet is certain to hit it as the city defenders are directing their fire on the men concealed by the road bank.

Jack arranges with the General for us to proceed down the river, an orderly being sent to notify the outposts not to fire upon us and to let us pass unmolested. We accept this statement as being capable of enforcement but experience proves that the outposts are not notified and could not be in all cases because of their isolation. We work our way again behind hills and through ravines to the boats. We cast off into the middle of the current and are scarcely started before shots come from the shore we have just left. The bullets spout spray as they hit the water near us. Soldiers come running down to the water's edge so we try to turn back but the current takes us downward in sight of the city before we can touch land and explain to the outposts the order of their general. Evidently he is permitting us to inform his outposts. The sentinels allow us to depart so we start again and reach the other side, closer to the walled city but on the opposite shore from it, and perhaps 600 yards away. We dock and then firing comes from both sides of the river at us as we jump ashore. The crew flee in such haste that I must aid the boatmaster to set the anchor firmly while the family run for the shrubbery among the sand dunes.

We hasten behind some sand ridges and find a rounded bamboo mat shelter where we hold a hurried consultation. Jack, Terris, and I decide that we must contact the outposts and leaders on this side in order to secure permission to proceed down river and also to halt the bullets which are whistling overhead. It is possible we may be attacked by an assault party from outlying troops. Louise and the children are sheltered in the low tumbled down mat-shed which is surrounded by dunes so that it cannot be seen until one is almost upon it. Richard Burdsall agrees to stay with them in this spot which is protected from fire on all sides and still is within sight of the boat. Our servants and boatmen are also nearby.

Jack, Terris and I then start across the wide sandy waste toward the hills opposite the city from where bullets are still coming. As we walk, the walled city defenders who belong to the war party within Kiating, continue to fire at us until we are out of sight and range. Our new friends are of the forces of Liu Hsiang. Forces from both sides of the river fire at us but the troops on the shore we have just left are soon outdistanced. From this side of the river the new friends we are trying to contact shoot too high, too wide or too short as we keep walking toward them as nonchalantly as possible. This indifference puzzles them and finally one sentinel stands up on the hillside about 500 feet distant, fires a time or two and then holds his fire as we persistently walk toward him without any menacing gesture. The shots die out and we breathe more freely. The sentinel keeps his gun pointed at us as we approach. We are glad the Chinese have little training in shooting.

We cross a small stream by a foot bridge and as we draw near the sentinel commands us to put up our hands which we promptly do. When we arrive in front of him he has us turn around and slaps us for pistols. Terris and I are unarmed and Jack's revolver has never left its holster since the trip began. The sentinel compels Jack to unfasten his gun and hand it to him. Other sentinels hove into view coming in from their posts. Our guard motions us to go uphill and another soldier pokes Jack's gun into his back to encourage him. We struggle up the hill. I soon let my hands drop and I think the others did also but being in front I cannot see them. We climb the hillside in single file and dip over a tiny divide to find ourselves in a hollow from whose southern watershed now streams a file of the most villianous Chinese I have ever seen. We wait and the newcomers surround us, pointing their guns so close and thickly that with the wrong move we can be riddled. We make no move. Their captain, standing on the outside, begins to talk to us. My throat is dry and I begin to think our time is up. I try to answer, as Chinese believe a foreigner tells the truth and at first they will not believe Jack is an American. However, they do not understand me properly and Jack asks me to let him do the talking. I am glad to turn things over to him. It is a long parley but finally the Captain orders his men to lower their rifles so we breathe easier. They think that we are Russians in the employ of the other army and that we are leading a landing party to attack them in the rear. We learn later that this Captain and many of his men were former bandits who have been taken into the service of Liu Hsiang in order to fight Liu Wen Hui. Naturally they are highly excited over the prospect of becoming casualties in being sent to stop the supposed landing party and the Captain, a stout man, is not happy in finding his puffing and worry is baseless. Reinforced by my assurances that Jack is an American, the Captain finally believes my story that we are merely going down river to the extent that I am to go back with an officer and bring the boats downstream but Jack and Terris are to be held as hostages for my good behavior and fulfillment of our statements.

Jack and Terris are marched off as prisoners back to their army headquarters while I start out with a young lieutenant who is to accompany me to the boats. The lieutenant is very apprehensive as we walk along lest I may be leading him into a trap and after I have several times assured him that I am telling him the truth I clinch my words with the oath given often by Chinese that "he can cut off my head if I am not telling the truth." These words, we of course have been talking in Chinese, eases his mind that there are no soldiers in our boats. I start asking him questions about his education after telling him I am an educational missionary and gradually he relaxes. I find he is a graduate of a mission high school located near Canton and that he has recently joined Liu Hsiang's forces. He says he is not happy as the Captain is a former brigand and he is not. He becomes more friendly as we walk leisurely but his fears are not totally dispelled until we arrive at the shelter where my family and Richard Burdsall have waited with no harm but considerable anxiety about us. Outpost guards had found them and were standing guard but Tsang Wen Chin is fluent in diplomacy and had satisfied the soldiers so that all is peaceful when we reach them. At the sight of the foreign woman and children the lieutenant drops his apprehension and we also are relieved at their safety.

We hastily board our boats and an outpost sentinel is placed upon each one. The lieutenant assures me that their men will not shoot at us but no sooner have we pulled anchor then their forces in the walled city, with a few shots from everywhere, begin to fire. The officer and his soldiers hold up their right hands but to no avail, although they stand in the bow of the boat calmly leaning on their guns. I stand beside the sentinel so the presence of a foreigner may reassure those firing that there is no cause for shooting and also if they must fire to draw their aim at us rather than at the family who are lying flat on the deck beneath the bunks where I ordered them when the bullets sang. The current is swift and we stay close to the left bank which is a fairly steep cliff, so most of the shooting comes across the river from the city distant not only by the width of the water but also by a broad stretch of shingle, not less than four hundred yards and a moving target which causes them to miss us entirely except one shot which sinks into the timber near the bow of the boat. The swift current, running about eight miles an hour, and the frantic rowing of the crew brings us quickly past the city and around a curve out of sight where we pull into the shore on the left bank. Here we are happy to see Jack and Terris. They board their boat but none of us are permitted to depart.

Jack and Terris had been brought here to await the coming of the boats and meanwhile the general in command had been informed of their presence. The general sends an aide to buy a pair of field glasses from us. I had told the Gongkar boys to hide anything they wanted to keep but Richard had left his field glasses hanging around his neck where the officers had seen them. Fortunately all of our guns are in cases stowed in the hold except Jack's pistol which he has not yet recovered. Jack informs Richard that the commanding officer wishes to buy his field glasses and since our position is precarious urges Richard to sell at a fair price. I also strongly recommend this deal, telling him he is lucky to get money for them and if he is not paid we will share the loss. Richard is reluctant to part with them as they are a prized gift from his father. But sensing that he cannot refuse and that if both Jack and I should bring out ours we all will undoubtedly be compelled to part with them, Richard states the American price and hands over the field glasses.

Our boats are now ordered downstream a short distance where we enter a forested cove on the left bank. Here the commanding general has his headquarters in a small village. We land and are graciously treated by officers who give us decent quarters for our cots and our mess. The general sends us his apologies but declares the widespread fighting makes it too dangerous for us to proceed. Evening is approaching and the day's events have tired us so we retire soon after our evening meal. We have a good night's rest broken by one humorous interlude. About midnight we four men are awakened by the arrival of officers from the general with the money for the field glasses. They enter so rapidly that we receive them in our night clothes which for the other three men consisted of baggy woollen underwear. Afterwards down river I never tired telling friends in the presence of the three Gongkar boys, how they, dressed in their formal underwear, had greeted, counted the field glass money (mostly in depreciated twenty cent pieces) and then bowed their high ranking hosts to the outer gate.

We are informed by the general that troops will leave the cove about daybreak to cross the river and drive away the attacking forces of Liu Wen Hui. Confusion and danger in the turmoil which might sway up and down the river with alternate defeat and victory will prevail. We take the hint, rise at four A.M. and leave the crowded cove in the grey half light of dispelling darkness, gratefully dropping down the river in the rapid current which soon takes us safely on our way (Photo No. 93). Later the news filtered through that the early morning assault was not made as the attacking forces of Liu Wen Hui had withdrawn from Chien Wei Hsien during the night. The siege of Kiating was soon abandoned temporarily by Liu Hsiang but not long afterwards fell in a new assault by his soldiers.

The sun rises dull and red through the heavy mist which soon lifts from the muddy sullen waters whose rumbling gurgles are the voice of summer floods. Even our crew is silent, perhaps not fully awake and perhaps still numbed by the risk which working for the crazy-thinking foreigners had caused them to undergo. Maybe these risks can be used as a talking point for extra tea money at the end of the voyage. Whatever the reason the day's run is quiet and restful as are most days after a battle when men have died and the living are exhausted.

At night we tie up at a village along the shore far from last night's fear and worry. A short run in the morning and soon after noon we dock at Ipin. Seeing a steamer at the wharf we rush ashore for tickets and find the vessel is leaving the next morning which gives us time to move our luggage aboard to the deck space we have bought. Tsang Wen Chin and his wife, Dendru Lhamo, are left to set up the cots and guard everything we have on the Kiafoo which is a Chinese steamer about a hundred feet long and drawing five feet of water. We take rickshas to the homes of the Baptist missionaries where we arrive in time to watch Dr. C. E. Tompkins save the life of a Chinese woman who had taken opium to work on the face of her husband when he refused to take her with him on a new military assignment. Dr. Tompkins worked constantly one and a half hours in the resuscitation. Then we have tea at Chester F. Woods and following this refreshment the five of us take baths, some in one home and some in another. After a fine evening meal and a long talkfest Mr. Wood orders a sedan chair for Louise and the three children. Then he leads us in an enchanting walk first through a part of the city and then outside the city walls in a clouded moonlight, bringing us to the ship at midnight. We go on board to our cots at once.

It is about 4:30 A.M. when I am awakened as the Kiafoo swings out into the mighty Yangtze, now a saturated yellow torrent, but the same river we had left almost five months previously at Batang. We arrive upon the afternoon of the second day at Chungking. It is the 19th of December, 1932. A pleasant stay at the Canadian Mission hostel with Gordon Jones and his wife, as charming hosts, with whom we spend Christmas. A few days afterward we begin once more the trip through the gorges of the Yangtze where, if we could have seen the black bellowing yak upon the thinly shrubbed banks, we would often have visualized ourselves as once more on the highlands of Tibet. As we had left the yak behind so we soon leave the Yangtze to reach our American home in April of 1933.

Figure 93
Boat, similar to our own, containing the Boh Gongkar party, as our two craft
leave the cove where we were held captive by a Chinese warlord

Figure 94
My wife with her Tibetan orphans of the Batang orphanage including helpers

Figure 95
The Batang Mission school with teachers

Figure 96
Mrs. Minnie Ogden with Batang church school

Appendix No. 1

ITINERARIES OF ROUTES

Explanation of Symbols and Abbreviations

(1) Pop. means population which is based on a personal count of houses and tents and figuring five persons to each unit. When there are two lines of figures the upper line indicates the number of persons from the previous point to this one; and the lower one the population of the stopping place. N means nomads. Figures opposite monasteries under Pop refer to number of monks or nuns.

(2) M means monastery and letters after names of monasteries indicate sect, as follows:—G is Gelugpa; Ga is Gahdanpa; K is Kahgyupa; Ka is Karmapa; N is Nyingmapa; and S is Sakyapa.

(3) Ele. is elevation in feet above sea level, determined by harmonizations of aneroid barometer, boiling point readings, and/or eye estimations from vantage points of previously fixed elevations, also, considering snow lines and vegetation. All elevations are approximate as temperature, etc., was ignored.

(4) Dis. is distance in miles measured in time by the caravan marching, estimated as moving one and a half miles an hour uphill and two miles an hour on other grades.

(5) Temp. is temperature in Fahrenheit degrees read every A.M. about eight o'clock from a high grade maximum and minimum thermometer placed in shade outside house or tent.

(6) Weather data:—C is clear and CL is cloudy. C followed by dash and CL, refers to clear in morning and cloudy in afternoon and vice versa. Many prior years of measurements and calculations of rainfall in Batang enabled me to approximate the rainfall estimations. D is drizzles and all sprinkles up to one sixteenth of an inch. Wind direction in obvious abbreviations is that most prevalent during the day. Precipitation is rain unless otherwise stated and in inches.

(7) Names of places west of Tachienlu on the Tibetan Plateau are the Tibetan ones with the Chinese names of important places in parenthesis.

(8) On dates. Rest days are not included nor indicated.

Date	Place	Pop.	Ele.	Dis.	Temp. Max.	Min.	Sky	Rain or Snow	Wind	Remarks
Sept. 1935										
	Leaving Sept. 8th From Tachienlu (Dartsemdo) (Kangting)	12000	8500							
	Seven Monasteries	1500								
8	Jethoh, via	250 125	11500	10	67	48	CL	1/16	E	

Date	Place		Pop.	Ele.	Dis.	Temp. Max.	Min.	Sky	Rain or Snow	Wind	Remarks
	Je Pass	to		14500	10						
9	Teezuh	to	20 N	13300	2	74	45	CL	1/16	E	
10	Chorten Karpo	to	25 50	12750	10	79	48	CL	1/16	SW	
11	Dongoloh	via	25 50	12750	7	78	50	CL	1	W	
	Karzhi(M)G	over	150	13500							
	Karzhi(2) Passes	to		15000	3						Western—15000 Eastern—14650
13	Orongzhee	to	25 N	13000	9	73	38	CL	D	W	
14	Orongzhee Podrang	to	25	11500	8	77	46	CL	1	W	
15	Nyahchukha	over	100 1000	9000	10	66	52	CL	D	W	
	Nya(Yalung) River	to		9000							
18	Magendrong	over	50	12000	9	65	29	CL	D	E	
	Rama(3)Passes	to		15500	6						Eastern—14750 Central—15000 Western—15500
19	Manlamgang	to		14000	2	64	25	C		W	
20	Ngoloh	to	50	12500	8	75	30	C	D	W	
21	Jangkarkhoh	over	15 60	13750	8	70	38	C		SE	
	Kharsa(3)Passes	&		15000	5						Eastern—15000 Central—14750 Western—15000
	Bongo			14500	1						
22	Thangkar	over	50N	14000	2	64	35	CL		W	
	Jeri Pass	to		14625	7						
23	Horchukha	over	50N	14000	2	63	33	CL	1/2	W	
	Hor Chu	over		14000							
	Tsasha Pass	to		14800	6						
24	Litang(Lithang) past (Lihwa)		25N 1500	13800	3	68	46	CL		S	

ON MOLASHEE TRIP

Date	Place		Pop.	Ele.	Dis.	Temp. Max.	Min.	Sky	Rain or Snow	Wind	Remarks
	Champachoskor Ling(M)G	to	4000	13800							
28	Pehma	to		14000	8	72	40	CL		S	
29	Thraloi Dzong	to		13000	8	74	36	CL	D	S	
Oct.											
1	Deemdokhoh	to	10N	12750	4	72	31	CL	1/16	SE	
4	Rijyakhoh	to		14000	5	72	27	CL	1/16	SE,NW	
5	Litang	to		13800	15	72	36	CL	1	E	Hail size of Peas.

ON BATANG TRIP

Date	Place		Pop.	Ele.	Dis.	Temp. Max.	Min.	Sky	Rain or Snow	Wind	Remarks
15	Chukhuhdo	to		13900	10	65	34	C		S	
16	Banyathang	over	1675N	14000	14	62	35	CL	1/4		Hail. (100 monks in tent service.)

Date	Place		Pop.	Ele.	Dis.	Temp. Max.	Min.	Sky	Rain or Snow	Wind	Remarks
	Li Chu	to		14000							
18	Asehchu	to	1200N								
			200N	14100	6	62	33	CL	D	S	
19	Sharitsathang	over		14200	9	61	19	C-CL	D	S	snow falls on mountains.
	Shari Pass			16200	5						Basic rock is granite
20	Sharingohthoh	over		15500	2	63	23	C-CL	D	NE	snow falls on mountains.
	Bahrongdah Chu	to		14000							
21	Janglungdah	over		14500	10	60	15	C-CL		W	
	Tshongpen Pass	to		16500	8						Basic rock is dolomite
22	Ganohdorjhe	to		14750	4	64	18	C		W	
23	Meliting	to	20	11000	8	75	19	C		W	
24	Batang (Bathang)		25	8500	8	67	37	C		W	
	past (Bah)		2500								
Jan.	From Batang and										
	Bahshehdrupendi		1000	8500							
	Ling(M)G	past									
	Rituh Lhakang										
	(M)G	to	50	8550							
20	Bajungshee	to		10900	8	58	22	C		SW	
21	Ganohdorjhe	over		14650	8	40	13	C		SE	
	Tshongpon Pass	to		16500	5						
22	Dolungdah	to	150N	14000	8	43	10	C		calm	
23	Melongdrohthoh	over		15000	10	36	—3	CL		SW	
	Shari Pass	to		16200	5						
24	Tshachukha	to		14100	5	38	—3	CL		W	
25	Pangvartoh	over		14200	10	40	1	CL		W, E	
	Li Chu	to		14300	5						
26	Pangyarchungtsang-			14400	2	37	3	C-CL		W	Bitter 30 mi. an hr. wind all day
	toh	over									Snowing on mountains
	Chungtsang(2)										Northern pass 15000
	Passes	to		15500	4						Basic rock is granite
27	Trangtohkhoh	over	250N	14500	8	38	5	CL		N,W,S	Bitter winds Snow falls on mts.
	Ba Chu(Batang River)	to		14700	4						
28	Manlungpa	over		15500	12	33	—17	CL		NW	Our bitterest day. Basic rock is dark red limestone.
	Manlung Pass	to		16500	4						
29	Posheekhoh	over	15N	14500	6	39	+2	C		N,NW	
	Lamar(2) Passes	over		16500	3						Southern Pass—16000 Basic rock is blue and yellow limestone
	Tama Pass	to		14500	3						
30	Samar	past	250	11500	6	53	8	C-CL		S	
	Samar(M)	to	50								
31	Zhosothang	past		11000	10	56	3	CL		S	
Feb.	Darche	and	125	10750	5						
	Darche(M)	to	50	12250							

Date	Place		Pop.	Ele.	Dis.	Temp. Max.	Min.	Sky	Rain or Snow	Wind	Remarks
1	Deneh	past	125	10250	7	57	18	C-CL		NW	Snow falls on mts.
	Khamzhung(M)	and	60	10500							
	Gotse Dzong	to		10000	4						
2	Zhangdothang	over		13500	8	50	20	CL		N	snow falls on mts.
	Man Pass	to		15500	3						
3	Chyimdah	to	90	12500	10	52	—4	C-CL		calm	Snow is 1½ in. on shady ground.
	Pehyee(M)N	and	400	11250							
4	Pehyee	to	75 125	11000	12	53	1	C-CL		calm	
5	Yangtze River		375	9750	4	44	21	CL		calm	Snow lies on mts.
	back	to									Limestone gorge
6	Pehyee	over		11000	4	63	18	C-CL		NE	
	Ngeezo(2)Passes	to		16300	12						Northern Pass—15500
7	Kathoh(M)N	over	2000	13500	4	51	16	CL		calm	Snow lies 3 in. on ground and 1 ft. in drifts.
	Dzin Chu	past		10500							
	Rajah(M)	to	500								
8	Horbu	to	100	10500	7	62	9	C-CL		calm	
9	Sothang	to	1000 25	10050	13	61	19	CL	slight snow	S	tent felled by wind
10	Lhagethang	past	750 25	10100	12	50	19	CL	slight snow	calm	hail falls. Deep 300 ft. limestone canyon
	Gangthohdrukha	over	50	10150	8						Skinboat ferry is located here
	Zhee Chu	near									50 ft. wide and 3 feet deep.
	Degepabam(M)Ka	to	2000								
11	Jangra(M)S	to		10600	6	63	15	C		N	
12	Dege(M)S	to	850	11000	8	54	8	C-CL		N	600 monks, 250 Lay
17	Khorlomdo	and	500 10	12000	16	50	25	CL		calm	no snow on mts. 6 mi. limestone gorge and high
	Khorlo(M)S	past	60								
	Galeh(M)S	to	60	12500	4						
18	Pahchungdah	over	100	13750	11	54	16	CL	light snow	SE	heavier snow falls on mountains.
	Zee Pass	to		14250	5						
19	Mahrong	to	15 10N	12750	7	50	13	CL	1/2in. snow	SE	blizzard at night.
20	Gohzer(M)S	over	500 300	12250	8	52	18	C-CL		SE, E	
	Man(2)Passes	to		12750							
21	Namjyeh Ling (M) K	over	60	12000	10	53	8	C-CL		W	
	6 major and 2 minor divides	to									see this road retraced June 23rd
	Kahphur(M)Ga	to	50	11500							
22	Tankhoh	with	1500 600	11250	14	54	14	CL		W	Bitter wind all day

Date	Place		Pop.	Ele.	Dis.	Temp. Max.	Min.	Sky	Rain or Snow	Wind	Remarks
	Drehma Lhakhang										
	(M)Ga	at	100								
	Chungkhor(M)G		200								
	and 2 monasteries										
	(M)Ga	to	100								
28	Ngoja	over	50	13500	15	55	23	CL		S	Snow falls on mts.
			75N								Limestone canyon
Mar.											lines road.
	Chutsuh Pass	to		15300	5						
1	Chunahkhar	to		14850	5	38	—5	CL	1/2 snow	S, N	
2	Jyur(M)G	to	500N	14000	15	46	—3	C-CL	1 snow	S, N	Snow in night.
6	Dza Chu(Yalung										
	River)	to		13000	10	34	5	C	1/2 snow	S	Snow in night.
6	Jyur(M)G	over	50	14000	10						
6	low ranges	to		14750							
8	Dzazhungdo	over	750N	13000	10	40	4	C		S	
	Dza Chu(Yalung)	to		13000							2 branches, 35 ft. wide,
											3 ft. deep
	Getse(M)N	over	50	13100	6	54	—13	C		N	
	Garchen Pass	to		14000	3						
9	Garchen	to		13600	3						reddish shale rocks
11	Zhachunyandra	to	250N	13500	6	50	—3	C-CL		S, W	
12	Minahlong	over		13750	7	48	—4	CL		S,N	
	2 ranges	to		15000							
13	Yachuzha	over		14500	10	42	2	CL		W	
	Yachu Pass	over		15500	2						our farthest north
	Dza Chu(Yalung)	to									2 ft. deep, 30 ft. wide
14	Garchen	over	65N	13750	13	54	—4	C		S	
	Garchen Pass	over		14750							
	Dza Chu(Yalung)	to		13000							
15	Wather(M)	up	300	13000	9	63	2	C		SW	tent monastery
	Dza Chu and	over		13100	5						
	six ranges	to		14750							
16	Jyur(M)G	over	50	14000	15	61	9	CL		S.	
	2 Passes	to		14500							
19	Sershee(M)G	to	1250N	13250	18	55	15	C-CL		W, SW	ten incarnations
			400								in monastery.
20	Zhu	over		13500	11	54	15	CL	1/2 snow	W	east & west valley
	Ngangpa Pass	to		14500	10						
21	Zhewa	past	250N	12250	9	56	—3	C-CL		W, SW	
			250								
	Torkon(M)S	and	50	12300							
	Drizhung(M)K	and	50	12200							
	Bahgon(M)K	and	25	12000	4						
	Gawo(M)K	to	25	11800	1						
22	Dripomdah	over	500	11700	6	54	19	CL		S	
			25								
	Yangtze River	past		11650	1						cross on ice 100
											yds. wide & deep
	monastery-K	past	75	12000							
	Jyeku(M)S	to	500	12350							
23	Jyekundo	over	2000	12250	20	66	19	C		W	
			1000								

Date	Place	Pop.	Ele.	Dis.	Temp. Max.	Min.	Sky	Rain or Snow	Wind	Remarks
Apr.	Lajyan Pass to		14200							
12	Lanyeepa over		14000	6	42	30	CL	1 snow		calm
	Thangbumdah Pass to		14500	2						
13	Sajyahsumdo past	15 5	13000	4	48	6	CL-C		W	strong wind
	Thangbumdah near	125								
	Ranyah(M)Ga and	125 400								
	Bumten(M)K and	100 200								
	Denda to	125 125								
14	Dzindah and	150	11750	8	68	14	C-CL		SE	Yangtze 150 ft. wide
	Dzindah(M) to	25								
15	Lamdah near	625	11775	6	64	27	C-CL		SE	crossed Yangtze by ferry—3 min. to cross
	Tharlung(M)S to	200								
16	Parlalatsar over		12500	8	52	29	C-CL	1/2 snow NW		hail falls.
	Par Pass and		13500	2						
April	Gonsar(M)S and	300								
	Dungtrih(M)S to	100								
17	Trindo Camp over	1000 250	12500	6	54	23	CL-C	1 rain 1/4 snow	NE, S	
	Pass to		14000	4						
18	Drijyuh(M)K to	250N 200	13400	6	46	11	C-CL		W	
20	Dzachumdo to	375N	13700	8	55	22	CL	1/4 snow & hail	S	
30	Kharongtsar to	125N	14000	4	44	16	CL	1/4 snow & hail	E, W	
May										
1	Drjyuh(M)K over		13400	11	48	19	CL	3 snow	W	crossed Yalung R. on ice bridge
	Pass and	75N	13750							
	Gangdzom Pass to above		14500							
4	Loh Monastery past		13000	13	56	21	CL		W,S,N	
	Loh(M)G and	500	12750	4						
	Tharlung(M)G and									
	Lamdah over		11725							
	Yangtze River to									1½ ft. higher 5 min. to cross Yak 2 min. to swim
5	Thangdah, on former route to	125	11760	7	59	19	CL	3/4 snow	W	
6	Sajyasumdo, over former passes to		13000	13	58	31	CL		NE,SW	
7	Jyekundo past		12250	12	69	22	CL	1 snow	NE	

Date	Place		Pop.	Ele.	Dis.	Temp. Max.	Min.	Sky	Rain or Snow	Wind	Remarks
June											
	Tranggoh(M)K	and	200	12350							
	Pehchen(M)K	to	150	12750							grass plain 15 mi. by 2 mi.
17	Pehchen	over	200N 100	12750	18	73	46	CL-C		1 W	snow above 14,500
	Trao Pass	to		13500	7						
18	Kharsa	past	300N 100	12000	6	65	39	CL-C	D	SE	
	Jyonggon(M)K	and	50	11750							
	Jyongchun(M)G	and	50	12000							
	Ponglon(M)S	to	75								
19	Dangthoh(M)S	over	775 75	11450	9	62	44	CL-C	1/2	SE	200 ft. high rock walled Yangtze canyon
	Pass	past		13500	5						
	Dronthoh(M)K	to	75								
	Drumda Drutsha	over		11300	10						
	Yangtze River	to		11300							3 min. to cross Yangtze in skin boat. Round trip 20 min.
20	Gehsar	past	500 50	11350	1	75	46	CL-C	1/2	SE	snow above 14,500 ft.
	Rajyah(M)S	to									
21	Tankhoh	past	525 600	11250	17	76	45	C-CL	1 1/2		Limestone cliffs.
	Chohra(M)S	and	40								
	Trongthoh(M)G	and	40								
	Kahphur(M)Ga	to	50								
23	Bahzhah	over		12500	12	74	49	C-CL	3/8 S,N,W		
	Man Passes(2)	to		12750							
24	Gohzer(M)S	past	25N 300	12250	21	79	44	CL-C		W	
	Jhachu(M)K	over	50								
	Latse Kehring Pass	to	650	14000	14						
25	Dzohchen		250N 175	13000	16	76	46	CL-C	1/2	E	Hail
Short trip northwest from											
Sept.	Dzochen	past									
	Lolang(M)N	and	50								Forded three rivers 3 to 5 ft. deep and 50 ft. wide, in flood
	Jhoru(M)G	to	100								
3	Jhoru Nomad camp	to	400N	13500	26	63	41	CL		SE	Tsatsa & Gotsar two (M)G in this area.
	Caravan enroute and	back to		13750	4						

Date	Place		Pop.	Ele.	Dis.	Temp. Max.	Min.	Sky	Rain or Snow	Wind	Remarks
4	Johru Nomad Camp			13500	4	61	40	CL	1½	NW	Snow above 15,000 ft.
		over									
	Jho Chu	to									75 ft. wide, 3-4 ft. deep.
5	Jhochutsar	to	100N	13250	15	53	42	CL	2¼	NW	Snow above 15,500 ft.
6	Dzohchen	past		13000	17	59	37	CL	1/2	SE	Wind up valley
June	Continuing June										
	25 above										
	Dzohchen(M)N	over	500	13100							
	Muri Pass	to		15250							
26	Yeechutsar	past	250N	13000	20	74	47	C-CL	3/8	SE,	Hail falls twice
	Yahzer(M)N	to	75							NW,E	
June											
27	Yeelung	over	225N	12750	10	68	39	C-CL		SW	Yee Plain—16 mi.
			25								by 1 mi.
	Lahnah Pass	to		13000							
28	Rongbahtsa	past	150N	12000	21	62	50	CL	1	SE,N,E	Snow above 15,000 ft.
			100								400 monks in 3 monasteries nearby
	Darjeh(M)G	to	1000		1						
	Lingtsang	to	900		3						
	Bero	past	1000	11850	7						
			500								
	Nyara(M)S	and	500								
	Guluh(M)N	and	75								
	Bero(M)G	over	600								
	Yalung River	to		11700							
29	Gangdzi	and	1750	11750	10	63	48	CL-C	1 1/2	SE	Snow above 14,500 ft.
			1250								Bridge over Yalung R
	Gangdzi(M)G	and	3000								
July											
	Khomma(M)G	and	250								
	Zihja(M)G	and	50								
	Dothoh(M)S	and	75								
	Nunneries(2)G	and	80								
	Tsesee(M)G	to	150								
4	Lozhung	over	2100	12000	8	74	50	CL-C	1 5/8	W	
			75								
	Latse Pass	past		13000	9						
	Jhori(M)G	to	300								
5	Kharsar	over	150N	12000	4	77	44	CL	2	W	
			125								
	Bu Chu	to			2						
	Drewu	past	1000	11850							
			250								
	Zhaleh(M)S	to	50								
6	Bahmdah	past	1875	11500	10	78	36	C-CL	5/8	W,NW	
			10								
	Jola(M)S	and	50								
	Nunnery G	to	50								
	Drango	past									Junction of Zhi and Bu rivers.

Date	Place		Pop.	Ele.	Dis.	Temp. Max.	Min.	Sky	Rain or Snow	Wind	Remarks
	Drango(M)G	and	1000		11						
	Getsang(M)G	over	100								
	Rama Pass	to		13000							
7	Yesu	over	3700	11400	4	72	31	C-CL	D	NW,SE	
			100								
	Zhe Chu	to			3						150-200 ft. wide & 10 ft. deep
8	Chahjya	past	3800	11250	12	77	37	C	D		
			50								
	Zhe Chu bridge	and			10						River 180 ft. wide
	Bolung(M)G	and	25								
	Nyeetsho(M)G	to	1500								
9	Dawu	past	1000	11000	3	83	43	C	D	SE,NW	
			2000								
	An Hermitage,G	&	25								
	Chapoh(M)	to	75								
10	Chapoh	over	2925	11500	13	63	51	CL	1/4	SE, NW	
			50								
	Mijhi Pass	past		13000	6						
	Louhthang(M)N	&	50								
	Mijhi Dzong	and	10	12850	4						
	Garthar(M)G	to	400	12000							
11	Garthar	past	1150	12000	10	60	46	CL	1 1/4	SE,NW	
			375								
	Pahmeh	and	125	11750	4						
	Sakhunggo(M)N	&	50								
	Jelung(M)S	to	50								
13	Bahodrang	over	250	12750	12	74	44	CL-C	1/4	SE,NW	
			10								
	Drepa Pass	past		14000							
	3 small(M)	and	125								
	8 shoulder passes	to	200N	13750							
14	Nahjhapuh	over	325	13000	15	72	46	CL		SW	
			50								
	Jethoh Pass	to	75N	14500	6						
15	Tachienlu	to	375	8500	13	67	51	C			
			12000								
Aug.											
19	Suthohlungpa	to	575	11000	12	65	55	CL	1/8	S	
			10								
20	Latsar	over	100	14000	11	63	53	CL	1/2	S	200 gold diggers near
	Zhara Pass	and		14750	2						Zhara Peak 20,000 ft. on west side.
	Pass	to		13000	11						
21	Garthar			12000	4	62	44	C	1 3/4	NW,E,NE	fearful lightning

TRIP FROM BATANG TO GARTHOK AND RETURN AS DESCRIBED IN CHAP. VII

Oct.											
	From Batang	to	2500	8500							
10	Li	via	50	8300	7						includes Nushi— a village nearby
			60								

Date	Place		Pop.	Ele.	Dis.	Temp. Max.	Min.	Sky	Rain or Snow	Wind	Remarks
	Druwalung	over	190	8200	8						Downstream by boat 1½ hours.
	Yangtze River	to									
11	Gora	via	450	8450	8						
			50								
	Degoteng	over	30	9750	4						
			75								
	Khungtsekha Pass	to		13000							
12	Khungtseteng	past	100	12500	4						
	Two Monasteries		50								
	one G and one N		25								
13	Pumteh	over	625	12250	8						
			25								
	Pang Pass	past		13500	2						
	Two monasteries G		50								
		to	40								
14	Lhandee	past	140	11900	2						
	A monastery G	over	25	11950							
	Sherepetse Pass	past		14000	5						
	A monastery G	to	25								
15	Pangda	over	140	11600	2						
			125								
	Phu Pass	past		14000	5						
	A monastery G	to	50								
	Phula	to	165	11725	2						Other 225 pop. below Phula in valley.
			85								
16	Garthok	past	325	12400	7						
			300								
	Garthok(M)G	to	200								
	Lhora(M)G	to	100		8						
28	Chunohnong	over	50	12900	6						
	Four Passes	near		13500							
				13900							
				14500							
				15450							
	Two monasteries one G and one N, to										
29	Dzongshee	over	50	10250	16						
	Laguchume Pass	to		15500	10						
30	Kundeedrahphuh										
		over		14500	5						
	Thoh Pass	to		15200							
	Shisonggong	over	50	12000	12						
	Yangtze River	to									
	Li	to	60	8300	5						
31	Batang		50	8500	7						
			2500								

Date	Place		Pop.	Ele.	Dis.	Temp. Min. Max.	Sky	Rain or Snow	Wind	Remarks

TRIP FROM TACHIENLU TO YEELUNGSHEE AND BACK TO TACHIENLU—
CHAPTER XIII

Date	Place		Pop.	Ele.	Dis.	Temp.	Sky	Rain or Snow	Wind	Remarks
Sept.	From Tachienlu	to	12000	8500						
27	Jethoh	to	250	11500	8		CL			a chilly day
			125							
28	Jethohkhoh	via		14500	10		CL	2-snow & hail		a cold day
	Jethoh Pass	and		14600	1					very cold on pass
	Laneepar Pass	to		15600	3		C-CL			
29	Yeelungshee	Valley								
		to		14300	8		C-CL			
30	Jalaphodrang	via	175N	13650	9		CL	1/16		
			150	other						
Oct.			25							
	Sobu	to	35N	12875	5			hail & rain 1/2		Past (Ga) temple and 5 stone towers
			10							
1	Meje	via	200							
			10	12800	4					
	Lelekhuthe	to		11700			CL	1/16		
2	Serurong	to	60	11675	10					Past 2 temples (Ga.), 50 monks each
3	Zhohlu	to	5N	11550	12		C-CL	1/4		
			35							
4	Trundo	to	40	11600	15		C-CL			50 monks in temple up ravine near Li R. bridge
			5							
5	Athedrong	via	720	12600	15		C-CL			Passed two temples
	Aje Pass	and		15400	2					
	Jethoh Pass	to		14600						
6	Tachienlu			8500	14		C-CL	1/16		

Appendix No. 2

Mph—miles per hour Temperatures in Fahrenheit
in.—inches   Precipitation in inches (10 in. snow=1 in. Rain)
No.—number   This includes expeditions with returns
hrs.—hours   from many places at various altitudes (Summary)

1927-35	J	F	M	A	M	J	J	A	S	O	N	D	Total	Yrs.
Mean Max.	51.9	55.9	61.2	66.9	75.5	79.1	80.8	78.8	69.8	65.3	59.1	53.9		6-8
Mean Min.	23.8	26.8	32.6	41.2	49.2	56.3	58.1	57.0	48.3	41.8	32.4	25.4		6-8
Mean	37.9	41.4	46.9	54.1	62.3	67.7	69.4	67.9	59.1	53.6	45.8	39.7		6-8
Highest Temperature Any One Day	63.5	70.0	80.0	84.0	90.0	95.5	96.0	98.0	83.0	77.0	75.0	66.0		3-5
Lowest Temperature Any One Day	-17	-3.5	-13.0	3.5	6.0	38.0	32.0	35.5	25.0	14.5	20.0	15.0		3-5
Total inches Precipitation Any One Day	0.06	0.2	1.5	1.31	2.27	10.31	12.63	12.69	14.63	4.38	0.56	0.05		3-5
Maximum in 24 hrs. Any One Day	0.06	0.06	0.5	0.6	0.75	1.50	2.00	2.00	2.25	1.00	0.50	0.05		3-5
Average No. of Days over 0.1 in. Rain	0	0	0	3.75	5.25	11.0	11.0	12.5	14.8	3.7	1	0		3-5
Average No. of Days Below Freezing	28.3	19.25	9.75	6.5	1.75	0	0	0	1.2	2.7	17.5	26.5		3-5
Average No. of Days Dust Storms	4	6.75	2.5	2	1.25	.75	0	0	0	0	0.25	4.25		3-5
Average No. of Days Clear	11.25	6.25	8.75	3.75	5.50	4.50	5	3.75	2.6	17	14.25	15.75		3-5
Average No. of Days Partly Cloudy	15.0	12.5	15.75	20.25	20.5	21.25	20.75	19.75	17.4	6.7	12.75	13.50		3-5
Average No. of Days Cloudy	4.75	9.25	6.5	6.0	5	4.25	5.25	7.5	7.8	7.3	3.75	1.75		3-5

1927-35	J	F	M	A	M	J	J	A	S	O	N	D	Total	Yrs.
Average No. of Days Wind over 10 mph.	7.25	9.75	8.25	8.50	8.75	4.50	3.50	2.75	1.4	4.7	2.25	5.50		3-5
Average No. of Days Wind under 10 mph	13.0	13.25	16.25	19.75	19.25	25.75	23.50	22.0	21.4	11.0	17.25	11.25		3-5
Dominant Prevailing Wind Direction	SW	SW	SW	SW	SW	SW	SW	SW	W	SW	SW	SW		3-5

BATANG ONLY—ALTITUDE 8500 (30 N. 99 E.)

	J	F	M	A	M	J	J	A	S	O	N	D	Total	Yrs.
Mean Max.	52.2	56.1	63.5	69.9	76.9	80.6	82.1	79.6	71.7	65.0	59.1	53.9		5-6
Mean Min.	25.8	29.3	36.7	45.2	51.6	58.4	59.3	57.5	53.1	43.6	32.4	25.4		5-6
Mean	39.0	42.7	50.1	57.5	64.3	69.5	70.6	68.6	62.4	54.3	45.8	39.7		5-6
Highest Temperature Any One Day	63.0	70.0	80.0	84.0	90.0	95.5	96.0	94.0	83.0	77.0	75.0	66.0		5-6
Lowest Temperature Any one Day	15.0	14.5	24.0	34.0	42.0	48.0	49.0	45.0	38.0	29.0	20.0	15.0		5-6
Total Inches Precipitation Any one Month	0.06	0.06	1.50	1.31	1.69	5.44	12.63	12.69	12.38	1.56	0.56	0.05		2-4
Maximum in 24 Hours Any one Day	0.06	0.06	0.50	0.50	0.75	1.50	1.50	2.00	1.50	0.50	0.50	0.05		2-4
Average No. Days Over 0.1 In. Rain	0	0	2.67	3.75	4	8.67	10.67	11.0	15.0	1.50	1	0		2-4
Average No. of Days Below Freezing	29	16⅔	4	0	0	0	0	0	0	0	11	26.5		2-4
Average No. of Days Dust Storms	5.33	8	.67	0	0	0	0	0	0	0	0	4.25		2-4
Average No. of Days Clear	9.33	7.33	9.00	4.33	8.67	5.67	5.0	4.5	3.0	17.5	13.5	15.75		2-4

1927-35	J	F	M	A	M	J	J	A	S	O	N	D	To-tal	Yrs.
Average No. of Days Partly Cloudy	17.67	12.33	17.33	22.33	22.0	21.67	21.33	18.5	20.0	8.0	11.25	22.5		2-4
Average No. of Days Cloudy	4.33	8.67	4.67	3.33	3.0	2.67	4.67	8.0	7.0	5.5	5.25	1.75		2-4
Average No. of Days Wind over 10 mph.	8.33	11:0	7.67	11.0	10.0	4.0	4.0	2.5	2.0	1.5	1.25	5.5		2-4
Average No. of Days Wind under 10 mph.	8.33	13.67	15.0	17.67	17.33	28.67	21.67	15.5	16.5	6.5	17.75	11.25		2-4
Dominant Prevailing Wind Direction	SW	SW	SW	SW	SW	SW	SW	SW	NW	SW	SW	SW		2-4

AT BATANG — ALTITUDE 8500

1927-35	J	F	M	A	M	J	J	A	S	O	N	D	To-tal	Yrs.
1927														
Mean Maximum				75.4	84.4	78.3	77.6	68.0	60.9	54.9	49.1			
Mean Minimum				49.1	58.7	57.0	57.2	51.8	40.3	29.4	21.5			
Mean				62.3	71.6	67.7	67.4	59.9	50.6	42.2	35.3			
Highest Temperature				84.0	92.0	86.0	86.0	81.0	74.0	61.0	55.0			
Lowest Temperature				42.0	54.0	51.0	50.0	46.0	29.0	22.0	15.0			
1928														
Mean Maximum	51.7	55.6	61.7	71.2	74.2	78.6	82.5	74.2	73.0	61.8	53.4	52.9		
Mean Minimum	26.0	28.4	37.4	44.6	51.4	59.8	57.9	53.3	54.2	46.4	30.3	26.2		
Mean	38.9	42.0	49.6	57.9	62.8	69.2	70.2	63.8	63.6	54.1	41.9	39.6		
Highest Temperature	63.0	70.0	71.0	75.0	85.0	89.0	89.0	81.0	79.0	75.0	60.0	65.0		
Lowest Temperature	15.0	20.0	27.0	34.0	42.0	48.0	49.0	45.0	51.0	30.0	20.0	19.0		

1927-35	J	F	M	A	M	J	J	A	S	O	N	D	To-tal	Yrs.

BATANG

1929

	J	F	M	A	M	J	J	A	S	O	N	D	To-tal	Yrs.
Mean Maximum	50.8	51.7	62.9	64.8	74.2	77.8	78.2	79.4	70.3	64.8	57.2	56.1		
Mean Minimum	26.6	27.3	35.6	45.3	50.6	56.3	57.5	57.8	50.5	43.7	32.7	29.3		
Mean	38.7	39.5	49.3	55.1	62.4	67.1	67.9	68.6	60.4	54.3	45.0	42.7		
Highest Temperature	61.0	66.0	72.0	73.0	85.0	87.0	87.0	85.0	79.0	75.0	63.5	64.0		
Lowest Temperature	16.0	19.0	27.0	37.0	43.0	51.0	54.0	55.0	38.0	37.0	23.0	21.5		
Precipitation Total inches											0.31	0.05		
Precipitation Max. in 24 hrs.											0.13	0.05		
No. of Days over 1/10 in. Rain											1	0		
No. of Days Below Freezing											10	20		
No. of Days Dust Storms											0	13		
No. of Days Clear											21	23		
No. of Days Partly Cloudy											5	4		
No. of Days Cloudy											4	4		
No. of Days Wind over 10 mph											4	13		
No. of Days Wind under 10 mph											4	4		
Prevailing Wind Direction											SW	SW		

BATANG

1930

	J	F	M	A	M	J	J	A	S	O	N	D	To-tal	Yrs.
Mean Maximum	52.2	56.5	62.8	72.7	79.9	80.1	86.6	82.4	73.2	65.5	61.6	53.6		
Mean Minimum	26.9	27.7	37.3	45.7	54.0	58.6	63.0	59.8	54.5	43.5	33.6	26.5		
Mean	39.6	42.1	50.1	59.2	67.0	69.4	74.8	71.1	63.9	54.5	47.6	40.5		
Highest Temperature	59	65	71	84	90	90	96	94	80	76	75	66		
Lowest Temperature	17	17	25	34	43	52	53	56	50	33	23	22		
Precipitation Total inches	0	0	1.50	1.31	1.69	4.06	5.19	12.69	8.31	1.56	0.56	0		
Precipitation Max. in 24 hrs	0	0	0.50	0.50	0.75	1.13	1.50	2.00	1.50	0.50	0.50	0		
No. of Days over 1/10 in. Rain	0	0	4	4	4	6	8	14	13	3	1	0		

1927-35	J	F	M	A	M	J	J	A	S	O	N	D	To-tal	Yrs.
No. of Days Below Freezing	27	20	3	0	0	0	0	0	0	0	12	27		
No. of Days Dust Storms	10	12	1	0	0	0	0	0	0	0	0	3		
No. of Days Clear	12	11	21	4	15	11	9	5	6	17	13	21		
No. of Days Partly Cloudy	10	16	6	21	12	16	16	11	17	8	12	10		
No. of Days Cloudy	9	1	4	5	4	3	6	15	7	6	5	0		
No. of Days Wind over 10 mph	19	13	5	8	5	3	1	3	2	1	0	2		
No. of Days Wind under 10 mph	2	6	14	20	20	26	21	18	10	4	19	3		
Prevailing Wind Direction	SW	SW	NE	SW	SW	SW	SW	SW	NW	SW	SW	SW		

BATANG

1931	J	F	M	A	M	J	J	A	S	O	N	D	Total	Yrs.
Mean Maximum	54.5	62.0	65.6	72.5	80.3	86.0	84.5	84.4	74.0	71.8	60.9	54.6		
Mean Minimum	25.7	35.5	38.4	46.0	53.1	58.5	58.5	59.5	54.4	44.0	31.6	25.6		
Mean Temperature	40.1	48.8	52.0	59.3	66.7	72.3	71.5	72.0	64.2	57.9	46.3	40.1		
Highest Temperature	63.0	67.0	80.0	79.5	88.0	95.5	95.0	89.5	83.0	77.0	72.5	62.0		
Lowest Temperature	17.0	22.5	27.5	39.0	46.5	50.5	55.0	55.0	49.0	38.5	26.0	20.5		
Total inches Precipitation	0	0	0	1.00	0.69	4.06	12.63	10.25	12.38	0.19	0.25	0	41.45	
Maximum in 24 hrs	0	0	0	0.50	0.19	1.50	1.50	2.00	1.50	0.06	0.13	0		
No. of Days over 0.1 in. Rain	0	0	0	3	3	9	16	8	17	0	2	0		
No. of Days Below Freezing	27	4	2	0	0	0	0	0	0	0	18	29		
No. of Days Dust Storms	5	10	0	0	0	0	0	0	0	0	0	0		
No. of Days Clear	9	11	5	8	5	5	2	4	0	18	13	11		
No. of Days Partly Cloudy	19	14	17	19	26	23	25	26	23	8	13	19		
No. of Days Cloudy	3	3	9	3	0	2	4	1	7	5	4	1		
No. of Days Wind over 10 mph	4	17	10	11	13	5	2	2	2	2	1	3		
No. of Days Wind under 10 mph	9	11	15	14	14	24	27	13	23	9	19	11		
Prevailing Wind Direction	SW	SW	SW	SW	SW	SW	SW	SW	NE	SW	SW	SW		

1927-35	J	F	M	A	M	J	J	A	S	O	N	D	To-tal	Yrs.

*From Aug. 22nd en route home at same latitude but going eastward at varying higher altitudes until Tachienlu on Sept. 23rd and end of record then

BATANG, SIKANG PROV. TIBETAN PLATEAU

1932

	J	F	M	A	M	J	J	A	S	O	N	D	Total	Yrs.
Mean Maximum	51.8	54.7	63.9	68.3	77.9	76.5	82.2	80.9	61.4					
Mean Minimum	23.6	27.5	35.0	43.6	51.5	58.7	61.8	58.4	44.5					
Mean Temperature	37.7	41.1	49.5	56.0	64.7	67.6	71.5	69.7	53.0					
Highest Temperature	55.5	63.5	75.0	81.5	89.5	89.0	89.0	98.0	80.0					
Lowest Temperature	15.5	14.5	24.0	36.0	44.0	52.0	58.0	35.5†	37.5					
Total inches Precipitation	0.06	0.06	0.63	1.00	1.69	5.44	3.19	6.94	10.81				29.82	
Maximum in 24 hrs	0.06	0.06	0.13	0.25	0.50	1.00	.50	1.00	2.00					
No. of Days over 0.1 in. Rain	0	0	4	4	5	11	8	10	14					
No. of Days Below Freezing	30	25	7	0	0	0	0	0	0					
No. of Days Dust Storms	1	2	1	0	0	0	0	0	0					
No. of Days Clear	7	0	1	1	1	1	4	3	0					
No. of Days Partly Cloudy	24	7	29	27	28	26	23	21	18					
No. of Days Cloudy	1	22	1	2	2	3	4	7	5					
No. of Days Wind over 10 mph	2	3	8	11	12	4	9	3	2					
No. of Days Wind under 10 mph	14	24	16	19	18	26	17	26	20					
Prevailing Wind Direction	SW	SW	SW	SW	SW	SW	SW	NE	W					

†At Litang 14,000 ft.

On the road or lodged in Tachienlu, Litang or Batang, this last place Oct. 24th to end of year. Altitudes from 8,500 to 14,500 but at practically same latitude

1934

	J	F	M	A	M	J	J	A	S	O	N	D	Total	Yrs.
Mean Maximum									71.0	66.7	66.8	57.2		
Mean Minimum									37.7	32.6	37.0	23.2		
Mean									54.4	49.7	51.9	40.2		
Highest Temperature									81.0	75.0	74.0	64.5		
Lowest Temperature									25.0	14.5	27.0	16.0		

1927-35	J	F	M	A	M	J	J	A	S	O	N	D	To-tal	Yrs.
Total inches Precipitation									6.19	4.38	0	0		
Maximum in 24 hrs									1.0	1.0	0	0		
No. of Days over 0.1 in. rain									9	8	0	0		
No. of Days Below Freezing									3	8	4	30		
No. of Days Dust Storms									0	0	0	1		
No. of Days Clear									5	16	7	8		
No. of Days Partly Cloudy									14	4	15	21		
No. of Days Cloudy									7	11	8	2		
No. of Days Wind over 10 mph									0	11	0	4		
No. of Days Wind under 10 mph									25	20	29	27		
Prevailing Wind Direction									W	SW NE	SW	SW		

After 24 days in Batang the record goes northward to Jyekundo and then southeast to Tachienlu back beyond Kanze and winds up its last 4 days at Tachienlu

1935	J	F	M	A	M	J	J	A	S
Mean Maximum	50.2	54.0	50.1	52.0	65.5	70.3	73.1	72.4	67.1
Mean Minimum	14.2	14.4	12.1	22.2	35.0	43.2	51.2	52.9	39.1
Mean	32.2	32.2	31.1	37.1	50.3	56.8	62.2	62.7	53.1
Highest Temperature	63.5	63.0	66.0	68.0	75.0	80.0	84.0	83.0	75.0
Lowest Temperature	−17.0	−3.5	−13.0	3.5	6.0	38.0	32.0	41.0	27.0
Total inches Precipitation	0	0.2	0.6	1.6	2.27	10.31	7.88	12.69	14.63
Maximum in 24 hrs	0	0.05	0.2	.6	0.38	1.5	2.00	2.00	2.25
No. of Days over 0.1 in. Rain	0	0	0	0	9	18	12	18	21
No. of Days Below Freezing	29	28	27	26	7	0	0	0	3
No. of Days Dust Storms	0	3	8	8	5	3	0	0	0
No. of Days Clear	18	3	8	2	1	1	5	3	2
No. of Days Partly Cloudy	7	13	11	14	16	20	19	21	15
No. of Days Cloudy	6	12	12	14	14	9	7	7	13

1927-35	J	F	M	A	M	J	J	A	S	O	N	D	To-tal	Yrs.
No. of Days Wind														
over 10 mph	3	6	10	4	5	2	2	0	1					
No. of Days Wind														
under 10 mph	27	12	20	26	25	27	29	31	29					
Prevailing	SW	W	W	W	W	W	NW	E	SE					
Wind Direction			S						SW					

Appendix No. 3

CHYAHTSHAN OR HAND SIGNS

Symbolism of Hand Signs in Tibetan Lamaistic Ceremonies

Religious ceremonies conducted by Tibetan monks are featured by:— (a) chanting of texts either from memory or from the printed leaves held upon their knees as they sit cross-legged in rows in temple or tent; (b) symbolical motions of hands with dorje, and flexing of fingers in various positions; and (c) orchestral use of musical instruments as the bell, drum, flute, conch-shell and trumpets.

The method of grasping the instruments is stabilized. The dorje is held inside the right clasped hand and the bell by the thumb and forefinger of the left hand. The thumbs must clasp the dorje and bell all of the time the manipulations of the fingers are taking place.

The hand motions are symbols of acts of worship and a deity is in mind or actually present such as an idol figure, when the ceremony is performed. The ceremony is known as "offering reverence" or "conducting worship" either to the idol or the tutelary deity.

The chanting proceeds by consecutive steps. The first eight steps are preceded by reading of scripture and groaning. Then the eight steps are pronounced, winding up with the ringing of bells, the beating of drums and clanging of cymbals. Following this orchestral salute the monks read scripture and then go into the five steps. These rituals of hand symbolism may be repeated a number of times in the ceremony.

Monks who eat meat can perform this ritual except when the object or recipient of the ceremony is for the White Drolma (goddess saving from rebirth) or for the mystical goddess Namjyehma who has three faces and eight arms. In these two ceremonies only vegetarians are permitted to participate and some of the hand symbols are different from those used in the regular hand-symbolistic rites.

The position of the palms is very important, for instance showing the inside of the hand is indicative of peace and friendship. The palms are always held upward or toward the face of the chanter if possible. The motioning of the hands and the sounding of the instruments are interpolated decisively with the chanting which rises and falls in tone in harmony with the meaning of the text. All of the motions of the hands are substitutes for the actual acts of adoration to the god and the instruments are aids in securing the attention of the deity or coercing him to favor the worshipper.

The performance may take place in a temple, in a tent, in a home or out under the open sky. The eight different steps are outlined below in regular order and with the furniture as mentioned.

Step 1. Offering blood to the tongue of idol.
        Both palms in offering the bowl of blood to the idol clasp
the bowl so the open palms face the chanter.

Step 2. Offering cleansing to feet of idol.
        Left palm facing and right palm sweeping over top of bowl
are the tokens of this step.

Step 3. Offering flowers to head of idol.
        With palms facing him the chanter snaps fingers off thumb
to symbolize placing a circlet of flowers on head of idol.

Step 4. Offering incense to feet of idol.
        With thumbs toward chanter's face and extended fingers in
pairs; commencing with forefingers slowly closing only the fingers indicate
the offering of incense.

Step 5. Offering butter lamp to eyes of idol.
        Palms facing chanter's face and fingers half-closed with fore-
finger against thumb making a circle.

Step 6. Offering sweet-smelling stuff to idol's heart.
        Two palms facing outward and thumbs touching indicate
this offering.

Step 7. Offering food to idol's tongue.
        With palms toward chanter's face the little fingers touch-
ing, or the whole sides of hands in contact and thumbs folded inward represent offering of food to idol's tongue.
        At this point the bell is rung and the instruments are
sounded.

Step 8. Offering sound instruments to idol's ears.
        Thumb of left hand in palm which is toward face and held
still, while the right hand with palm toward face is swung outward to left in
half circle with palm then turning to face outward. The tips of the fingers
go inward then down and out.
        The second series of five steps below follow the first eight after all in-
struments of the orchestra have sounded off.

Step 1. Offering a mirror to the body of idol.
        The left hand with palm upward is placed with the little
finger touching the right arm halfway between the elbow and the hand. The
right hand meanwhile is upright with palm outward and thumbs in boths
hands holding the regulation instruments of bell and dorje. This enables
idol to see himself.

Step 2. Offering all instruments to sound for idol's ears.
        Now the bell is rung and all instruments sounded. The left
thumb, while the left palm is facing outward, is held motionless toward the
face; and the right hand with its palm toward the face is swung outward to
left in a half circle. This movement thus causes the right palm to face outward and the points of the fingers go inward then down and outward.

    Step 3.   Offering perfumed water to idol's nose.

        The two palms, when faced outward with the thumbs touching, represent such an offering.

    Step 4.   Offering food to idol's tongue.

        Chanter's palms toward his face, with little fingers or the whole side touching and thumbs folded inward, portray the presentation of food.

    Step 5.   Offering of clothes to idol's body.

        The hands are held with palm outward, and thumbs with forefingers in circle holding onto dorje and bell.

    Lamaistic scriptures are now chanted in unison.

Appendix No. 4

Chart and Transliteration of Tibetan Place names into English Letters

Vowels

ཨ་	to a	=	Italian A
ཨི་	to i		short i as in "it"
ཨུ་	to u		short u as in "put"
ཨེ་	to e		short e as in "get"
ཨོ་	to o		long o as in "go"

Consonants imply a following a (Italian A).

ཀ་	Ka	K as g in garbage (as pronounced in southern U.S.A.)
ཁ་	Kha	as kh in block-head
ག་	Ga	as g in gone, give, etc.
ང་	Nga	as ng in coming on.
ཅ་	Ja	as J in jack, Japan, John, etc.
ཆ་	Cha	as cha and ch in chart, larch
ཇ་	Jha	as j in jar, jeer, etc
ཉ་	Nya	as nui in nuisance.
ཏ་	Ta	as d in dick

ཐ་	Tha	as t in tart, torn, pat-hard, etc.
ད་	Da	as d in dare
ན་	Na	as n in nest, not, etc.
པ་	Pa	as b in bear
ཕ་	Pha	as p in peer, stop-here pronounced as one word, etc.
བ་	Ba	as b in bond, bawdy, etc.
མ་	Ma	as m in man, march, etc.
ཙ་	Tsa	as ts in weights.
ཚ་	Tsha	as "pats hard" prounced as one word, potshot, etc.
ཛ་	Dza	as dz in "dead zone" pronounced as one word.
ཝ་	Wa	as wa in water.
ཞ་	Zha	as az in azure
ཟ་	Za	as z in azalea
འ་	Ah	as ah in rah
ཡ་	Ya	as ya in yacht
ར་	Ra	as r in rat
ལ་	La	as l in linger, lake, etc.
ཤ་	Sha	as sh in shout, shah, etc.
ས་	Sa	as s in sink, sahib, etc.

ཧ་   Ha   as h in hand, hah, etc.

ཨ་   A   as a in father.

ཇ་ཇ་ཇ་ཇ་   Jya as in giant

ཇང་   Jyang

ཁ་ཆ་Chya   as ch in chivy

ཉ་   Nya   as the previous Nya

ཀ་ག་ད་ད་ད་ད་   Dra as in dramatize

ཁ་ཐ་Tra   as in trap

ན་   Na   as in previous Na

མ་   Ma   as in previous Ma

ཤ་   Sha   as in previous Sha

ས་   Sa   as in previous Sa

ཧྲ་   Shra   as shr in shrubbery

ལ་ལ་ལ་ལ་ལ་   La   as in previous La

ད་   Da   as in previous Da

ལྷ་   Lha   as in Lhasa, and "La" in larch, etc.

ད་ before ཝ་ is Wa   as in previous Wa

ད་ before ཡ་ is Ya   as in previous Ya

Initial letters as well as the superadded ཪ་ ཨ་ and ཨ་ are not transliterated. These coincide with the pronounced basic letter and can be recovered by search in the Das Tibetan-English Dictionary.

Final consonants modify the sound in most instances and present the most difficulty in transliteration. The author is not satisfied with his usage, as here indicated:—

For   ག་ད་བ་ཨ་   "H" is added to the vowel letter

For   ང་   "Ng" is added to the vowel letter

For   ན་   "N" is added to the vowel letter

For   མ་   "M" is added to the vowel letter

For   ར་   "R" is added to the vowel letter

ཨ་ and ཨ་   radically modify the vowel and are

handled accordingly, sometimes "EE" long ee, again by "Eh", other times by "H", etc.

ཨ་ which is used as a second final is not transliterated.

Carried sounds such as ཨ་ and ན་ as initials in second syllables add "M" and "N" to the pronunciation and transliteration of the previous syllable as in དར་རྩེ་མདོ་ Dartsendo and ཆབ་མདོ་ Chamdo.

Diacritical marks useful and sometimes indispensable in indicating the correct pronunciation are not used as they are easily lost in printing and also most readers do not understand their meaning.

Finally, transliterations such as Lama, Yak, Chorten, La, etc., regardless of their Tibetan characters, having become stabilized in English spelling, are retained. For the same reason an attempt has been made to retain the most commonly used spelling of religious terms such as Gelugpa, Drolma, etc., so as not to confuse the scholarly reader.

Appendix No. 5

PERSONAL NAMES OF TIBETANS

Tibetans do not have a surname or family name but are called by their given name and said to be from such and such a house or as being the son of so and so. The wealthy have house names but the poor either belong to that house as servants, or to a certain monastery, or live in a certain named quarter of the city. Villages may take their name from the lord who has the principal house. In Batang one is known as being of such a household or from a certain section into which the town has been divided.

Personal names regularly contain four syllables but in everyday usage they may be shortened to two syllables or even a nickname. More often the nickname, which relates to a physical or other characteristic of the individual, is added to the commonly used two-syllable name. A person who has one eye is called for instance—One-eyed Lozong.

The syllables of the name always mean some admirable physical, mental, or moral quality unless given the name of a goddess or of some deity. Search into the qualities most desirable in the list below reveal that Long Life, Fortune, Power, Victory, Goddess, and the use of Drolma who is the goddess that saves from transmigration, are the most popular attributes selected in names. These terms are juggled in many different combinations subject to the laws of euphony, ease of utterance and economy of effort.

While there seems some slight effort to give a male names which indicate supposedly masculine qualities, and also to the female designations of supposedly womanly attributes, yet the only sure indication of sex is in the terms:—goddess, name of a goddess or the word Mo which means woman; one or more of these terms are usually found in the name given to a female.

List of Names used by Men	*List of names used by Women*
1. Life Long Prosperity	1. Life Long Melody Possessing
2. Life Long Power Increase	2. Life Long Melody Drolma
3. Completely Victorious Life Long	3. Life Long Goddess Life
4. Religious Service Life Long	4. Life Long Goddess
5. Luck Good Life Long	5. Luck Good Goddess
6. Luck Good Power Increasing	6. Luck Good Power Woman
7. Luck Good Morality	7. Luck Good Drolma
8. Luck Good Deeds	8. Luck Good Goddess Happy
9. Luck Good Business accomplished	9. Luck Good Religion Happy
10. Divine Wisdom Life Steadfast	10. Divine Wisdom Goddess
11. Divine Wisdom Light Ray	11. Divine Wisdom Goddess
12. Divine Wisdom Size Lake	12. Divine Wisdom Goddess Lake
13. Sun Victorious Banner	13. Divine Wisdom Religious Lamp
14. Blessed Complete Victory	14. Blessed Melody Possessed

15. Blessed Life Long
16. Blessed Work Accomplished
17. Blessed Power Good
18. Virtuous Way Increase
19. Virtuous Power Increase
20. Work Accomplished Banner
21. Mind Good Banner
22. Mind Religious Glory
23. Mind Good Power Possessed
24. Mind Good Perfected
25. Mind Good Thought
26. Mind Good Splendid Treasure
27. Moon Complete Victory
28. Victorious Banner Religious Increase
29. Victorious Year Work Accomplished
30. Life Steadfast Power Rich

15. Precious Goddess
16. Goddess Ranking High Lady
17. Bright Place 100,000 Lights
18. Virtuous Goddess
19. Paradise Clear Profound
20. Work Accomplished Goddess
21. Mind Good Goddess
22. Mind Good Religious Drolma
23. Virtue Possessed Good Woman
24. All Beings Good Woman
25. Universal Good Woman
26. Holy Religion Glorious Lamp
27. Moon Drolma
28. Life Long Lady
29. Sceptred Drolma
30. Absolute Wisdom Drolma

INDEX

A

Aden, 94, 158

Ajedrong, 266, 267, 268

Aki, 81

Aku Tseden, 148, 162

Amban, 148

Amdo, 225, 230

Animals,
    Antelope, 77, 194, 230
    Blue Sheep, 167, 169
    Deer, 245
    Leopard, 104
    Lynx, 86
    Marmots, 81, 125, 236, 237
    Ochotona, (Mouse hare), 122, 125, 192
    Steppe Bears, 192, 209 to 215
    Steppe Foxes, 190, 229, 243
    Weasels, 122, 192, 209
    Wild Asses, 191, 192, 194, 203
    Wolves, 190, 209

Astrology, 116, 205

Athedrong, 265, 266

Atring (Gegen Atring) (Gezong Tsering), 117, 127, 163, 164, 170,
    180, 217, 243, 244, 245, 246

Azong, 174

B

Bahmdah, 234

Bahodrong, 238

Bahzhah, 221

Ba Lama, 116, 148, 163, 165, 174

Bare, Dr. and Mrs. N. H., 107, 115, 139, 150

Date Due

DEC 0 4 2005			

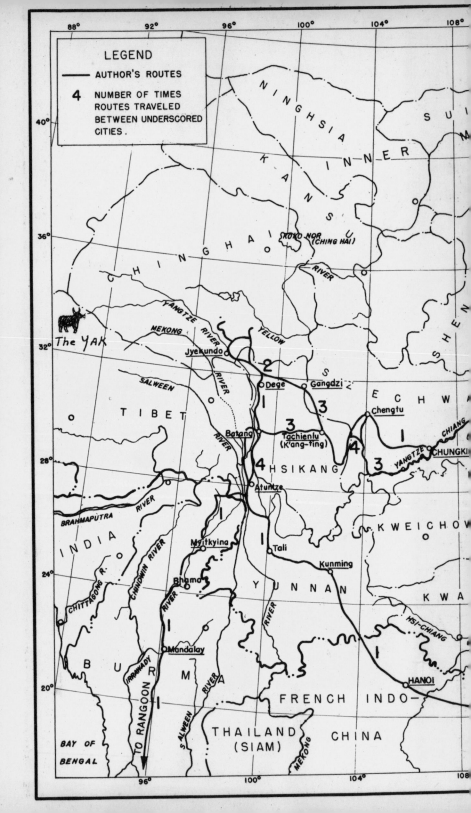